PACIFIC-ASIA AND THE FUTURE OF THE WORLD-SYSTEM

PACIFIC-ASIA AND THE FUTURE OF THE WORLD-SYSTEM

EDITED BY
Ravi Arvind Palat

STUDIES IN THE POLITICAL ECONOMY OF THE WORLD-SYSTEM
Immanuel Wallerstein, SERIES ADVISER

CONTRIBUTIONS IN ECONOMICS AND
ECONOMIC HISTORY, NUMBER 142

GREENWOOD PRESS
Westport, Connecticut • London

Library of Congress Cataloging-in-Publication Data

Pacific-Asia and the future of the world-system / edited by Ravi
   Arvind Palat.
      p. cm.—(Contributions in economics and economic history,
   ISSN 0084-9235 ; no. 142) (Studies in the political economy of the
   world-system)
      Includes bibliographical references and index.
      ISBN 0-313-28401-6 (alk. paper)
      1. Pacific Area—Economic conditions. 2. Pacific Area—Economic
   integration. 3. Pacific Area—Politics and government. I. Palat,
   Ravi Arvind. II. Series. III. Series: Studies in the political
   economy of the world-system.
   HC681.P24 1993
   337.9—dc20   92-18384

British Library Cataloguing in Publication Data is available.

Library of Congress Catalog Card Number: 92-18384
ISBN: 0-313-28401-6
ISSN: 0084-9235

First published in 1993

Greenwood Press, 88 Post Road West, Westport, CT 06881
An imprint of Greenwood Publishing Group, Inc.

Printed in the United States of America

The paper used in this book complies with the
Permanent Paper Standard issued by the National
Information Standards Organization (Z39.48–1984).

10 9 8 7 6 5 4 3 2

CONTENTS

SERIES FOREWORD

Immanuel Wallerstein

The Political Economy of the World-System section of the American Sociological Association was created in the 1970s to bring together a small but growing number of social scientists concerned with analyzing the processes of world-systems in general, and our modern one in particular.

Although organizationally located within the American Sociological Association, the PEWS Section bases its work on the relative insignificance of the traditional disciplinary boundaries. For that reason it has held an annual spring conference, open to and drawing participation from persons who work under multiple disciplinary labels.

For PEWS members, not only is our work unidisciplinary but the study of the world-system is not simply another "specialty" to be placed beside so many others. It is instead a different "perspective" with which to analyze all the traditional issues of the social sciences. Hence, the themes of successive PEWS conferences are quite varied and cover a wide gamut of topics. What they share is the sense that the isolation of political, economic, and socio-cultural "variables" is a dubious enterprise, that all analysis must be simultaneously historical and systemic, and that the conceptual bases of work in the historical social sciences must be rethought.

ACKNOWLEDGMENTS

All the papers assembled in this volume were presented at the Fifteenth Annual Conference on the Political Economy of the World-System, held at the University of Hawaii at Manoa, March 28–30, 1991. I would like to thank all the participants, including those not represented here, for making the conference a lively and intellectually stimulating experience.

Organized under the auspices of the Political Economy of the World-System section of the American Sociological Association, the conference was generously supported by the School of Hawaiian, Asian, and Pacific Studies, the departments of Political Science and Sociology, and the Pacific-Asian Management Institute of the University of Hawaii and by the Institute for Economic Development and Policy of the East-West Center. I am particularly grateful to my colleagues on the organizing committee—Hagen Koo, Mimi Sharma, Alvin So, Bob Stauffer, and Terence Wesley-Smith for their invaluable assistance. Thanks are also due to Yvonne Yamashita of the University of Hawaii Conference Center and to Alyson Turner for their help in organizing the conference; to the Asian Studies support staff, especially Jane Martin, Linda Miyashiro, Iris Odo, and Wendy Taira; and to Patricia Lane for assistance in editing this volume.

PACIFIC-ASIA AND THE FUTURE OF THE WORLD-SYSTEM

PART I

RECASTING PACIFIC-ASIA

INTRODUCTION: THE MAKING AND UNMAKING OF PACIFIC-ASIA

Ravi Arvind Palat

> [T]he Pacific Ocean will have the same role as the Atlantic has now and the Mediterranean had in antiquity and in the Middle Ages—that of the great water highway of world commerce; and the Atlantic will decline to the status of an inland sea, like the Mediterranean nowadays.
>
> Marx and Engels (1978: 266)

By the late seventies, when one of the lesser-known prophecies of Marx and Engels appeared imminent with the eclipse of the trans-Atlantic trade by that of the Pacific, policymakers and business leaders, scholars and journalists, were all quick to proclaim the dawn of a new era—the Age of the Pacific. This prognosis was seemingly confirmed in the eighties by the high rates of economic growth registered by Japan and the "Four Dragons" (South Korea, Taiwan, Hong Kong, and Singapore) amid the collapse of most other low- and middle-income states and the rapid industrialization of several Southeast Asian states (Malaysia, Thailand, and Indonesia). Additional corroboration for this thesis came from the growth of industries based on new technologies along the Pacific seaboard of North America and the concurrent de-industrialization of the Midwestern and Northeastern regions of the United States. Finally, the chronological simultaneity of the rise of export-oriented economies along the shores of the Pacific with the collapse of autarkic, centrally planned economies—and the concomitant end of the Cold War—appeared to confirm the proposition that we are standing at a major geopolitical turning point in world history.

Despite widespread consensus on these issues, there is considerable ambiguity and confusion in conceptualizing the nature, constitution, and future directions of an impending Pacific Century. On the one hand, the very ease with which we can locate booming economies and plot the complex economic and political networks on maps endows the concept with an aura of obviousness (Harris,

1989: 409). On the other hand, the very unity of lands along the shores of the Pacific, which "appears concrete with reference to the region's physical delineation on maps, is revealed as an abstraction when viewed in terms of human activity" (Dirlik, 1991: 6). As Bruce Cumings and Gary Gereffi suggest in their contributions to this volume, the most widely used terms to describe this geographical area—*Pacific Rim, Pacific Basin, Asia-Pacific,* and *Asian-American Pacific*—are all inadequate, since they either focus exclusively on the perimeters of the ocean or else include some 70 percent of the world population. Whether by forsaking most of the people within the area or by collapsing the enormous social heterogeneity within it, the concept is emptied of analytical coherence. Further, despite the apparent egalitarianism of the fourth term, discussions habitually exclude most of "peasant Asia" (Afghanistan, Burma, China, India, Vietnam, etc.), Australia, New Zealand, the Pacific Islands, and all of Central and Latin America.

Explanations for the economic dynamism of states located on Asia's Pacific perimeters are equally inadequate. Invocations of the shared Confucian heritage of Japan and the Four Dragons as the cause for their rapid growth stress that a positive cultural emphasis on hard work, respect for authority, paternalistic concern for subordinates, and loyalty fosters cooperation between political elites, entrepreneurs, and laborers for their mutual benefit (Morishima, 1982; Pye, 1988; Redding, 1988; Wong, 1988). Such interpretations scarcely amount to more than an idealization of contemporary capital-labor relations in these states while ignoring the complex, conflict-ridden evolution of these relations (see Gordon, 1985; Garon, 1987; Deyo, 1989). In addition, the emphasis on Confucian values glosses over the cultural heterogeneity of these states, which also have rich Taoist and Buddhist heritages, as well as Christian and even Hindu (in the case of Singapore) influences. Moreover, it is paradoxical that the Qing Empire's inability to resist the expansionary thrust of the capitalist world-economy in the nineteenth century has often been attributed to the very same Confucian values that are now said to be the fount of economic success in twentieth-century East Asia (Rozman, 1991).

At the same time, neoclassical economists, eschewing cultural specificity, attribute the tremendous economic vitality of the Four Dragons to their steadfast adherence to export-oriented, market-governed development strategies, combined with minimal government intervention (e.g., Balassa, 1981: 1–26; Hughes, 1988). In their strident advocacy of the principles of *laissez faire* and comparative advantage, the neoclassical economists who prescribe these policies as a panacea for all the ills that plague other low- and middle-income states ignore the actual record of the East and Southeast Asia's newly industrializing countries (NICs)— another name for the Four Dragons. Detailed analyses of the development strategies pursued by these states indicate that their governments had initially implemented import-substituting industrialization (ISI) policies (Gereffi, 1990c), and often intervened to distort market forces gravely (Amsden, 1989; Wade, 1990). Further, neoclassical economists typically discount the importance of the size of the states involved, as well as ignore that entrepôts like Singapore and Hong Kong can hardly be said to have "industrialized," since no transformation from an agricultural base ever occurred in those cases (Amsden, 1989: 4).

The growing recognition of the centrality of government policies has led some analysts to focus on the rise of a "developmental state" as the key ingredient in the economic success of the East and Southeast Asian NICs (Johnson, 1982, 1987). While this concept is a major advance over neoclassical universalism and cultural particularism, writings on the developmental state have tended to be descriptive rather than analytical. Moreover, their exclusive focus on the administrative apparatus precludes a recognition of the wider political context of industrial planning and, at least implicitly, suggests that the installation of similar bureaucratic methods of industrial guidance will lead to a replication of East Asian patterns of growth in other low- and middle-income countries (Friedman, 1988: 5, 30).

Dependency theorists, who have characterized the rapid economic growth rates in South Korea and Taiwan as a variant of "dependent development," represent another strand of interpretation (Gold, 1986; Lim, 1986). In this view, the structural dependence of East and Southeast Asian NICs on foreign capital and external markets represents a major constraint on, and distorts the pattern of, their future development. While this explanation has the great merit of locating South Korean and Taiwanese trajectories of growth within a wider context, in most cases it merely amounts to an uncritical extension of the model of the "triple alliance" between state, multinational corporations (MNCs), and local capital as devised by Peter Evans (1979) for Brazil. Consequently, the explanation tends to obscure the reasons that Taiwan and South Korea have been able to withstand the economic collapse of most low- and middle-income states in the eighties. Similar objections attend Alice Amsden's (1989) interesting argument that the distinctive characteristic of "late industrialization" is its basis in "learning" rather than on invention or innovation, since it lumps together such diverse states as Argentina, Brazil, India, Japan, Mexico, South Korea, Taiwan, and Turkey.

These conceptual and methodological problems in defining and explaining the causes for the robust economic growth of states along the Pacific shores of Asia raise several important questions. First, how are we to study the increasing density and interconnectedness of relational networks across and along the perimeters of the Pacific Ocean without diluting the sociohistorical diversity within this geographical arena? Second, how can we distinguish ephemeral and transitory gains from a more enduring process of upward mobility in the global divisioning of labor? Third, what are the contextual determinants of the development strategies employed by Japan and the Four Dragons to increase their share of the benefits accruing from the axial divisioning of labor, and how have these strategies changed the patterning of relational networks along Asia's Pacific shores? Fourth, is it possible for other low- and middle-income states to replicate these successes by adopting similar developmental policies and institutional structures, thereby implying an eventual negation of the polarizing tendencies of core-periphery relations, as suggested in much of the literature on the several Asian "miracle" economies? Fifth, how has rapid economic growth affected political structures and social movements? Finally, will states located along the Pacific perimeters of Asia continue to enjoy their salience in the global economy well into the twenty-first century?

All the chapters presented in this volume bear upon one or more of these questions, either from a shared world-historical perspective or, in the case of Sankaran Krishna, from the standpoint of a friendly critic of the outlook that the others share. This common approach—a world-systems perspective—does more than merely recognize the importance of the international context to national trajectories of sociohistorical change, making selective comparisons of sets of individual states or policies and arraying and tracking the development of these states by criteria such as their rates of industrialization. Rather than taking states as self-evident units of analysis that are then related to each other through trade, investment flows, and labor exchanges, world-systems scholars view these units as being constituted and continually reconstituted by the relations between and among them. By shifting the focus of attention to temporal and spatial changes in the patterning of multiple, interconnected relational networks, world-systems analysts seek to interpret the trajectories of individual states as integral parts of an ongoing restructuring of a singular, capitalist world-economy. The result is a fundamental reconceptualization of both the economic success of the East and Southeast Asian NICs and the prospects for their future development.

In this vein, Bruce Cumings dissects the term *Pacific Rim* to reveal its amorphous nature and conceptual vacuity, and he considers whether Japan is on its way to becoming a new hegemon. Defining economic success as a state's ability to increase—and retain over time—its share of the benefits accruing from the global divisioning of labor, Giovanni Arrighi, Satoshi Ikeda, and Alexander Irwan trace the success of East and Southeast Asian NICs to the specific strategies devised by Japanese MNCs to ride out the global economic crisis of the seventies and eighties. They argue that while the spread of hierarchically linked Japanese subcontracting networks to locations in East and Southeast Asia led to robust growth, there are reasons to be skeptical of future patterns of development. Gary Gereffi examines the garment, automobile, and personal computer industries and demonstrates that the increasing dispersal of manufacturing operations to low-income states has profoundly transformed circuits of production. Less skilled operations are farmed out to low-wage areas, while the more skilled and technologically intensive activities in the same industries and product lines continue to be concentrated in the core. He also suggests that the transnational integration of production has had an adverse impact on the ability of state machineries to intervene in economic affairs.

Approaching the issue from another angle, Stephen Bunker and Denis O'Hearn analyze the different strategies employed by economically ascendant powers—the United States and Japan—to secure reliable supplies of essential raw materials. They demonstrate that the Japanese strategy of encouraging resource-rich low- and middle-income states to expand their mineral processing operations through joint ventures significantly impaired the capacity of peripheral producers to affect prices by rapidly expanding supplies without corresponding increases in demand. While industrial restructuring along the Pacific shores of Asia has received considerable scholarly attention in recent years, Philip McMichael points out that a parallel process of agricultural restructuring is also proceeding apace. He argues that the globalization of the U.S. agro-industrial model and the emergence of several rival exporters of agricultural products have led to a major restructuring of agricultural production along the perimeters of the Pacific under the aegis of Japanese capital and in accordance with Japanese taste preferences.

In sharp contrast to the chapters in Parts I and II, which analyze the changing patterns of relational networks along Asia's Pacific perimeters as integral parts of the ongoing restructuring of the capitalist world-economy, chapters in Part III examine the individual trajectories of two Asian giants—India and China. Krishna argues that the large domestic market, the substantial resource endowments, and the geopolitical importance of the Indian state have insulated it from U.S. pressures toward private enterprise. Consequently, he suggests, that the Indian state, by shrewdly playing its nonaligned card, was able to secure substantial assistance from both superpowers for a state-led industrialization drive, strongly biased toward the heavy industrial sector. Michael Hsiao and Alvin So examine the consequences of the assimilation of Hong Kong and Taiwan into the People's Republic of China (PRC). They contend that political integration of these three jurisdictional entities will present a unitary Chinese state with an avenue for upward mobility in the axial divisioning of labor. The chapters by Krishna and by Hsiao and So also cast in bold relief the distinctive experiences of Japan and the Four Dragons.

The chapters in Part IV explore how changes in the patterning of production processes have shaped the antisystemic movements in the eighties. Mark Selden ascribes the failure of the 1989 student movement in the PRC to the socioeconomic consequences of the Maoist mobilizational model. He argues that the growing chasm between town and country during the period of centralized economic planning fundamentally weakened the student movement, since it ruptured the links between the students and revolutionaries on the one hand and the peasants on the other. Finally, Robert Schaeffer attempts to place the rise of democracy movements in Latin America, East Asia, and Eastern Europe within the context of the contradictory development of the capitalist world-economy. Despite their broadly similar outcomes, he suggests that these movements were responses to the differential impact of a variety of pressures, emanating from the global restructuring of relational processes, on institutional structures in these very different areas.

Instead of recapitulating the arguments of individual contributors in greater detail, it is perhaps more useful to develop some of the underlying premises on which they are based. This procedure will serve to highlight how a world-systems perspective diverges sharply from other interpretations and provides a contextual background to the major themes addressed in this volume.

PACIFIC-ASIA AS A REGION OF THE WORLD-ECONOMY

Recognition of the growing interconnectedness of economic relationships across the Pacific and along its perimeters—and the sheer simplicity of locating the increasing density of these networks on a map—lead to "a tendency to view the region as a geographical given, a physically delineated stage, as it were, upon which human beings play out their activities". (Dirlik, 1991: 1). The underlying assumption—that geographical proximity automatically engenders the expansion of circuits of production and exchange—ignores, even violates, the historical structuring of the area as a sphere of human activity.

While acknowledging the importance of recognizing the historical constitution of the Pacific as a realm of human activity, my purpose here is not to trace these complex processes and the marginalizations, suppressions, and even physical annihilations of entire peoples that they have entailed (see Spate, 1979, 1983, 1988; Dirlik, 1991). Rather, my central concern here is to argue that the increasing integration of relational networks across, and along the shores of the contemporary Pacific—far from being the natural outcome of an expansion of the circuits of exchange within and between its constituent parts—is rooted in the concrete conditions of capital accumulation and of the relative weakness of Japanese capital during the era of U.S. hegemony. It follows that this patterning of relational networks is likely to unravel with the decline of U.S. hegemony and the growing ascendancy of Japanese capital. In short, the current preoccupation with the rise of a Pacific Century is the result of a short-sighted focus on a particular configuration of relational dependencies, divorced from the larger context of the evolution of capitalism as an historical social system.

Once we abandon the cartographic bias inherent in the notion that the Pacific is a self-evident entity, we can begin to explore the processes by which "the greatest blank on the map became a nexus of global commercial and strategic relations" (Spate, 1979: xi). As Oskar Spate has insisted, the ocean was constituted as an entity on the world map as a result of the global expansion of capitalism, which involved the reorganization, naming, and symbolic appropriation of vast spaces. While atomistic societies on the islands, "lost over its blue expanse like a handful of confetti floating on a lake," certainly interacted with each other long before the intrusion of European interlopers into these waters and while the inhabitants on the Pacific's continental shores undertook impressive maritime expeditions, these circulatory networks and the peoples' consciousness of them were not pan-Pacific but littoral or thalassic in nature (Cumberland, 1956: 5; Spate, 1979: 2). The lineaments of the ocean were charted, after all, not by indigenous peoples but by Europeans and their transplants in the Americas. To insists that the Pacific was a Euro-American invention is not to assert that its construction was determined solely by outsiders. The characteristics of the indigenous inhabitants and their resistance to external domination, as well as the activities of migrants from its continental coasts, were equally crucial determinants (Spate, 1988: 211; Dirlik,

Natas

1991: 5-17). None of this activity was, however, unique to the Pacific. Africa, the Americas, Asia, and Australia all share similar, though differently nuanced, histories.

The incorporation of Asia and the Pacific into the capitalist world-economy implied neither their constitution as distinct entities that were integrated through trade, capital flows, and labor migrations to form a consolidated nexus of relational networks, nor the construction of densely interwoven circuits of exchange linking the Pacific perimeters of Asia (with the exception of the Philippines) to the Pacific seaboard of the Americas. Far from producing greater linkages within and between newly subordinated zones, incorporation denotes a restructuring of production processes and political relations within these zones, such that they become integral parts of the axial divisioning of labor and the interstate system of an expanding world-economy. It does not necessarily entail the spatial integration of circulatory networks within incorporated areas. On the contrary, the installation of core-periphery relations—leading to the elimination of local manufactures, the growth of export-cropping, and the increasing coercion of labor—more often than not has led to a disarticulation of preexisting relational networks within incorporated territories.

From this perspective, an examination of relational networks along the Pacific coasts of Asia prior to the outbreak of the Second World War reveals two distinct patterns of core-periphery relations. The transformation of locations along the southeastern coasts of Asia into monocultural export economies and their firm integration within increasingly rigid imperial trading structures denoted the initiation of a nexus of circuits of exchange that linked peripheral producers in these territories to core capital in Europe (Dixon, 1991: 86-121). This was also largely the case along the coastal regions of China, where Great Britain (including British capital based in Hong Kong) remained the largest foreign investor, dominated the all-important cotton textile sector, and controlled the most important trade links until the Japanese occupation of Manchuria in 1931 (Feuerwerker, 1983: 118-19, 125-27). Despite formal similarities between these relational networks and the set of core-periphery relations linking the northeastern coasts of the continent and Taiwan to Japan, there were substantive differences between the two matrices. Instead of extracting raw materials from the colonies for manufacture in the metropole, the Japanese set up industries and built the necessary infrastructure in their colonies (Cumings, 1987: 53-55).

This patterning of relational dependencies was decisively fractured after the Second World War. The geopolitical context of the Cold War and the dismemberment of the Japanese colonial empire led to an unraveling of the earlier patterning of core-periphery relations that had linked locations in East and Northeast Asia to Japan. At the same time, U.S. plans to reconstruct these economies under its tutelage as a bulwark against communism were predicated on the revival of a demilitarized Japan as a second-rank economic power (Cumings, 1987; McMichael, 1987). Shorn of its colonial empire, however, Japan could act as a surrogate for the hegemonic power (the United States) only if assured access to both raw materials in East and Southeast Asia and to high-income markets in North America. With the PRC, North Korea, and North Vietnam remaining outside the U.S. sphere of influence, these requirements entailed severing relational networks that had hitherto tied production processes in Southeast Asia to core locations in Europe and installing a new set of networks oriented toward Japan. To achieve these ends, as Bunker and O'Hearn have demonstrated, the United States required European metropolitan powers to dismantle the controls over investments and resources in their colonies in return for reconstruction assistance. The relaxation of colonial controls over raw materials in resource-rich colonies and in newly independent states was also welcomed by nationalist leaders eager for large infusions of foreign investment.

It is this spatial reorientation of preexisting core-periphery relations along new axes within a geographical arena that denotes the emergence and consolidation of a distinct region within a unitary world-economy. Rather than being a mere cartographical nomenclature or a designation based on a number of characteristics common to a particular area of the globe, 'region' in our usage refers to "the development of a specific matrix of core-periphery relations within a previously subordinate area of the world-economy" that is marked by multiple political jurisdictions (Martin, 1986: 117). It is important to recognize that the constitution of regions within the world-economy does not entail a withdrawal of these regions from wider supraregional relational networks.

Indeed, the consolidation of U.S. hegemony in the world-system was central to the reformation of core-periphery relations along new axes not only on the Pacific shores of Asia but also in southern Africa (Martin, 1986) and, for very different reasons, in Eastern Europe (including the erstwhile Soviet Union, see Wallerstein, 1991a, 1991b: 90). The significance of the political and military aspects of U.S. hegemony in the formation of regions is obvious even in northeast Asia where Japanese capital had created a nexus of core-periphery relations akin to the imperial trading blocs of the European colonial powers by the 1930s. While Taiwan's independence was guaranteed by the U.S. military presence in the Pacific, South Korea's existence as a distinct jurisdictional entity would have been eradicated in the summer of 1950 but for the intervention of U.S.-led United Nations forces. The Korean War not only preserved the postwar partition of Korea, but also provided a powerful stimulus to the Japanese economy. Moreover, that conflict offered the excuse for excluding labor and the left from effective political participation in Taiwan, Korea, and Japan.

The postwar settlement under U.S. tutelage also conferred relative autonomy on the state machineries of those three states. U.S.-sponsored land reforms eliminated the resistance of major landholders to the subordination of agriculture to industry. Together with the availability of ample cheap wage goods through the PL 480 scheme, high levels of economic and (in the cases of South Korea and Taiwan) military aid from the United States and the relaxation of colonial controls over raw materials, this change facilitated the formation of a regional subunit of the world-economy along the Pacific perimeters of Asia. While the adoption of ISI policies by most newly independent states implied that relational linkages within the region remained tenuous till the mid-1960s, access to raw materials from Southeast Asia fostered labor-intensive industrial production in Japan for sale in North American markets.

Despite the importance of the political and military aspects of U.S. hegemony, it was the mode of integrating the world market under U.S. leadership that was central to creating regional formations in select geographical arenas. Whereas the former hegemonic power, the United Kingdom, had integrated the world-economy through a policy of free trade, the United States achieved a far greater degree of integration through the promotion of a free enterprise system—the freedom to invest across state boundaries (Arrighi, 1990a). The U.S. policy of promoting direct investment rather than free trade as the preferred means to consolidate the world-economy under its leadership enabled core capital to bolster its competitive position "not by expanding the scale of production in their original locations, but by developing a complex *organizational* network of productive and service activities *across* national boundaries" (Arrighi, 1982: 76, emphasis in the original).

This transnational expansion of capital provided the institutional and organizational scaffolding on which distinct regions could arise in select geographical arenas. The virtual elimination of colonial trading blocs meant that U.S. (and subsequently European and Japanese) MNCs could greatly diversify their sources of raw materials and thereby further undermine preexisting core-periphery relations. At the same time, the MNCs were freed from earlier restrictions on expanding their operational networks to exploit wage and cost differentials between and among different segments of the global markets for labor and commodities. In some cases, relocation of manufacturing operations could guarantee them privileged access to actually or potentially lucrative markets.

The wartime destruction of industrial plants and physical infrastructures in Europe and Japan had ensured that the transnational expansion of capital would be confined largely to U.S.-based MNCs in the short term. By the mid-1960s, however, the reconstruction of the economies of Western Europe and Japan began to erode the competitive advantage of U.S.-based MNCs, while rising labor costs in the most dynamic sectors of advanced capital precipitated a corresponding fall in the global rate of profit. Pressures on core capital were intensified further by attempts by peripheral states to nationalize extractive industries within their jurisdictions and by the emergence of several peripheral and semiperipheral states as exporters of agricultural products. Core capital responded to these tendencies by rapidly escalating its investments in manufacturing operations in low- and middle-income states in a bid to secure reliable supplies of raw materials and to counteract rising wages in their home bases. This spectacular increase in direct foreign investment (DFI) from the core to the low- and middle-income states from the mid- to late seventies was facilitated by two other factors.

Constraints imposed by narrow domestic markets on the pursuit of ISI strategies in many peripheral and semiperipheral states paralleled the intensification of competitive pressures in the core. At the same time, moderate nationalist leaders of peripheral states had realized that their earlier enthusiasm for foreign investments in extractive industries was misplaced, since these had not delivered the expected benefits. In addition, the creation of a supranational money market through the hoarding of the profits of MNCs in specially denominated bank accounts (Eurodollars) and their use in short-term speculation led to a prodigious increase in the liquidity of major financial institutions in the core. This encouraged both a rapid increase in DFI and a flow of cheap credit to the low- and middle-income states.

These global conditions of accumulation and the distinctive attributes of Japanese capital proved conducive to an increase in the density and interconnectedness of relational linkages within the Pacific-Asian region between the late sixties and the late seventies. Labor shortages and rising wages in Japan, as well as an appreciation of the yen, steadily undermined the competitive advantage of the Japanese economy in labor-intensive, light industrial production while their growing dependency on exports made Japanese manufacturers increasingly vulnerable to protectionism. The coincidence of these developments with the adoption of outward-looking, export-oriented industrialization (EOI) strategies by several low- and middle-income states in the late sixties favored a transfer of labor-intensive segments of Japanese light industries to other locations in East and Southeast Asia. What was peculiar about the transnational expansion of Japanese capital was that it was undertaken by small- and medium-scale firms, rather than by large, vertically integrated MNCs, as was the case in the contemporaneous expansion of U.S. and European capital (Ozawa, 1979: 25–30). More specifically, the expansion of Japanese capital was primarily an extension of its multilayered subcontracting networks to the Pacific perimeters of Asia (excluding the PRC, North Korea, and Indo-China) in order to exploit and reproduce wage differentials between different segments of domestic and world labor forces. Further, since this transnational expansion of Japanese subcontracting networks typically took the form of joint venture projects, it did not involve foreign majority ownership in production facilities and was therefore more politically palatable to the host countries.

This pattern of transnational expansion can be attributed to the relative weakness of Japanese capital. In contrast to the large MNCs that dominated the geographical expansion of U.S. capital, the small- and medium-scale industries that spearheaded the transborder expansion of Japanese capital did not have the financial resources and technical competence to operate fully owned subsidiaries overseas. Moreover, unlike the large U.S.-based multinationals, the comparative advantage of Japanese capital stemmed from labor-intensive, light industrial production rather than from innovation, product differentiation, and technological sophistication. This fact implied that the technological differences between Japanese investing firms and their overseas partners were relatively small (Ozawa, 1979: 58–69). Finally, while U.S. mineral processors were especially vulnerable to peripheral nationalism (because of their large investments), Japanese firms were well positioned to take advantage of the shift in bargaining power away from the MNCs toward resource-rich low- and middle-income states. As Bunker and O'Hearn have argued, Japanese capital sought access to reliable supplies of raw materials by encouraging a number of peripheral states in Asia and Latin America to expand their mineral-producing capacities through joint ventures. Participation in joint ventures, however, increased the exposure of host governments to risk and debt while reducing their capacity to regulate foreign investors. In short, although the relative weakness of Japanese capital prevented Japanese investors from insisting on majority control over overseas projects, it had become apparent by the early seventies that joint venture projects with minority ownership better served their needs in any case.

By the mid-1970s, growing concern over the social and environmental costs of an industrialization drive based on heavy and chemical industries triggered a further outward expansion of Japanese capital. Signaling a shift toward "clean" and "knowledge-intensive" industries within Japan, this involved a transfer of "pollution-prone" and "resource-consuming" industries primarily to South Korea and less significantly to Taiwan (Ozawa, 1979: 18–19, 85–90). At the same time, in response to rising wages and to accommodate these new industries, South Korean and Taiwan-based capital began to extend their own subcontracting networks to Hong Kong, the Philippines, Indonesia, Malaysia, and Thailand through a transfer of labor-intensive manufacturing operations.

This massive extension of multilateral subcontracting networks has been responsible for the high rates of industrialization registered by several states within the region. There was, however, nothing exceptional about these levels of industrialization. The unprecedented increase in global liquidity by the early seventies through the creation of a large, supranational money market and the consequent availability of cheap credit spurred a wave of industrialization in several low- and middle-income states—most notably in Argentina, Brazil, and Mexico in the Americas, in Poland and other centrally planned economies in Eastern Europe, and in Iran and some other oil-exporting states.

The exceptional nature of industrial growth along the Pacific perimeters of Asia became evident only during a further phase of regional consolidation. In the late seventies, the adoption of high interest rates by the Federal Reserve to resolve the rapidly escalating national debt in the United States led to a sharp reduction in American and European DFI to low- and middle-income states. This sudden and drastic decline and the concurrent elimination of cheap credit in the early eighties has had extremely deleterious consequences for almost all the low- and middle-income states. The ability of states in the Pacific-Asian region, with the exception of the Philippines, to register high rates of growth in the midst of this general collapse of peripheral and semiperipheral states was rooted in the unabated extension of subcontracting networks based in Japan, South Korea, Taiwan, and Hong Kong. In contrast to the earlier wave of transnational expansion of Japanese capital, which primarily involved the transfer of light industrial production, Japanese investments in the eighties increasingly involved more technologically sophisticated capital goods (e.g., industrial machinery and electronics components) and high-income consumer products (e.g., automobiles). This shift in patterns of investment—first by Japanese capital and later by capital based in South Korea, Taiwan, and Hong Kong—was a response to the increasing demands for intermediate industrial goods in the NICs, the enforcement of local content requirements by several states, and as a means to circumvent restrictions on imports from Japan and the Four Dragons to markets in Europe and North America (Ozawa, 1985). It was this ability of states along Asia's Pacific perimeters to withstand the general collapse of low- and middle-income states that spawned the burgeoning literature on the "miracle" economies of the "Pacific Rim."

In short, the emergence of a distinct region of the world-economy along the Pacific perimeters of Asia was initially based on U.S. attempts to resurrect the Japanese economy by ensuring access to markets and raw materials for its light industries. The subsequent consolidation of the region served to link peripheral producers in East and Southeast Asia to consumers in the core through the mediation of corporations in Japan, South Korea, and Taiwan. This pattern of core-periphery relations was achieved primarily through a spatial expansion of hierarchically linked Japanese subcontracting networks to East and Southeast Asia and, less significantly, by a similar expansion of networks originating in Hong Kong, South Korea, and Taiwan. It is this transfer of low value-added manufacturing operations to Malaysia, Indonesia, Thailand, and more recently, to Shenzhen and other 'special economic zones' in the PRC that has led to the rapid industrialization of these territories in the seventies and eighties.

By thus focusing on the changing temporal and spatial patterning of relational networks, a world-systems perspective enables us to chart the historical structuring of a Pacific-Asian region within a unitary world-economy. This reconceptualization of the region, while indicating the contextual determinants of developmental strategies, does not address the issue of whether these strategies have enabled these states to negate the polarizing tendencies of core-periphery relations, as alleged in much of the literature on the "miracle" economies of East and Southeast Asia.

INDUSTRIALIZATION IN A WORLD-HISTORICAL CONTEXT

The factory and the machine have symbolized economic progress ever since the "Industrial Revolution" transformed England into the "workshop of the world." The imagery of growth associated with these symbols has been so pervasive that, despite their differences, both modernization and dependency theorists agree that the economic performance of states and territories ought to be assessed by gauging the spread of industrial activities within their boundaries—by indicators such as industrial production as a percentage of their gross domestic product (GDP), the percentage of their working population employed in manufacturing operations, the ratio of manufactured goods to their total exports, and so forth. Similarly, the unquestioned acceptance of ordinal rankings of states and territories by these criteria and their classifications as "industrial market economies" or "newly industrializing countries" by scholars of widely differing ideological persuasions has reinforced the premise that industrialization is synonymous with "development."

There are, however, reasons to be skeptical of the ubiquitous acceptance of the axiomatic equation of industrialization with development in the late twentieth century. While a certain mix of activities (e.g., highly mechanized manufacturing operations, the export of industrial products embodying high-wage labor, and the import of primary products embodying low-wage labor) may have allowed particular states to seize an unequal share of the benefits accruing from the global divisioning of labor at any given time, the installation of identical production processes in other states does not necessarily imply that they too will be able to reap similar competitive advantages. On the contrary, as illustrated by the case of the textile and steel industries, the spatial diffusion of "leading sectors" has inevitably led to their peripheralization, since it intensified competitive pressures. This phenomenon indicates that the gains that originally accrued from the installation of these production operations have grown correspondingly smaller over time.

Methodologically, an *a priori* identification of industrialization with economic progress does not take into account significant technological differences between manufacturing processes that are deemed similar. For instance, the installation of production complexes associated with the manufacture of steel, automobiles, and heavy machinery has often been taken as an index of upward mobility in the axial divisioning of labor. Thus, after inspecting the installation of such production operations in states like the PRC and India, scholars have charted the ascent of these countries to the middle range of states in the global divisioning of labor. Such procedures do not allow for the enormous technological chasm between, for example, automobile production in India and Japan: The first is technologically obsolescent, while the other is the world leader.

Further, in the context of the concurrent deindustrialization of the core, continued adherence to a virtual identification of "development" with industrialization is analogous to maintaining that the industrialization of low- and middle-income states has narrowed the differentials in wealth, power, and welfare separating them from the core (Arrighi 1990b: 11–12). There is, however, no indication that the recent industrialization of low- and middle-income states has corroborated this assumption. On the contrary, the data presented by Arrighi, Ikeda, and Irwan suggest that despite the achievement of high rates of growth, the income gap separating most of these states (excluding the Four Dragons) from the core has continued to widen in the 40 years between 1948 and 1988.

These observations pose several questions regarding the nature of industrialization in the late twentieth century. First, is industrialization still tantamount to upward mobility in the axial divisioning of labor, as implied in much of the literature on economic development? Second, what are the distinctive attributes of industrialization in low- and middle-income states during the current restructuring of the capitalist world-economy? Finally, how have these processes affected political movements and state structures in these states? Since a detailed analysis of the issues raised by these questions is far beyond the scope of an introductory chapter, I will attempt to outline briefly how these questions can be addressed from a world-systems perspective.

The major impetus towards the rapid industrialization of low- and middle-income states in the Pacific-Asia region, as we saw in the previous section, stemmed from a search by core capital for low-wage labor and was accomplished primarily through a transborder expansion of subcontracting networks originating in Japan. In conditions of global economic contraction, an intensification of competitive pressures tends to have a disproportionate impact on "leading sectors," since their greater profitability attracts an increasing number of firms. Consequently, in order to retain their competitive advantages, enterprises in these industries have usually sought to relocate their production facilities to areas where wages are significantly lower than in their original sites. Thus, in itself, the relocation of industries from the core to semiperipheral (or from semiperipheral to peripheral) zones is not uncommon (Wallerstein, 1982: 17–18).

What is peculiar about the process of rapid industrialization experienced by most low- and middle-income states in the Pacific-Asia region since the late sixties is the global context in which it occurred. In particular, the implementation of a series of innovations over the last two to three decades—the automation, computerization, and robotization of production, the lowering of freight costs through containerization, and the development of satellite communication systems—has facilitated an increasing fragmentation of production processes. This tendency has, in turn, greatly enhanced the propensity towards the progressive geographical decentralization of industrial activities—particularly labor-intensive, low-skilled, and pollution-prone operations—to low- and middle-income states. The consequent replacement of the pattern of "national segmentation" of production by a pattern of "transnational integration," as Gereffi argues in chapter 4, has not been accompanied by a corresponding redistribution of global income. On the contrary, the greater globalization of production networks has been marked by the increasing concentration of capital in the core (Harvey, 1990: 152–60; Sassen, 1991: 19–63).

Under these conditions, the geographical dispersal of industrial production has derived from a search by core capital for low-wage labor, while the benefits accruing to the host countries have been much fewer than in the past. Though the "international vagabondage" of capital, as Folker Fröbel (1982: 548) has nicely put it, may have led to an increase in *real* incomes for some groups of the inhabitants of these states (most notably for the middle-level managerial and technical strata), in most cases a rise in *cash* income has not meant an increase in *real* income. On the contrary, through selective labor-recruitment policies (e.g., the employment of young women), capital has sought to hire part-time proletarians and thereby shift the costs of the reproduction of labor to households and to the "subsistence" sector. Further, the enactment of special labor laws—often a condition for DFI—has removed many impediments to a more optimal accumulation of capital. Thus, governments in low- and middle-income states, competing fiercely to attract foreign investments (following the collapse of their ISI strategies), have enacted legislation to extend the working day by permitting extensive shift working, placed severe restrictions on labor organizations, refrained from regulating health and safety conditions, and removed barriers to the repatriation of profits and investments. Moreover, the increasing use of subcontracting arrangements has enabled MNCs and their primary subcontractors to stabilize wage costs for periods of up to ten years by fixing piece-work rates. Finally, the growing fragmentation of production processes has meant that industrialization has generally not led to a transfer of advanced technology to the low- and middle-income states in the region.

In this context, the exceptional ability of the East and Southeast Asian NICs to withstand the general collapse of most low- and middle-income states is related not only to the expansion of Japanese subcontracting networks but also to the relative autonomy enjoyed by their state apparatuses in the post-World War II era and to the geopolitical strategies employed by the United States to contain the spread of Soviet and Chinese influence in the region. These geopolitical conditions, particularly the enormous infusion of U.S. aid to Taiwan and South Korea and their privileged access to high-income markets in North America, enabled those states to resist the polarizing tendencies of core-periphery relations in the post-World War II era. Since their export of commodities that embodied low-wage labor in exchange for commodities that embodied high-wage labor from the core was competitive in the sixties and early seventies, they were able to increase their share of the benefits flowing from the global division of labor relative to the core over time (Arrighi, 1990b: 13–14). As more and more low- and middle-income states sought to replicate the achievements of the Four Dragons by attempting to industrialize on the basis of low-wage labor, however, the terms continued to worsen for all, especially since the increasing fragmentation of production processes has led to an unprecedented expansion of alternative sites for investment (Fröbel, 1982: 540). Briefly put, whatever benefits the process may have conferred on industrializing states in the nineteenth and early twentieth centuries, industrialization cannot be taken as an indicator of upward mobility in the global divisioning of labor in the late twentieth century.

Consequently, instead of identifying "stages of development" with comparative rates of industrialization or other arbitrary measures, world-systems analysts view core-periphery relations as a continually varying combination of diverse productive activities. Taking our cue from Marx and Joseph Schumpeter, we perceive innovations in production processes to be the motor force that generates and sustains competitive pressures in a system of capitalist production. Rather than defining any particular production process or set of processes as inherently core-like or peripheral-like activities, this conception of capitalism as an evolutionary system argues that core-periphery relations are the systematic outcomes of the continuous struggle to appropriate disproportionate benefits from the global divisioning of labor.

Though the dispersal of industrial activities to low- and middle-income states has not shifted the distribution of the spoils from the axial divisioning of labor in their favor, the "new international division of labor" has had profound implications for political struggles within their borders. The rapid industrialization and deepening integration of these states within global production networks have enhanced the social power of their industrial proletariats to a level matched only by "that previously enjoyed by the proletariat of the core but in a national context of relative deprivation long forgotten (if ever experienced) in core states" (Arrighi, 1990b: 26). Manifestations of this social power of labor include the extensive bouts of labor unrest and civil strife experienced by most low- and middle-income states in the eighties and nineties, as well as the revival of religion-based oppositional movements, regional and ethnic conflicts, and movements for greater democracy and human rights.

The common thread that unites these movements by ethnic and religious groups, the working class, and the urban poor is the attempt by core and local elites to shift the human and social costs imposed by developmentalist ideologies and practices onto the shoulders of these groups (see also Walton, 1987). Instead of being directed against élites in the core, however, these movements have typically taken aim at the most visible agents of oppression—state élites, privileged ethnic and religious groups, and domestic bourgeoisies. In this context, it is ironic that élites in the core have often supported democracy and human rights movements, not out of concern for the underprivileged masses, as Schaeffer has pointed out in chapter 10, but to endow peripheral and semiperipheral governments with greater legitimacy in order to impose the austerity measures necessary for core capital to recover its loans.

Squeezed by the core and pressured from below, state and business elites in the low- and middle-income states are confronted with an increasingly untenable position. These tendencies are felt particularly acutely in those states where the process of rapid industrialization has exhausted the supplies of unwaged labor. Implementation of the type of austerity measures prescribed by the World Bank and the International Monetary Fund will only aggravate domestic tensions, while raising wages will hasten a flight of capital in search of reservoirs of unwaged labor still untapped in "peasant Asia" and Africa or in the vast pools of trained laborers freshly available in Eastern Europe and in the former Soviet Union for exploitation by the MNCs. While an examination of the implications of these tendencies falls beyond the scope of this introductory chapter, the concluding section will briefly examine the short-term prospects for the further consolidation of the Pacific-Asian region within the context of the ongoing restructuring of the capitalist world-economy.

FUTURE PROSPECTS

As we have seen, the construction of core-periphery relations between Japan and Southeast Asia was fundamental to the emergence of a distinct region centered along the Pacific perimeters of Asia. The expansion of the Japanese (and subsequently, the South Korean and Taiwanese) multilayered subcontracting systems to other locations in East and Southeast Asia was predicated on the fact that these locations enjoyed as privileged an access to U.S. markets as Japan did. In this context, it was advantageous for Japanese small- and medium-scale enterprises to transfer low value-added operations in the sixties and early seventies, when high wages and the rising value of the yen made Japanese light manufactures increasingly uncompetitive.

These conditions no longer obtain for several reasons. First, the increasing expansion of manufacturing operations in the Four Dragons, as well as in Malaysia, Thailand, and Indonesia, has led to a steady rise in wages in these states. Paralleling this rise in wages, vast pools of low-wage labor in Vietnam, Laos, Cambodia, China, India, and elsewhere are increasingly being made available to the MNCs. As the limitations of autarkic ISI strategies become apparent, this phenomenon could imply a shift in investments in favor of the latter group of states. Second, the spectacular growth of Japanese capital over the last two decades has meant that the agents of Japanese DFI are no longer the small and medium enterprises, but large MNCs that are able to organize production operations anywhere on the planet. Whereas the earlier waves of Japanese transnational expansion were produced by the need to counteract labor shortages and rising wages at home, the growing financial resources of large Japanese MNCs, especially in the context of a global shortage of liquidity, have shifted the bargaining power away from potential host governments in favor of the MNCs. Third, the growing protectionist sentiment in the United States and especially the impending formation of a North American Free Trade Association (NAFTA) no longer guarantees privileged access for East and Southeast Asian states to U.S. and Canadian markets. In this context, it may be more advantageous for Japanese MNCs to exploit low-wage producers in Mexico and the Caribbean—or, through the emergence of ''telecommuting'' and the revival of sweatshops and home working, in the United States itself—than to continue their manufacturing operations in East and Southeast Asia.

Under these circumstances, it is not implausible to expect that the density and interconnectedness of relational linkages along the Pacific perimeters of Asia may unravel in the future as new matrices of core-periphery relations develop, reflecting the maturity of Japanese capital and the changed geopolitical realities of the times. While it is impossible to predict the specific spatial orientation of these relations, several trends—the growing protectionist sentiment in North America and the European Community, the new possibilities for investment in Eastern Europe presented by the end of the Cold War, the availability of vast reserves of low-wage laborers in ''peasant Asia'' and elsewhere, and the comparatively high levels of wages in many East and Southeast Asian states—suggest that the Pacific-Asian region is likely to disintegrate. The coincidence of this process with the disintegration of other regional formations in southern Africa and Eastern Europe implies that the construction of regions within a unitary world-economy was a characteristic feature of the era of U.S. hegemony, rather than a distinctive attribute of the capitalist world-economy.

As far as individual states within the Pacific-Asian region are concerned, we may plausibly expect that the reorientation of Japanese investment will lead to a deepening peripheralization of Indonesia, Malaysia, the Philippines, and Thailand. Rising wages in the manufacturing sector, combined with the withdrawal of privileged conditions of entry to the high-income markets of North America and Europe, support this inference. The impending return of Hong Kong to Chinese sovereignty and the political integration of Taiwan with the PRC (envisioned by So and Hsiao) will obliterate these states as jurisdictional entities. In any case, given the demographic mass of the PRC, their absorption will scarcely change the location of a unitary Chinese state within the axial divisioning of labor. The comparative weakness of state and domestic capital in Singapore, evident since the failure of its "Second Industrial Revolution" in the mid-1980s (Bello & Rosenfeld, 1990a: 297–300), combined with its relatively high level of wages spell equally dismal prospects for the tiny city-state. South Korea, the largest of the Dragons, with its large, diversified business corporations (the *chaebol*) would seem to have the most promising prospects. Even in this case, however, there are several reasons for skepticism. The increased militancy of labor and the growing assertiveness of the middle class—two groups that have long been excluded from political participation—have steadily undermined the legitimacy of the ruling elites. At the same time, since a major reason for the upward mobility of South Korea has been the strategic shop-floor focus of its firms, which enabled them to make incremental improvements in product quality (Amsden, 1989), the increasing peripheralization of industrial production is rendering this strategy progressively obsolete. While the *chaebol* may have the resources to counteract these tendencies towards peripheralization aggressively through innovation, it ought to be remembered, as noted by Arrighi, Ikeda, and Irwan, that the contemporary South Korean economy is roughly comparable to the Japanese economy in 1938. It remains to be seen whether, in the post-Fordist era, this largest of the Dragons will be able to replicate the Japanese success. For now, suffice it to say that depictions of South Korea as "Asia's Next Giant" are premature.

Paradoxically, the increasing peripheralization of Pacific-Asian states may result in improving the welfare of the mass of inhabitants of the region, who have long been excluded from the benefits of economic growth, through a "democratization of poverty." The increasing social power of labor and support for human rights and democracy movements by core states and world financial institutions (see World Bank, 1991: 128–47) have eroded the legitimacy of authoritarian ruling elites to such an extent that a redistribution of income and political power in favor of the vast majority of the inhabitants of the region is a real possibility.

NOTE

I gratefully acknowledge the helpful comments of Giovanni Arrighi, Hagen Koo, Mimi Sharma, Bob Stauffer, and Faruk Tabak on earlier *avatars* of this chapter.

2

THE POLITICAL ECONOMY OF THE PACIFIC RIM

Bruce Cumings

> The bourgeoisie, by the rapid improvement of all instruments of production,
> by the immensely facilitated means of communication, draws all, even the
> most barbarian, nations into civilization. The cheap prices of its commodities
> are the heavy artillery with which it batters down all Chinese walls.
>
> *The Communist Manifesto*

> Capitalism always runs ahead of the critique.
>
> Jean Baudrillard

My original title for this paper was "The Pacific Rim in the twenty-first century,"
but as I thought about the literature clustered around that theme, I decided that
I did not want to contribute to it—except perhaps in facetious prognosis. In any
case, Murray Sayle has done the latter better: Here's what he said about "the
Pacific Rim in the twenty-first century":

Britain and Ireland could respectively be Japan's Hong Kong and Macao, well placed for
the European entrepôt trade, the United States will be Japan's fabulously wealthy India,
terre des merveilles, while Australia can be Japan's Australia, land of rugged adventure
and heavy drinking, the appropriate place of exile for Japanese dissidents and remittance
men. This would leave only table scraps for the others: Holland, perhaps, for the Indonesians,
France for the Vietnamese. (Sayle, 1989)

How to explain the currency of the term "Pacific Rim"? The first answer is, simply,
currency. In the late 1970s, a hue and cry suddenly arose about the dawning era
of the Pacific, especially up and down the West Coast of the United States among
academics trying to find some way to interest donors in funding Asian or international
studies. "Pacific Rim" was a discourse searching out its incipient material base,
targeted toward exporters with Asian markets or importers of Asian products.

The Henry Jackson School of International Studies at the University of Washington (where I taught for several years) is a good example. Founded in 1978 (although not named for Senator Jackson until 1983) and funded by Boeing, Weyerhauser, and other corporations, it is based in a Seattle that was otherwise sleepwalking into the Pacific century. So is the newer School of International Relations and Pacific Studies at the University of California, San Diego, but by now we have many other academic centers of "Rim Studies."

"Pacific Rim" is not an academic subject so much as it is a field for academics working in the present and looking toward the future and for transnational technocrats and policymakers. According to the director of the San Diego School, Peter Gourevitch, Pacific Rim inquiry is important for the "two communities who have a need to know: the community of social scientists . . . and the community of policymakers (Gourevitch, 1989: 9). That is an apt summary of one meaning of "Rim Studies": our academic pundits' and government policymakers' need to know (but to know *what?*).

This kind of Rimspeak is a recent phenomenon. "Pacific Rim" was a construct of the mid-1970s that revalued East and Southeast Asia, as Westerners (mostly Americans) had recognized and defined it, in ways that highlighted some parts and excluded (or occluded) others. The centerpiece in the region was Japan, a newly risen sun among advanced industrial countries—indeed, "Number One," according to Ezra Vogel's perfectly timed book, *Japan as Number One: Lessons for America* (1979). Organized into the region were "miracle" economies in Japan, South Korea, Taiwan, Hong Kong, Malaysia, and Singapore, with honorable mentions for Thailand, the Philippines, Indonesia, and post-Mao (but pre-Tiananmen) China. The miracles were "NICs" (newly industrializing countries), and various books proliferated about the Asian miracles (Johnson, 1982; Gold, 1986; Gereffi & Wyman, 1990).[1]

"Miracle" is one trope that is always found in the Rimster's repertoire. Another is "dynamism," as in Gourevitch's "dynamism of East Asian-North American relations," or Staffan Linder's "Asia-Pacific Dynamism" (Gourevitch, 1989; Linder, 1986). The miracles of the Rim, of course, have no truck with Joseph Schumpeter's notion that capitalism's dynamic is through waves of creation and destruction: It is all on the up and up, a whoosh of progress transforming the region.

Rimspeak is a curious discourse with a half-life of months or years, depending on the source. To believers situated in the dynamic present and facing a yet more dynamic future, all things seem possible—until something like the Tiananmen bloodletting demolishes the incorrigible optimism of this genre and sends a handful of recent books to the instant oblivion of secondhand stores, where they fetch 50 cents. Rimspeak peers into the future, but it also clouds one's perspective on the present. Consider this statement that leads off a new book entitled *Pacific Rising* (admittedly one of the more interesting and thoughtful texts in the genre):

Rarely indeed is one fortunate in being able to live through times in which a major shift in the world's history can be seen to be taking place. . . . One such event . . . came about when the fifty-odd countries now grouped around the Pacific Ocean seemed to take the torch of leadership from those hitherto grouped around the Atlantic. (Winchester, 1991: xiii)[2]

A torch passed from Atlantic to Pacific, but into whose hands? Fifty countries, including the Sultanate of Brunei? Those of the Four (or is it Five) Tigers? A Japan that went catatonic at the mere hint that it might do something significant about Iraq's invasion of Kuwait? And when exactly was that torch passed? (The answer is, of course, that the flame still burns brightly along the Atlantic rim.)

In the subterranean text of all this palaver about "dynamism," Saint-Simon meets the theory of the Asiatic mode production, as in: "I thought that they were vegetating in the teeth of time over there in Asia. But suddenly they make better cars than we do: Behold, a miracle has occurred." Tropes of dynamism and miracles also say this: Capitalist universalism is the only thing I can see; thus I discover the Pacific Rim.

The latter point is not facetious, but precise: The people of the Pacific Rim did not know that they inhabited a bustling new sector of the world-system until they were told, just as our "Indians" did not know that they were in America (or "West India") until Columbus told them so. "Rim" is an American construct, an invention just like the steam engine, incorporating the region's peoples "into a new inventory of the world" (Dirlik, 1991: 14). "Pacific" is a Euro-American name in itself, measuring, delineating, and recognizing living space for the people who live there (see Dirlik, 1991). That these are Western social constructions does not mean that the natives think them unimportant or have self-confident definitions themselves. For example, former Chinese premier Zhao Ziyang invited certified twenty-first-century Rimster Alvin Toffler to lecture at the Academy of Sciences in 1983, to audiences who "listened to him as if he were an oracle" (Mendelsohn, 1988, quoted in Woodside, 1991).[3]

In the second tier of the Rim, we find candidates for inclusion: pre-NICs, near-NICs, would-be NICs, miracles-in-the-making if they "do the right thing." Bit of a basket case, the Philippines; not sure if they know their comparative advantages. Digging itself out of decades of irrationality China was, but with enlightened leadership under Deng Xiaoping (after his resurrection and his reforms in 1978), the new China might make it. In 1991, the newest of the NICs was Thailand, "doing the right thing" by exporting cheaply made goods (and by allowing an ocean of Japanese capital to slosh around since the mid-1980s). Defined out in the 1970s were North Korea, Mao's China, and Indochina—especially Vietnam, which had just won its 30-years' war, only to find itself in the pale of "the Rim." "OINKS," they were sometimes called: old industrialized kountries. Certain Latin American countries are sometimes included in the Pacific Rim, usually by Latin Americanists: post-Allende Chile, *maquiladora* Mexico, even Atlantic Rim Brazil, but only in its pre-debt-crisis phase of miracle growth.

In other words, the phrase "Pacific Rim" painted the entire region in different colors than it had been since 1945. "Paint it Red," the pundits said until 1975.

"Paint it black" inspired post-1975 artistry. Hollywood followed suit, with a number of films in the late 1970s and 1980s seeking "to put Vietnam behind us." This was Francis Ford Coppola's stated goal for *Apocalypse Now*; another film that parodied America's "Vietnam syndrome," Stanley Kubrick's *Full Metal Jacket*, ends with The Rolling Stones singing "Paint it Black." "Pacific Rim" heralded a forgetting, a hoped-for amnesia, in which the decades-long but ultimately failed American effort to obliterate the Vietnamese revolution would at last enter the realm of Korea, "the forgotten war."

When East Asia was "painted Red," it held an apparent outward-moving dynamic whose core was Beijing: "400 million Chinese armed with nuclear weapons," in Dean Rusk's 1960s scenario, threatened nations along China's rim with oblivion: South Korea, South Vietnam, Taiwan, Indonesia, Thailand, and, the big enchilada, Japan. Another secretary of state, Dean Acheson, had drawn a "defense perimeter" through island Asia in 1950. China and North Korea were among the most rapidly growing industrial economies in the world in the 1950s and early 1960s, "success stories" to be contrasted sadly with basket-case South Korea (as Agency for International Development people always called it up through the mid-1960s), running sore Indonesia (with its formidable internal communist "threat" until 1965), incompetent South Vietnam, mendicant Philippines, and Lucian Pye's hopelessly obtuse and retarded Burma.

"Pacific Rim" revalued all that. Suddenly the Rim had became the locus of dynamism, bringing pressure on the mainland of Asia. The "basket cases" were now any countries still foolish enough to remain committed to self-reliant or socialist development (from Burma to North Korea), while the "success stories" were any countries that sought export-led capitalist development. The new discourse was deeply solicitous of the benighted and laggard socialist economies, however, and therefore sought a formal end of ideology: "Pacific Rim" invoked a newborn "community" that anyone, socialist or not, could join . . . as long as they were capitalist. Rimspeak, of course, continued to talk with curiosity, if not disdain, about anyone who did not privilege the market (but only *sotto voce*).

With hindsight, we see that the decade from 1961 to 1971 was the critical turning point toward Rimspeak. In 1961, Soviet Chairman Nikita Khrushchev fashioned a voluntarist, programatic, ideological vision that anticipated the overcoming of capitalism on a world scale within a few decades. At about the same time, Mao's "East is Red" theme placed socialist Asia in the van, and the Great Leap Forward sought to overtake England within fifteen years. At Bucharest in 1961, however, the socialist camp openly split. Mao's private writings laid the cause of the failure of world socialism at Khrushchev's feet: The Soviet leader's revisionism consisted of replacing two world-systems within a single planet with one world-system, which the Soviets wished to join (symbolized by his talks with Eisenhower at Camp David in 1959) and through which they would exploit other socialist-bloc nations in an international division of labor. State capitalism in Moscow prefigured Russia in the capitalist world-system, according to Mao (see Cumings, 1979).

W. W. Rostow joined the John F. Kennedy administration in 1961, bringing his "noncommunist manifesto" of capitalist growth by stages, a view deeply influenced by technological determinism. One of his first projects was to get South Korea and Taiwan moving toward export-led policies and to reintegrate them with the booming Japanese economy. Facing America's first trade deficits, the Kennedy administration sought to move away from the expensive and draining security programs of the Eisenhower years and toward regional pump-priming that would bring an end to the bulk grant aid of the 1950s and make allies like Korea and Taiwan more self-sufficient. The economism of the Kennedy years inaugurated the phase of export-led development, but this approach was short-circuited by the Vietnam War. Richard Nixon later revived these ideas through his Guam Doctrine and opened relations with mainland "Red" China; policies that were in place by 1971 thus completed the Kennedy agenda. "Pacific Rim" was now ready to happen, as Nixon hinted in an influential 1967 article:

The United States is a Pacific power . . . Europe has been withdrawing the remnants of empire, but the U.S., with its coast reaching in an arc from Mexico to the Bering Straits, is one anchor of a vast Pacific community. Both our interests and our ideals propel us westward cross the Pacific, not as conquerors but as partners. (Nixon, 1967: 112)

The many working-class and antisystemic movements of the region in earlier decades suddenly became poxes, irrationalities that illustrated immature "political development" in the Rim. Standing above all else was the nearly instantaneous revaluation of China. The very real slaughters of Mao's failed Cultural Revolution—many directed against the intellectual class—became for American intellectuals the signifier to rename and parenthesize the entire history of the Chinese Revolution and also occasioned a vast rewriting of scholarship on the China field. But the same thing has happened throughout the Rim: For example, when South Korean students protested the pipe-beating murder of an activist by police in the spring of 1991, many American editorials greeted this news with exclamations of sheer amazement that students or workers should be "radical" in a world where—as all agreed—the role model was democratic and market-driven America, led by George Bush and Dan Quayle. The logic seems to be this: Stalinism has palpably failed, therefore why should we have daycare centers?

"Pacific Rim" has a class-based definition of Asia. The "community" is a capitalist archipelago, based on indigenous labor power and purchasing power—although, until recently, mainly labor power. It has thus been the "workshop of the world," using cheap and efficient labor to manufacture exports for other regions that have consumer buying power; the vast American market has been and is its mainstay. The archipelago runs through but also divides the Pacific and Asian region.

Capitalist classes, obviously, are organized into the archipelago. Dense, developed, highly differentiated urban nodes are in; the two most important are Tokyo and Los Angeles, but city-state nodes, like Hong Kong and Singapore, are also critical. Peasant Asia (Vietnam, Kampuchea, much of India, Indonesia, and China) is out. China's old treaty ports and new Special Export Zones like Shenzhen are in; vast reaches of interior China are out. South Korea is in, North Korea is out (unless Kim Il Sung "does the right thing"). In other words, the majority of the populations in Asia are either out or participate only as unskilled or semi-skilled laborers.

This class-based archipelago is also a hierarchy, not just the core urban nodes, the peripheral peasantries, and the intermediate zone of strivers ("NICs" and "OINKS"), but also a virtual pyramid of power according to the C. Wright Mills' model (in *The Power Elite*, 1956): at the top, a transnational power elite, intertwined in various networks and educated at top-rated American or British universities; then an echelon of urban middle and working classes; and, finally, a vast mass at the bottom. The level to which terms like democracy and pluralism refer encompasses at best a decile or two of the stratification but legitimates the whole. In *The German Ideology*, Marx said that the bourgeoisie views the world as if in a *camera-obscura*, that is, upside-down; a narrow echelon claims its particular view to be universal and thus paints the whole in its hue (Marx & Engels, 1970).

This hierarchy reproduces itself throughout the region. Los Angeles is the perfect example: first, in its current polyglot Hispanic, black, and Asian masses, its putatively universal Yuppie lifestyle, and its world-class elite drawn from financial, industrial, and mass culture industries; second, in its sanitized history, which paints black a homegrown Asiatic mode of production and paints white an élite liberalism.

That is, Los Angeles was created through hydraulic engineering, which brought water to the arid coast and the city to the water, and through vast suburbanization by Anglo-Saxon despots who corruptly utilized their privileged public position to make vast private fortunes in real estate; this history was collapsed but not violated in the film *Chinatown* (see Davis, 1990). The interior history of Los Angeles capitalism up into the 1940s was one of a "private sector" distant from the central state that took upon itself innumerable works of irrigation, transportation, port-building (infrastructure and "social overhead"), and the like. These projects placed Los Angeles at the opposite pole from the "state-dominant" capitalism of Japan and energized a free-market myth that deeply influenced (among other things) Ronald Reagan and his furious deregulation in the 1980s.

In the film *Chinatown*, John Huston plays Noah Cross, a man who owned the city water system and then gave it up to "public" control by nepotistically inserting his son-in-law as head of Water and Power; here is Oriental despotism in our own backyard. The film ends with the knowing detective being led away from a scene of incestuous murder by his friend: "Forget it, Jake, it's Chinatown." This might be the perfect metaphor for the history of Anglo-Saxons in the Pacific Rim.

MANIFEST DENSITY: "PACIFIC RIM" AS ANGLO-SAXON LAKE

Roland Barthes (1982) used Japan as a system of difference to develop a radical critique of the West and its assumptions, instead of as a mirror to reflect to the

West what is good and true here and is sadly lacking there. Barthes developed a means that offers a parallax view or a salutary boomerang with which to question ourselves. As he said, Japan afforded him "a situation of writing . . . in which a certain disturbance of the person occurs, a subversion of earlier readings, a shock of meaning" (Barthes, 1982: 4). Further, "Someday we must write the history of our own obscurity [or provincialism]—manifest the density of our narcissism" (Barthes, 1982: 4).

Friedrich Nietzsche used the term "emergence" (*entstehung*) to mean "the principle and the singular law of an apparition." Emergence does not mean "the final term of a historical development"; "culminations" are "merely the current episodes in a series of subjugations." "Emergence is thus the entry of forces; it is their eruption, *the leap from the wings to the center stage* . . . emergence designates a place of confrontation" (Nietzsche, 1969: 15–23; emphasis added). An event (or an emergence) is not a decision, a treaty, or a war, but "the reversal of a relationship of forces, the usurpation of power, the appropriation of a vocabulary turned against those who had once used it." Hence, his conclusion: "the body [or history, or the descent, or the present] is molded by a great many distinct regimes" (Nietzsche, 1969: 77–78).

The insights of Barthes and Nietzsche helps us to ask the question, "where do tropes come from?" Whence come the dynamics and miracles of far-off Asia? They also help us to understand our own density and a history in which "Pacific Rim" and "Japan" seem to emerge suddenly and mysteriously, not just in the 1970s but at several points throughout the past 150 years. Both authors underline a central point in my argument: We have had "emergence," but we have not had "the reversal of a relationship of forces." The torch has not been passed. Throughout the Pacific industrial era—save for six years or so, from 1939 to 1945—Japan has been junior to Anglo-American hegemony. But we know what happened during these years, . . . and it does not go under the title of "Pacific Rim Community."

"Pacific Rim" was there from the beginning, soon after Commodore Matthew Perry's "Black Ships" arrived in a Tokugawa port. A famous secretary of state, William Seward, found in world history a movement of empire, making its way "constantly westward, and . . . it must continue to move on westward, until the tides of the renewed and the decaying civilizations of the world meet on the shores of the Pacific Ocean" (Drinnon, 1980: 271).

The high-tech conveyance of that era was the steamship, which was so much less expensive than the ongoing building of continental railroads that it rendered the Pacific a vast plane that traders could skate across toward the putative China market. These longings brought American ships to Hawaii, where more Noah Crosses subdued the natives and gave the islands over to pineapple and sugar production, and to Manila Bay in 1898, which was seen as the first important colonial way station to the treasures of the "Rim" itself.

Somehow, then as today, Japan was thought to be separate from the rest of the Rim—the honorary Westerner, the pearl of the Orient, the good pupil (or, as

Acheson called it in the 1940s, "the West's obstreperous offspring"). As another observer noted, "They are Asiatics, it is true, and therefore deficient in that principle of development which is the leading characteristic of those ingenious and persevering European races . . . but amidst Asiatics the Japanese stand supreme" (Lehman, 1978: 46).

The steamships skated toward Asian markets, but also toward a presumed earthly paradise possessing occult knowledge unavailable to the rational Westerner. That the second theme persists today is evident in the pages of *The Economist*; a recent article on "The Pacific Idea" is subtitled "There is a Better World." The Pacific idea, the article alerts us, "is important for the mental well-being of the world" because it stands for a "belief in the survival of innocence." The accompanying map centers the globe on various tropical islands in the middle and south of the Pacific (described in the article as "a village pond for the Seventh Fleet"), unwittingly placing Bikini at the epicenter—an island that the United States made uninhabitable with H-bomb tests in the 1950s. The British did the Americans one better, destroying an island called Christmas by the same means. The French still test nuclear weapons in the region, and the United States uses Johnston Island for the destruction of chemical weapons. Meanwhile, *The Economist* writes wistfully of Paul Gauguin's women, Herman Melville's *lory-lory*, and Marlon Brando's Tahiti, and then deposits the burden of Rim-exclusion on the natives themselves: "the places that people call Eden and Paradise can really become so, if only the Pacific islanders will heave themselves to their feet" [translation: get dynamic] (*The Economist*, March 16, 1991).

The Pacific Rim in the nineteenth century was a realm of formal empire for the European powers. In response, the United States enunciated the "Open Door" policy in 1900 to deal with other empires and made its effective, if informal, alliance with England in search of an Anglo-Saxon condominium. Japan was the Anglo-Saxon junior partner, in formal alliance with England from 1902 onward and also in informal alliance with Teddy Roosevelt's America.

Japan was also a junior partner in a hierarchical, product-cycle driven regime of technology (the productivist aspect of American and British hegemony). Viewed temporally, Japan has been a "late" industrializer, as South Korea and other NICs have been "late-late" (to use Albert Hirschman's term for mid-twentieth century industrialization), benefiting from the adaptation of core technologies. Japan has maximized its economic power in the one region not claimed by other imperial powers (except for Tsarist Russia)—Taiwan, Korea, and Manchuria—creating a closely linked, regional political economy that has promoted and skewed the development of East Asia ever since (Cumings, 1987: 44–83).

During Japan's first wave of industrialization in the 1880s, there were fish canneries in Hokkaido, the pioneer Kashima Cotton Mill, the huge Kobe Paper Factory, the first cigarette company, tanning and leather firms, the Osaka Watch Company, the Tokyo Electric Company with its own brand of light bulbs, even tasty Kirin Beer—and every last one was based on American technological start-ups or American expertise. We find that Japan's favorite economist in the 1880s was an American, Henry Carey. Marx thought Carey was the only original American economist, and inveighed against "English economics" (see his wonderful essay "Bastiat and Carey" in *The Grundrisse*, 1973: 883–93). Actually, Carey was a protectionist who learned much from Friedrich List, whose theories were also favored in Japan.

General Electric was dominant in the delivery of electricity, and, by the 1890s, Standard Oil had placed both Japan and China well within the world oil regime, which was increasingly dominated by American firms. Standard's comparative advantage was financial and technical, but it also resided in its innovative marketing schemes, based on monopoly on a world scale and creative ways to sell "oil for the lamps of China."[4] The joint British-American condominium is perhaps best symbolized by the British-American Tobacco Company, a subsidiary of Duke tobacco interests in North Carolina, which got Japan and China hooked on something else, a cigarette habit so deep that nonsmoking sections can hardly be found anywhere in either country today.[5]

Japanese textile firms, the leading sector in Japan's first phase of industrialization, for decades bought their machines from the famous Pratt Brothers of England. Around 1930, these firms came up with their own "high-tech" equipment and quickly became the most efficient textile producers in the world. They also became England's primary *bête-noire* of industrial dumping, market stealing, and general miscreance. A few years later, Japan's obsolescent machines were stoking Korea's first textile conglomerate, courtesy of "technology transfer" (Eckert, 1991).

During the halcyon days of the Anglo-Japanese alliance, however, Japan was a model of industrial efficiency for an England in incipient decline. As Phillip Lyttleton Gell said in 1904, "I shall turn Japanese, for they at least can think, and be reticent! [Witness] their organization, their strategy, their virile qualities, their devotion and self-control. Above all, their national capacity for self-reliance, self-sacrifice, and their silence!" (Holmes & Ion, 1980: 309). A Fabian put it this way in 1907: "Witness the magnificent spectacle of Japan today; the State above the individual; common good above personal good; sacrifice of self and devotion to the community" (Holmes & Ion, 1980: 321). By the 1930s, matters had descended from that sublime point, however, as British business publications vented their rage at "The wily Jap [who is] determined to stop at nothing in his efforts to bamboozle shoppers in this country [and is] STEALING OUR MARKETS!" [sic] (Asahi, 1939: 207).

JAPAN AS NUMBER TWO

What about today—is Japan the core power of the Pacific Rim? I don't know what the future will hold, but today the answer is not yet. However close Japan may be to hegemonic emergence, in "concrete reality" for this entire century, it has been a subordinate part of either bilateral American hegemony or trilateral American-British hegemony. Here is our metaphor for 1900–1991: *Japan as Number Two*.

An archaeology of Japan in the twentieth-century world-system unearths the following timelines:

(A) 1900–1922: Japan in British-American hegemony

(B) 1922–1939: Japan in American-British hegemony

(C) 1939–1945: Japan hegemonic in East Asia

(D) 1945–1970: Japan in American hegemony

(E) 1970–1990: Japan in American-European hegemony

Three of the periods (A, B, and E) are trilateral, and none are colonial or necessarily imperial. A bilateral regime is predictable in the temporary phase of comprehensive hegemony (1945–1970 for the United States), while a trilateral regime is likely in the rising and falling phases of transitional hegemonies.

Shortly after World War I ended, in 1922 to be overly exact, America came to be the major partner in the trilateral hegemony. This was the period when American banks became dominant in the world-economy (Schreiber, 1969; Parrini, 1969). In general, the Anglo-Japanese alliance had become tattered and the United States became more important than England in Japanese diplomacy. The Washington Conference was the occasion for this transfer of the baton, a "locking in," with the critical element of global military reach—the American Navy.[6]

Japan adapted to these trends with a very low-posture diplomacy throughout the 1920s. Meanwhile, it girded its loins at home for trade competition, inaugurating tendencies in its political economy that remain prominent today. Here was an early version of NIC-style "export-led development." Both Chalmers Johnson and William Miles Fletcher have dated Japan's national industrial strategy and "administrative guidance" to the 1920s, and both the Americans and the British were most receptive to Japan's outward-turning political economy (Johnson, 1982; Fletcher, 1989). Only between 1931 and 1945, and during the 1980s and 1990s has this strategy been perceived as a problem for the United States.

The Japanese Export Association Law of 1925 was an important turning point, stimulating industrial reorganization, cartels, and various state subsidies to exporters. Japan was careful to direct these exports to the noncolonial semiperiphery and not to the core markets of America and England.[7] The 1920s also inaugurated a period of import-substitution industrialization (Fletcher, 1989: 28) that went hand-in-hand with the exporting program, even though the policy became more pronounced in the 1930s when Japan accomplished its heavy-industrial spurt and its virtuoso mastery of the industrial product cycle.

From 1910 to 1931, Japan's "old" empire in Northeast Asia was the empire that the United States and England *wanted it to have*. Even when Manchuria was colonized in 1931, England and the United States chose to do little about it, save a lot of rhetoric about the "open door." The reason they did little was that Japan preserved a modified open door in Manchuria until 1941 and encouraged American and British investment—of which there was much more than is generally thought.

In the postwar period, from 1947 to the present, American planners have urged a modified restoration of Japan's position in Northeast Asia.

Acheson and George Kennan masterminded this repositioning of Japan in the world-system by deciding in 1947 to position Japan as an engine of the world-economy, an American-defined "economic animal," shorn of its prewar military and political clout. Meanwhile, the United States kept Japan in a defense dependency and shaped the flow of essential resources to it, in order to exercise a diffuse leverage over all its policies and to retain an outer-limit veto on Japan's global orientation. This strategy was articulated precisely at the time of the formal onset of the Cold War, in the spring of 1947. The postwar American empire has not rested upon territorial exclusivity like the old European colonial systems. It has been an "open-door" empire, policed by a far-flung naval and military basing system and by penetration of allied defense organizations (e.g., the prohibition on the use of military force in the Japanese constitution, the American command of the West German and Korean militaries; see Luckham, 1990: 2).

Japan would also need an economic region "to its south," in Kennan's words, and Acheson came up with an elegant "Rim" metaphor to capture this restoration: A "great crescent" from Tokyo to Alexandria linked Japan with island Asia, around Singapore, and through the Indian Ocean to the oil of the Persian Gulf. It was this "crescent" that lay behind Acheson's famed "defense perimeter" speech in January 1950 (Cumings, 1990). This definition was hammered out at the same time as the emergence of the Cold War, and it deepened as Japan benefited from America's wars to lock in an Asian hinterland in Korea and Vietnam.

Here we intuit a truth that Rimspeak would rather forget: The "Pacific Rim community" has been a region fashioned in warfare. America was "at war with Asia" from 1941 to 1975, to use Noam Chomsky's term. If Americans see Pearl Harbor in terms of original sin, Hiroshima and Nagasaki connote a cataclysmic rendering of "Japan as Number Two." The Korean War drew the Northeast Asian boundaries of Pacific capitalism until the 1980s, while functioning as "Japan's Marshall Plan" (Johnson's term); war procurements propelled Japan along its world-beating industrial path. In South Korea, too, original sin came on a Sunday morning, when Kim Il Sung's forces invaded, seeking to overturn a Korean original sin—the U.S. decision to divide Korea, carried out by Rusk at the request of John J. McCloy, in August 1945. Original sin was harder to determine in Vietnam: Ho Chi Minh resembled neither Tojo nor Kim. For some Americans, it was apparent in the Tonkin Gulf incident; for the Vietnamese, perhaps it was Acheson's decision to link Indochina to the revival of Japanese industry, bringing the United States in on the side of French imperialism (see Rotter, 1986).

In this era, which ran from the administrations of Harry S. Truman through that of Lyndon B. Johnson, Japan was a dutiful American partner, and the partner was tickled pink at Japan's economic success. As the American capacity to manage the global system unilaterally declined in the 1960s, however, a new duality afflicted the United States-Japan relationship: Japan should do well, yes . . . but not so well that it hurt American interests. Nixon was again the agent of change, with his neo-mercantilist "New Economic Policy," announced on V-J Day in 1971. American thinking about Japan remains firmly within that duality today, symbolized by the inability of elites to do more than oscillate between free trade and protectionism, between admiration for Japan's success and alarm at its new prowess.

In short, Japan has been thriving within the hegemonic net for 90 years, but it nonetheless "emerged" in the Western mind—leapt from the wings to the center stage—at three critical and incommensurable points: at the turn of the century, when it was a British *wunderkind* (but a "yellow peril" to the Germans); in the world depression of the 1930s, when it was an industrial monster to the British (but a *wunderkind* to the Germans and Italians); and in the 1980s, when it was a *wunderkind* to American internationalists and a monster to American protectionists. The Four Tigers, the Three or Four Cubs, and all the others tread the same path: Do well, please, but not so well that you threaten us (because at that point the tropes all reverse, and you move from miracle to menace, from market-driven dynamo to crypto-fascist upstart).[8] The main point is that there has been no fundamental reversal of relationships. No torches have been passed, and none are likely to be for "the near term."

THE NEAR TERM: TRILATERAL FUTURES

As I said earlier, I am not good at prognosis: I find it hard enough to predict the past. In the near term of the next couple of decades, however, I would hazard the guess that the world-system will have three nodal, central points, symbolized by New York, Tokyo, and Berlin, and a core point of hegemony, headquartered in Washington. New York will have a tendency to connect with Europe, Los Angeles with East Asia, and Washington will seek to manage a trilateral condominium. In other words, we are not on the eve of a regionalization of the world-economy, but still in a period of prolonged North-North cooperation propelled by a historic "peace interest," to use Karl Polanyi's term, on the part of high finance and the modal capitalist organization of our era, the transnational corporation (Cumings, 1991).[9]

The Pacific Rim is neither a self-contained region nor a community, but just that: a rim—peripheral and semiperipheral societies oriented toward both Tokyo and the American market. Consumer purchasing power there is still lower than in Western Europe or the United States, and labor cost advantage still orients the region toward assembly and finishing work using Japanese or American technology. It is still a region under dual economic hegemony, held by a unilateral American security network. No common culture unites the region: Japanese do not interact culturally with Koreans, Koreans have little noneconomic intercourse with the Filipinos, Indonesians do not mingle with Thais.

Instead the lineaments of "culture" run through Los Angeles and New York; Hollywood and the global center of television purvey American mass culture throughout the region. South Korea has three networks, of which one is the Armed

Forces Korea Network, broadcasting in English. The other two run dubbed versions of *Dallas* and *Miami Vice*, as well as Korean shows on similar themes. Most Americans have never seen a single Korean movie. Japanese films play in American art houses, if at all, while American films play throughout the region. The unrelenting seductions of Hollywood's vision of a universal bourgeois lifestyle are apparent in the ultimate failure of two scions of the antisystem to resist it: Mao's wife, Jiang Qing, watched *Gone With the Wind* in the Forbidden City, and Kim Il Sung's heir-apparent son, Kim Jong Il, reportedly has a personal library of 10,000 films, most of them American. Travelers even to remote Nepal report that street urchins tug at their sleeves, yelling "Michael Jackson, Michael Jackson." Japanese investors' recognition of the epicenter of late twentieth-century culture has led, of course, to their purchase of Columbia Pictures and MCA.

Since the mid-1960s, it is true, Japan has deepened its regional influence in Asia, with much higher levels of direct investment in Northeast and Southeast Asia. Its direct investment in the region has grown sixfold since 1985. Its trade with Taiwan tripled in the same period, and its manufactured imports from the Asian region as a whole more than doubled from 1985 to 1988 (contrary to pundits who argue that its economy is basically closed). Japanese investors have been especially active in Thailand; on average, one new Japanese factory opened every working day in 1989 (*Far Eastern Economic Review*, July 3 and August 20, 1990). The Pacific region, inclusive of Northeast Asia, the Association of South East Asian Nations (ASEAN), and Australia, will have a gross national product (GNP) of $7.2 trillion by the year 2000, according to current projections, which will be bigger than that of the European Community (EC); the number of effective consumers will be about 330 million, as large as the EC's, but not as affluent (*Far Eastern Economic Review*, August 7, 1990).

Japan has also been assiduous in breaking barriers to trade with the Asian socialist countries. It is North Korea's biggest capitalist trading partner (which does not say much) and may normalize relations with P'yongyang soon. It went back into China much more quickly than other investors in the wake of the Tiananmen bloodletting in June 1989. As the Asian "Berlin walls" crumble, Japan will be poised to pursue a "German" option; that is, to intensify its market position in socialist China, Korea, and Vietnam as Germany had been doing in the old semiperiphery of Eastern Europe. Indeed, Japanese experts have been asked to come back and renovate industrial technology in Manchuria and even to revive big gold mines in North Korea that were formerly owned by Japanese and American firms.

All this regional activity is grist for the mill of those who find a developing tendency toward regional economic blocs, but this outcome is unlikely short of a major world depression. A trilateral regime of cooperation and free trade linking Europe with the Far East and the Americas is much more likely, with the great markets of each region underpinning and stabilizing inter-capitalist rivalry in the world-system and encouraging interdependence rather than go-it-alone strategies that would be deleterious to all. Japan's regional investment hedges against exclusion from the EC after 1992, but it has other hedges as well in the form of direct investment in manufacturing in Britain and Eastern Europe. The United States is pressuring its European allies strongly not to exclude Japan from the post-1992 arrangements, in favor of trilateral cooperation.

Japan is also constrained regionally, in that "actually existing socialism" persists, above all in "the East." There is no break as yet in Asian communism, with the predictable exception of Soviet-aligned Mongolia. China has thus announced that "the center of socialism has moved East." With the demise of the "people's democracies" in Europe, the *Wall Street Journal* predictably ran an article under the title "The Coming Collapse of North Korea" (*Wall Street Journal*, June 26, 1990). It is therefore strange that the most recalcitrant outpost of communism today is in North Korea, which seems almost a museum of 1950s and 1960s revolutionary socialism. Today it is the most interesting communist nation, because it is the last unadulterated redoubt of what all the others used to be. It is the last communist. Furthermore, for 40 years, it has been a state organized as an anti-Japanese entity, an apotheosis of the resistance to Japanese penetration that exists throughout the Asian rim.

The simplest answer for the seeming anomaly of persistent Asian communism in the "Pacific Rim community" is precisely the Chinese claim that "the center of socialism has moved East." It is just that they are off by a few decades: It moved there after World War II or perhaps in the 1930s, when formidable revolutionary nationalist movements emerged in China, Korea, and Vietnam. Today octogenarians in China and septuagenarians in North Korea and Vietnam are guardians of that deep-running, anti-imperialist tradition. In China, of course, "Marxism-Leninism-Mao Zedong Thought" remains little more today than a justification for one-party rule. The post-1978, Rim-joining economic reforms are ranged along a spectrum, from a young, urban, coastal crowd, which follows the capitalist road blazed by the "Four Tigers," through an old crowd, whose preferred Marxism is the Stalinist variety (central planning, heavy-industry-first), and to the still vast peasantry, for whom nobody but Mao had a policy—other than that they should disappear as a class by becoming workers and urbanites, or according to the latest slogan, "getting rich." (In 40 years of industrialization, perhaps half a billion of them have done none of the above.)

Centrist national security elites in the United States have frankly promoted a reviving trilateralism. Internationalists are sure that they know which direction the United States-Japan relationship should take: more intense collaboration, moving toward a joint condominium, in which Japan will continue to play second fiddle.[10] A similar trilateral logic also expressed itself at the dawn of German reunification in the fall of 1989, when Henry Kissinger and David Rockefeller both journeyed to Berlin and Tokyo in September; Kissinger was second only to U.S. Ambassador Vernon Walters in announcing his support for German unity. By not opposing what soon became a *fait accompli*, American leaders succeeded in keeping Germany within the postwar settlement, and "containment" continues apace: not of the old enemy, the former Soviet Union, but of the old ally, Germany, just as American bases still dot Japan in spite of the end of the Cold War.

How long this situation will last is anybody's guess, but it makes the enormous American commitment to the Persian Gulf in 1990–1991 something less than the "first post-Cold War crisis." American forces were in the Gulf to shape the flow of resources to Japan, Germany, and the other industrial economies, in order to maintain the "outer limit," hegemonic lines that were central parts of the postwar settlement. (Imagine the reverse—a German or Japanese airlift of 500,000 troops to Saudi Arabia!)

The ultimate logic of trilateralism for the near term resides in Japan's being for the United States today what the United States was for England in the 1920s: the emergent financial and technological center, but a long way from assuming hegemonic responsibilities. As the recent Gulf War demonstrated, Japan (and Germany) will be content to "let George do it" for some time, since they have no interest in taking on an expensive security role as long as the United States is willing to do so and in the absence of major security threats from the Soviet Union or any place else.

North-North cooperation, including the Soviet Union (or whatever Russia and its allied republics will come to call themselves), is thus the order of the day in what is perhaps the most bourgeois era in world history. It is the Third World in our midst, the other archipelago running from Los Angeles through Seoul and Manila to the hinterland masses of China and Indonesia, that will find no way out in the "Pacific Rim community," save hard work at low pay.

The Third World is now dominated by the advanced countries in a way unprecedented since the colonial era, with no convincing antisystemic model to follow. It is outside the loop of the prosperity of recent years and is therefore the prime source of war, instability, and class conflict. Here, of course, is the explanation for George Bush's overweaning desire to make sure that the Gulf crisis had no negotiated end: A Panopticon-like display of high-tech military power was needed to remind the Third World of its contemporary impotence.

CONCLUSION: THE SIGNIFICANCE OF THE RIM

Is there a way of constructing and understanding "Pacific Rim" other than that which I have given to you in this chapter? Is there an indigenous path toward reconstituting Western Rimspeak? The people of the Rim have tried two ways before: the imperial pan-Asianism of Japan in the late 1930s and early 1940s, which was never very successful in gaining non-Japanese adherents, and the communist pan-Asianism of the 1950s, when Mao's China deeply influenced Korea, Vietnam, and various socialist movements in Asia. This approach had a brief heyday after North Korea and China fought the United States and its allies to a standstill in Korea, with the high point at Bandung in 1954. This way is as dead as dead can be today, when China courts "the NICs" and, like Russia, tries to wash its hands of North Korea and Vietnam.

Perhaps capitalism Chinese-style will provide an alternative model. Southeast Asia is not Northeast Asia, but both are part of "the Rim." It was a historic trading area for another world-economy, the Chinese, and was the centerpiece of England's "Pacific Rim" empire. It has been shaped recently by a number of anticolonial independence movements (Vietnamese socialism, Indonesian nationalism, Malayan and Filipino guerrillas, Burmese autarky, etc.) that make it less open to American and Japanese ministrations than Northeast Asia has been. Today Southeast Asia has an alternative organization of capitalism, the longstanding interstitial commerce of "island China," the Chinese diaspora. Some pundits think that this might provide a different way of organizing Rim capitalism, with Hong Kong and Vancouver, British Columbia, being principal nodes, patrimonialism and family-based entrepreneurship serving as the means, and Chinese being the *lingua franca*. A reorganization of the region under Chinese auspices seems remote, however, until the mainland itself is so organized; in the meantime, Chinese commerce will continue to operate in the pores of the system.

We are left, I think, with but one grand event that is symbolized by "Pacific Rim," and that is the rise to power of Japan. It is the only true entrant to the ranks of the advanced industrial core in the past century, with the possible exception of the (now deindustrializing) Soviet Union. It is the only non-Western entrant. If today it does not wish to be and cannot be the lodestone for an autonomous non-Western reorganization of the region, one day it will be. When that happens, an old soldier and charter Pacific Rimster, General Douglas MacArthur, Japan's benign American emperor, will have been right. In an address in Seattle back in 1951, MacArthur opined that:

Our economic frontier now embraces the trade potentialities of Asia itself; for with the gradual rotation of the epicenter of world trade back to the Far East whence it started many centuries ago, the next thousand years will find the main problem the raising of the sub-normal standards of life of its more than a billion people.

It is a classic piece of Rimspeak.

NOTES

1. According to Gary Gereffi, he and his coeditor wanted the title of their book to be *Manufactured Miracles*, but the press changed it (to go along with the trope).

2. Sociologists will be happy to know, even if East Asianists will drop to their knees in mortification to find out, that in Simon Winchester's view (1991: 487), Max Weber offered "the most complete, if not the most readable, account of Confucius" (in his *Religion of China*). Weber famously sought the source of East Asia's failure to develop capitalism in the absence of the Protestant ethic or its equivalent; generations of graduate students learned this as an explanation for why the West was dynamic and the East was not. But at least his version *was* readable especially compared to the East Asianist texts.

3. Alexander Woodside has noted that there are no Chinese, Indonesian, or Vietnamese Alvin Tofflers.

4. By 1894, American kerosene exports to Japan had reached 887,000 barrels of 42 gallons each. Standard entered the production field in Japan with its International Oil

Company, between 1900 and 1906, (Williamson & Daum, 1959: 675, citing *Sōritsu shichiju-shūnen kinen Nihon sekiyu shi* [seventieth anniversary history of Japanese petroleum] (Tokyo, Nihon Sekiyu K.K., 1958).

5. James B. Duke formed BAT in 1902, in league with a chief rival, the Imperial Tobacco Company; Duke held two-thirds of the stock. By 1915, BAT had almost $17 million in investments in China and was one of its two largest employers (Hunt, 1983: 282–83).

6. Although Akira Iriye's analysis is different from mine, he has demonstrated more the failure than the success of the "Washington system" and has underlined the upper hand that the United States now had in East Asian diplomacy (Iriye, 1965).

7. Gō Seinosuke, formerly head of the huge Oji Paper Company and director of the Tokyo Stock Exchange for 12 years, drafted a report in 1929 recommending, among other things, "a new national committee . . . to rationalize industrial production in order to 'aid industrial development' "; "Gō endorsed the principle of export planning—selecting products that might sell well abroad and fostering their growth." The plan led to the Export Compensation Act of May 1930 and to other measures to aid export industries; the plan was to help exports to Central America, Africa, the Balkans "central Asia Minor," and the Soviet Union, and it later expanded to include "the whole world except for Europe, the U.S., India, and the Dutch East Indies" (Fletcher, 1989: 59, 61–62).

8. By the 1990s, pundits were already beginning to suggest that Japan and South Korea might represent a different, "third" kind of political economy—"what we used to call fascism," in Jane Wanniskie's (1989) words. Karel von Wolferen, in an important book (1989), has hinted at a similar perspective with his discussion of the mysterious "system" at the core of Japan's political economy.

9. For Karl Polanyi's explanation of *"haute finance"* and the 100 years' peace (1815-1914), see Polanyi (1944: 3–19).

10. See for example, Zbigniew Brzezinski (1988), who advocated a U.S.-Japanese condominium called "Amerippon."

PART II

CHANGING CONTOURS OF PRODUCTION NETWORKS

3

THE RISE OF EAST ASIA:
ONE MIRACLE OR MANY?

Giovanni Arrighi, Satoshi Ikeda, and Alex Irwan

THE STYLIZED FACTS OF THE EAST ASIAN
ECONOMIC MIRACLE

When we speak of an East Asian "economic miracle," we are referring, implicitly or explicitly, to two main facts. On the one hand, we refer to the rise of several new centers of capital accumulation in East Asia—centers that have come to enjoy a command over world resources comparable to that traditionally enjoyed by the wealthier states of the capitalist world-economy. On the other hand, we also refer to the fact that this phenomenon is unusual—in fact, "miraculous"—in light of the predominant tendency in other low- and middle-income locations of the world-economy to lose ground, rather than gain, relative to traditionally wealthy states.

In order to gauge the extent and nature of this economic miracle, we shall use a very simple indicator: the ratio expressed as a percentage, of the GNP per capita of a region or jurisdiction to the GNP per capita of what we shall call the "organic core" of the world-economy. This ratio measures the income gap that separates that region or jurisdiction from the organic core—an aggregate defined here as consisting of all the states that over the last half-century or so have occupied the top positions in the global hierarchy of wealth and, by virtue of that position, have set (individually or collectively) the standards of wealth to which all other states have aspired.

These core states belong to three distinct geographical regions. The most segmented of the three regions, culturally and jurisdictionally, is Western Europe, defined here to include the United Kingdom, the Scandinavian and the Benelux countries, the former West Germany, Austria, Switzerland, and France. The states lying on the western and southern outer rim of the region (that is, Ireland, Portugal, Spain, Italy, and Greece) have not been included in the organic core because, for most or all of the last 50 years, they have been "poor relations" of the wealthier Western European states—poor relations that did not contribute to the establishment of a global standard of wealth but were themselves struggling more or less successfully to catch up with the levels enjoyed by their neighbors. The other two regions included in the organic core are less segmented culturally and jurisdictionally. One is North America (the United States and Canada); the other, small in population but large in territory, consists of Australia and New Zealand.

The percentage ratio of the GNP per capita of a given location to the GNP per capita of the organic core, as defined above, provides us with a measure of what we shall call the "relative economic command" of that location; that is to say, the figure expresses the average command of the inhabitants of that location over the human and natural resources of the organic core relative to the average command of the inhabitants of the organic core over the marketed human and natural resources of that location. Thus, when we say that in 1938 the GNP per capita of Japan was about one-fifth (20.7 percent) of the GNP per capita of the organic core (see Table 3.1), all we are saying is that the average command of the inhabitants of Japan over the human and natural resources of the organic core was five times less than the average command of the inhabitants of the organic core over the human and natural resources of Japan.

We would like to underscore that we do not consider the ratio in question to be a reliable indicator of the welfare or productiveness of the inhabitants of the particular region or jurisdiction to which it refers relative to the welfare or productiveness of the inhabitants of the organic core. We do, however, consider it the best indicator available of the position of that region or jurisdiction in the hierarchy of wealth of the world-economy. Whether this position is associated commensurately with the welfare and productiveness of its inhabitants is a question that we shall leave open.

With this in mind, let us examine the indicators shown in Table 3.1. These percentages refer to all the East and Southeast Asian jurisdictions for which we have comparable data, as well as to Taiwan—for which strictly comparable data are not available—and to the South Asian region as a whole. In parentheses, the table also shows the population of each location as a percentage of the total population of the organic core. While the main indicator measures the relative economic command of a location and its changes over time, the indicator in parentheses measures the relative demographic mass to which the main indicator refers.

The table provides a vivid picture of the nature and extent of the East Asian economic miracle. Its most noteworthy features include the following. The East Asian miracle is first and foremost a Japanese miracle. Our main indicator shows both the extraordinary economic distance "traveled" by Japan and the extraordinary speed with which that distance has been traveled. With a GNP per capita of slightly over one-fifth (20.7 percent) of the GNP per capita of the organic core, Japan in 1938 was firmly grouped in the middle-income ("semiperipheral") group of states. In 1988, in contrast, the GNP per capita of Japan was almost 20 percent higher than the average GNP per capita of the organic core. This increase

Table 3.1
Comparative Economic Performance in Asia

	1938	1948	1960	1970	1980	1988
I. East Asia						
I.1. Japan	20.7 (20.3)	14.5 (23.1)	23.2 (22.8)	52.1 (22.6)	76.3 (23.5)	117.9 (23.4)
I.2. S. Korea	n.a.	n.a.	7.7 (6.0)	7.2 (7.0)	12.7 (7.7)	20.2 (8.0)
I.3. Taiwan	n.a.	n.a.	[5.7] (2.0)	[8.2] (2.3)	[19.5] (3.4)	[31.1] (3.7)
I.4. China	4.1 (129.4)	n.a.	n.a.	n.a.	2.5 (196.9)	1.8 (208.0)
I.5. Hong Kong	n.a.	n.a.	16.4 (.7)	22.0 (.9)	39.5 (1.0)	51.7 (1.1)
II. Southeast Asia						
II.1. Thailand	n.a.	8.2 (5.2)	4.7 (6.5)	4.8 (7.9)	6.0 (9.5)	5.6 (10.4)
II.2. Malaysia	n.a.	n.a.	13.4 (2.0)	9.6 (2.4)	14.1 (2.8)	10.9 (3.2)
II.3. Singapore	n.a.	n.a.	21.2 (.4)	24.7 (.4)	38.6 (.5)	50.9 (.5)
II.4. Indonesia	5.3 (19.5)	n.a.	4.7 (22.9)	2.1 (25.2)	4.1 (29.5)	2.7 (33.4)
II.5 Philippines	9.6 (4.5)	4.1 (5.6)	12.5 (6.6)	5.1 (8.0)	6.3 (9.7)	1.7 (11.4)
III. South Asia	8.2 (109.6)	7.5 (123.3)	3.6 (131.6)	2.8 (149.1)	2.0 (173.4)	1.8 (200.3)

1. GNP per capita of state or region divided by the GNP per capita of the organic core, times 100. In parentheses, population of state or region as a percentage of the total population of the organic core.

2. The GNPs per capita have been calculated from data provided in Woytinsky and Woytinsky (1953) for 1938 and 1948 and from the World Bank (1982, 1984, 1990) for the other years. The data for Taiwan are from Economic Planning Council (1977, 1982, 1988). They are put in parentheses because they are not strictly comparable with the other data.

3. South Asia consists of Bangladesh, India, Pakistan, and Sri Lanka.

is all the more impressive in that, between 1938 and 1948, Japan's GNP per capita fell from 20.7 percent to 14.5 percent of the GNP per capita of the organic core. Thus, in just 40 years, Japan has caught up with and surpassed the standard of wealth of regions whose GNP per capita was almost seven times higher than its own.

No other economic performance in East and Southeast Asia bears even a pale resemblance to the Japanese. South Korea is often said to be on its way to replicating the exploit of Japan. This may well be so but, apart from the fact that the demographic mass involved in the South Korean miracle is only one-third that of Japan, the data of Table 3.1 suggest caution. South Korea, unlike Japan, began gaining ground relative to the organic core only in the 1970s and 1980s. Moreover, its ascent, as it were, started from a much lower level of per capita income than did Japan's. As a result, South Korea's position relative to the organic core in 1988 was almost exactly what Japan's position had been 50 years earlier in 1938. However impressive from other points of view, it follows that South Korea's economic ascent still has a long way to go before it can be said to have replicated Japan's exploit.

By our main indicator, the economic performance that comes closest to that of the Japanese in East and Southeast Asia is not that of South Korea but those of Taiwan and the city-states of Hong Kong (still a colony of the United Kingdom but soon to be a port-city province of China) and Singapore. The gains of these locations relative to the organic core over the last 30 years are remarkable. Still, relative to Japan, they all lost ground in the 1960s, and only Taiwan regained the lost ground thereafter. What is more, even if we add up the populations of all three locations, they still amount to an insignificant demographic mass—3.1 percent in 1960 and 5.3 percent in 1988 of the population of the organic core, and to a much smaller percentage of the population of East and Southeast Asia.

At the same time, the vast majority of the population of East and Southeast Asia has experienced either no improvement at all or a worsening in its economic command relative to the organic core. Even though the numerous gaps in the availability of comparable data, as well as the ups and downs in the comparable data that is available, make the identification and comparison of trends difficult, it would seem that Malaysia, with a slightly rising trend, has performed best, while the Philippines, with a sharply declining trend, has performed worst; the performances of Thailand, Indonesia, and China fall (in that order) somewhere in between the two extremes. If we exclude the catastrophic Philippine performance, however, the next worst performance of the East and Southeast Asian regions (that of China) has been much better than the performance of the South Asian region as a whole. It follows that the vast majority of the population of East and Southeast Asia has lost economic ground relative to the organic core but not to the same extent as South Asia—a region, be it noted, that accounts for a demographic mass larger than that of the whole of Southeast Asia and almost as large as that of China.

The nature of the East Asian economic miracle can be further elucidated by comparing Table 3.1 with Table 3.2, which provides indicators for other low- and

Table 3.2
Comparative Economic Performance in Other Low- and Middle-Income Regions

	1938	1948	1960	1970	1980	1988
I. Southern Europe						
I.1. Italy	32.0	22.8	37.0	50.4	60.9	74.8
	(12.6)	(13.2)	(12.1)	(11.6)	(11.3)	(11.0)
I.2. Spain	41.6	18.4	18.6	28.9	48.0	43.4
	(4.8)	(8.0)	(7.4)	(7.3)	(7.5)	(7.5)
II. Latin America	19.5	14.4	16.7	15.5	19.8	10.6
	(31.1)	(38.3)	(45.7)	(53.7)	(63.8)	(72.9)
II.1. Brazil	12.0	11.3	12.1	12.7	17.5	12.1
	(11.4)	(14.1)	(17.6)	(20.7)	(23.8)	(27.6)
II.2. Other	23.8	16.2	19.6	17.3	21.1	9.7
	(19.7)	(24.2)	(28.1)	(33.0)	(40.0)	(45.3)
III. Middle East & **North Africa**	n.a.	n.a.	11.5	8.1	11.1	7.1
			(19.6)	(22.5)	(27.5)	(32.0)
III.1. "Turkey & Egypt"	14.9	13.0	12.8	7.7	8.1	5.6
	(9.8)	(10.9)	(12.9)	(14.8)	(17.5)	(19.9)
IV. Subsaharan **Africa**	n.a.	n.a.	5.1	5.1	n.a.	2.5
			(46.9)	(53.7)		(81.2)
IV.1 Western & Eastern	n.a.	n.a.	3.6	3.4	4.7	1.6
			(36.8)	(42.3)	(51.7)	(65.1)
IV.2 Southern & Central	25.2	18.3	10.5	11.3	n.a.	6.1
	(6.9)	(7.6)	(10.1)	(11.4)		(16.1)

1. Same indicators and same sources as in Table 3.1.

2. Aggregate II consists of Argentina, Bolivia, Brazil, Chile, Colombia, Dominican Republic, Ecuador, El Salvador, Jamaica, Mexico, Paraguay, Peru, and Venezuela. Aggregate III consists of Algeria, Egypt, Libya, Sudan, Syria, and Turkey. Aggregate IV.1 consists of Benin, Burundi, Cameroon, Chad, Ethiopia, Ivory Coast, Kenya, Madagascar, Malawi, Mali, Mauritania, Mozambique, Niger, Nigeria, Rwanda, Senegal, Somalia, Tanzania, and Upper Volta. Aggregate IV.2 consists of South Africa, Zaire, Zambia, and Zimbabwe.

middle-income regions and jurisdictions of the world-economy, computed in the same way and from the same sources as the indicators of Table 3.1. The comparison suggests, first of all, that the closest parallel to the Japanese exploit lies outside of East Asia. The Italian trajectory, like the Japanese, decreased sharply between 1938 and 1948 and then increased steadily up through the 1980s. To be sure, the Italian trajectory refers to a smaller demographic mass and is flatter than the Japanese: it started at a higher level (32 as against 20.7 percent) and ended at a lower level (74.8 as against 117.9 percent). These differences notwithstanding, no other jurisdiction within or without East Asia—except for territories of insignificant demographic weight—comes as close as Italy does to the Japanese pattern.

The comparison also suggests that there is no parallel outside of East Asia for the South Korean and Taiwanese narrowing of the income gap that separates poor and rich countries. Even the celebrated Brazilian miracle of the 1970s appears as a blip on an otherwise perfectly flat curve. The indicator for the oil-rich Middle East and North Africa shows major ups and downs analogous to (and synchronous with) those of Malaysia and Indonesia, including, as in Indonesia, a slightly downward trend.

Although none of the regions and jurisdictions listed in Table 3.2 performed as disastrously as South Asia or the Philippines, on average they did worse than East and Southeast Asia. Even China improved its position relative to Latin America (excluding Brazil), to the "Turkey and Egypt" aggregate, and to Southern and Central Africa. It follows that even laggards within East and Southeast Asia have been doing better than the norm in low- and middle-income regions of the world-economy.

In sum, the East Asian economic miracle is a highly concentrated phenomenon. It consists, primarily, of the Japanese "great leap forward" from an intermediate ("semiperipheral") position in the hierarchy of wealth in the world-economy to its top position. It consists, secondarily, of a lesser "leap forward"—lesser, that is, in terms of distance covered and demographic mass involved—of the so-called Gang of Four or Four Little Dragons. Finally, it consists of a better than average performance by all but one (the Philippines) of the East and Southeast Asian states for which we have comparable data. These states have all lost ground relative to the organic core (let alone to Japan and the Gang of Four), but less ground than has been lost by the low- and middle-income jurisdictions of other regions of the world economy.

The temporal profile of this highly specific economic miracle is as important as its spatial unevenness, especially for the purposes of this chapter. From this point of view, three main features of the East Asian economic miracle require comment.

First, the East Asian miracle began only in the 1960s, and, for at least a decade, it remained an exclusively Japanese phenomenon. Although our data show a major increase in the indicator for Japan as early as the period from 1948 to 1960 (from 14.5 to 23.2 percent in Table 3.1), this increase cannot be taken to be symptomatic of an East Asian economic miracle in the making. For one thing, in the 1950s Japan simply recouped the position in the hierarchy of wealth in the world-economy that it had occupied in 1938. Moreover, up to 1960, the Japanese performance was almost exactly the same as that of Italy. As a matter of fact, its performance was slightly worse, with its GNP per capita relative to the Italian GNP declining from 64.7 percent in 1938, to 63.6 percent in 1948 and to 62.7 percent in 1960. If there was an economic miracle in the 1950s, it was not an East Asian miracle but a former Axis Powers' miracle—the expansion, that is, through which (West)

Germany, Italy, and Japan moved in that period with massive help from the new hegemonic power (the United States), and which brought them back to where they had been in comparative economic terms before their defeat in the Second World War.

The Japanese economic miracle, as distinct from a former Axis Powers' miracle, thus began in the 1960s, when Japan's ascent toward the top position in the global hierarchy of wealth gained momentum and began to outperform the slower Italian ascent by an increasing margin—the Japanese GNP per capita rising from 62.7 percent of the Italian in 1960 to 103.4 percent in 1970, to 125.3 percent in 1980, and to 157.6 percent in 1988. At the same time, there is no sign as yet of a more general East Asian economic ascent. The lack of comparable data for the first two decades of the half-century under examination prevents us from assessing the significance of the increases in our indicator for Taiwan, Hong Kong, and Singapore between 1960 and 1970. Nevertheless, these increases appear small in comparison with those shown not just by Japan and Italy but also by a country like Spain, which in 1960 had a per capita GNP of the same order as Hong Kong and Singapore and a demographic mass more than twice that of Hong Kong, Taiwan, and Singapore taken together.

More importantly, between 1960 and 1970, South Korea—demographically the largest by far of the future Gang of Four—experienced a slight decline in its position relative to the organic core. Although South Korea was at this time beginning to lose its previous reputation among practitioners and theorists of economic development of being a "basket case," no one would then have bet a farthing on the chances that in a decade or two South Korea would be hailed as a model of development for all poor countries. It was only in the 1970s that a reversal in the fortunes of South Korea and a speed-up in the advance of the three smaller Dragons would create the bases of an East Asian economic miracle that was not confined strictly to Japan.

This brings us to the second main feature of the temporal profile of the East Asian economic miracle—the sudden "take-off" of the South Korean ascent in the 1970s and the equally sudden acceleration in the ascent of Taiwan, Hong Kong, and Singapore. Taking the Gang of Four as a unit, its GNP per capita as a percentage of the GNP per capita of the organic core—which had increased very slightly (from 8.5 to 9.3 percent) between 1960 and 1970—almost doubled (from 9.3 to 17.7 percent) between 1970 and 1980. Thanks to this increase, the Gang of Four as a group even recouped part of its losses relative to Japan as its GNP per capita as a percentage of the Japanese GNP per capita rose to 23.2 percent in 1980, after declining from 36.6 to 17.8 percent between 1960 and 1970.

In the course of the 1970s, therefore, the rise of East Asia was no longer an exclusively Japanese phenomenon. Right up to the beginning of the 1980s, however, the narrowing of the income gap between poor and wealthy countries did not appear as a specifically East Asian phenomenon, as it would after 1982. As can be seen from Tables 3.1 and 3.2, between 1970 and 1980 all the regions and jurisdictions for which we have comparable data (with the exception only of

South Asia) were gaining ground relative to the organic core. Although the speed with which the Gang of Four was gaining ground was the highest (and that of Japan was higher than most), the difference seemed to be one of quantity rather than quality, and in some instances not even that.

The most important of these other instances was Brazil, whose GNP per capita as a percentage of the GNP per capita of the organic core increased only slightly less than that of the Gang of Four as a group (from 12.7 to 17.5 percent) but whose ascent involved a much larger demographic mass (almost twice as large as that of the Gang of Four as a whole). It was this ascent, rather than that of East Asia, that became the focus of developmentalist discourse in the 1970s. By and large, the rise of East Asia was taken as an important but by no means exceptional instance of a general "catching up" process within which the Brazilian economic miracle outshone all others.

The third and, for now, latest moment of the East Asian economic miracle has come in the 1980s, when all but a handful of the numerous other instances of "catching up" of the 1970s collapsed. Apart from Italy, the only examples of "catching up" that withstood the test of the great contraction of the 1980s were all East Asian: Japan, South Korea, Taiwan, Hong Kong, and Singapore. From the perspective of the early 1990s, the East Asian economic miracle thus looks pretty much like a miracle by default. In the 1970s, "many were called." In the 1980s, however, "only few were chosen," and these few were mostly East Asian countries.

It should also be noticed that the general collapse of the 1980s did not spare the jurisdictions in which the vast majority of the East and Southeast Asian population is concentrated. The collapse was most dramatic in the Philippines but it was quite drastic in China, Indonesia, and Malaysia as well. Our figures suggest that in Thailand, the contraction was comparatively mild, but it was sufficient to put this country in a category different from that of the Gang of Four. If Thailand is indeed going to be the South Korea of the future, as some maintain, that future is still to begin.

For now, the East Asian economic miracle—understood as a narrowing or closing of the income gap that has separated the peoples of the region from the standards of wealth of the organic core of the world-economy—has been a phenomenon limited to jurisdictions that account for no more than 10 percent of the total population of East and Southeast Asia. For all other jurisdictions, the "miracle," if any, is that, over the last half-century, they have lost ground relative to those standards less drastically than has been the norm for other low- and middle-income regions of the world-economy.

JAPAN'S MULTILAYERED SUBCONTRACTING SYSTEM

In trying to explain the spatial and temporal pattern of the East Asian economic performance outlined in the previous section, we shall depart from established lines of inquiry. Most inquiries treat the East Asian economic performance as the sum of multiple and basically independent developments based on particular state policies and strategies (which may or may not be traced to the particular social structures and social histories of the individual states), or on particular patterns of industrial relations and practices—what some French regulationists, following Henri Jacot (1990), now call "Toyotism" vs. "Fordism"—or on a particular world-view (Confucianism) or on some combination of the above. These lines of inquiry do elucidate one aspect or another of the East Asian economic miracle, but, in our view, they all miss its most central aspect, namely, its structural and conjunctural unity and integrity.

Our analysis follows in the footsteps of Bruce Cumings (1987) who has argued, first, that the East Asian region was structured into a single unit early in the twentieth century by the practices of Japanese colonialism in Taiwan and Korea, and, second, that after World War II this unity has been reproduced under U.S. hegemony right up to the present (on the latter point, see also McMichael, 1987). Like Cumings, we think that it is misleading to assess developments in any of these countries by abstracting from the regional pattern: "such an approach misses, through a fallacy of disaggregation, the fundamental unity and integrity of the regional effort in this century" (Cumings, 1987: 46). But whereas Cumings' analysis has focused on the power relations and product cycles through which Japan established lasting structural links between its domestic economy and the economies of its colonies, our main concern is with the particular system of interenterprise relations that has provided Japanese firms and some in a few East and Southeast Asian jurisdictions with a decisive competitive advantage in the course of the world-economic crisis of the 1970s and 1980s.

This system is the multilayered subcontracting system that originated in Japan and has expanded prodigiously since the late 1960s to encompass an increasing number and variety of East and Southeast Asian locations. Japanese capitalist enterprises are not the only core enterprises that have resorted to subcontracting nor has the expansion of the Japanese-centered subcontracting system in the 1970s and 1980s been limited to East and Southeast Asia. Nevertheless, the Japanese-centered subcontracting system has characteristics that differentiate it clearly from the subcontracting practices of capitalist enterprises of other nations; one such characteristic is precisely the heavy concentration of Japanese expansion in East and Southeast Asia. Let us briefly examine these characteristics.

First, the Japanese-centered subcontracting system relies upon and tends to reproduce a more decentralized structure of productive activities than do the subcontracting practices of capitalist enterprises in other core states. An indirect indicator of this more decentralized structure of production is the greater preponderance of small to medium-size corporations in the Japanese domestic economy in comparison with other core domestic economies. As Table 3.3 shows, the percentage of all corporations accounted for by small to medium firms is about the same in Japan as in the United States, the United Kingdom, and Germany. Significantly, the percentage of the labor force, of shipments, and of value added accounted for by small to medium firms is much higher in Japan than in the other three states.

Table 3.3
Weight of Small and Medium-Sized[†] Corporations in Different Core States

	Japan[††]	Japan[‡]	USA[‡]	W. Germany[‡‡]	UK[‡]
	(1986)	(1988)	(1982)	(1988)	(1986)
Percentage number	99.4	99.1	96.3	90.8	97.0
Percentage employment	80.6	72.9	46.9	38.3	39.2
Percentage shipment	n.a.	52.4	38.2	32.1[*]	n.a.
Percentage value added	n.a.	55.5	38.4	n.a.	33.3

[†]Japan: fewer than 300 employees; USA: fewer than 250; Germany: fewer than 300; UK: fewer than 200.
[††]Nonprimary sector. The size of small and medium corporations are: fewer than 300 employees for manufacturing, fewer than 100 for wholesale, and fewer than 50 for retail and service.
[‡]Manufacturing sector.
[‡‡]Manufacturing sector, excluding hand manufacturing.
[*]Total sales.
Source: These figures are calculated from various tables in the Agency of Small/Medium Size Corporations, 1990.

A large and, until recently, growing proportion of the Japanese small to medium manufacturing corporations has been integrated into subcontracting networks controlled by large corporations. Thus, small to medium corporations that subcontracted represented 53.2 percent of all small to medium corporations in 1966, 58.7 percent in 1971, 60.7 percent in 1976, 65.5 percent in 1981, and 55.9 percent in 1987 (Aoki, 1984: 26–27; Ministry of International Trade and Industry [MITI], 1990: 157). The percentages have actually been much higher than those suggested by the above figures in branches of activity that use a large number of parts and components in their products or that can operate efficiently on a small scale. Thus, in 1976 (when the average percentage stood at 60.7), the proportion of small to medium corporations that were integrated into subcontracting networks was well above 80 percent in "machines," "transport machines," and "electronics," on the one side, and in "textiles" and "apparel," on the other side (Shizuoka Ken Chishokigyo Seisaku Kenkyukai [SKCSK], 1979: 45).

Second, the Japanese-centered subcontracting system is highly stratified into multiple layers. The subcontractors are stratified into primary subcontractors (which subcontract the job directly from the ultimate purchaser, such as final product assemblers or distributors), secondary subcontractors (which obtain the job from the primary subcontractors), tertiary subcontractors (which obtain the job from the secondary subcontractors), and so on until the chain reaches the bottom of the pyramid formed by a large mass of households that subcontract simple operations.

As reported by JETRO (Japan's External Trade Organization), "[Behind] Japan's great industrial firms stands a loyal legion of 'independent' subcontractors without whose assistance Japanese big business would flounder and sink. Japanese automakers, for instance, have become the world's top auto exporters only with the support of thousands of subcontractors which supply them with parts. A single large automaker typically deals with as many as 170 primary subcontractors, which in turn consign parts manufacturing to 4,700 secondary subcontractors. The secondary concerns enlist the help of 31,600 tertiary subcontractors even further removed from the parent automaker'' (Okimoto & Rohlen, 1988: 83).

Below the third level, the subcontractors are too many to count as they come to include huge numbers of housewives who process tiny metal or electronic parts at home as piece-workers. Suffice it to say that, according to the Ministry of Labor in 1977, the total number of households where at least one member was working on a subcontracting basis at home was 1.4 million or about 4 percent of all Japanese households (Okimoto & Rohlen, 1988: 85).

Although large-scale manufacturers in the United States and Western Europe also use a large number of subcontractors, the degree of external sourcing in Japan is far greater in almost every branch of manufacturing. For example, in 1973 in the automobile industry, the gross value added to finished vehicles was 18 percent in Japan, 43 percent for the "big three" in the United States, and 44 percent for Volkswagen and Benz in Germany (Odaka, 1985: 391). More than anything else, this greater reliance on external sourcing enabled the Toyota Motor Corporation to turn out 3.22 million four-wheel cars in 1981 with only 48,000 employees, while General Motors needed 758,000 employees to turn out 4.62 million cars (Aoki, 1984: 27).

The discrepancy in the degree of external sourcing has been even greater in the case of the electronics industry. According to the Subcontracting Firm Research Group, the ratio of external sourcing in the automobile industry in the United States and Western Europe is about 50 percent and in Japan between 65 and 70 percent. In the electronics industry, by contrast, the ratio is 20 percent for the United States and Western Europe and between 70 and 80 percent for Japan (Shitauke Kigyo Kenyukai [SKK], 1986: 49–51).

Third, Japanese-centered subcontracting networks are far more stable and regulated than similar networks in the United States and Western Europe. In the United States and Western Europe, subcontractors have to renegotiate more often and under greater competitive pressure from other subcontractors or would-be subcontractors than do those in Japan. As a consequence, intentional cooperation aimed at the attainment of a common goal (such as the high quality or the low price of the final product of the subcontracting chain) across the organizational jurisdictions of enterprises situated at different levels in the multilayered subcontracting system is more problematic in the United States and Western Europe than in Japan; transaction costs for contractors and subcontractors are likewise higher. What is more, the length and stratification of the chain itself is affected negatively by the instability of interenterprise relations between the top layer and those next in command. As a matter of fact, the subcontracting practices of large-scale corporations in the United States and Western Europe seldom develop beyond a two-layered structure.

Instead of competing against one another, small and large firms in Japan cooperate through a specialization of techniques or processes in a pervasive subcontracting network that reproduces the widely dispersed structure over time (Eccleston, 1989: 31). This lasting partnership is idealized as a "family" relationship between "parent companies" and "child subcontractors." These affiliative relationships are so close that:

the hard and fast distinction between firms becomes very blurred [as] we find some supplier companies located within the plant of the parent firm, [as] the smaller company is managed by ex-employees of the larger one or [as] the bulk of the small firm machinery is handed down in second-hand sales from their principal buyer. . . . Close affiliative relations between firms are not confined to single level subcontracting but are typical of a hierarchical network of connections at several stages removed from the largest firm. Primary subcontractors will therefore transfer personnel, equipment and ideas about organization to their own subcontractors who in turn do likewise right down to the level of the single-person firm. (Eccleston, 1989: 34)

Continuity of subcontracting arrangements enables parent companies to economize on transaction costs with outside suppliers. These in turn willingly submit themselves and their employees to high rates of exploitation to the benefit of the parent company in exchange for the security of cash flows and material inputs afforded by the continuity of the relationship. These cooperative arrangements between parent companies and subcontractors are buttressed by cooperative arrangements among the parent companies themselves, in the form of semipermanent trading arrangements and intergroup stockholding.

Affiliative links between larger firms enhances the procurement of materials and smooths their pattern of marketing while inter-group stockholding prevents unwanted takeover bids and allows management to concentrate on long-term performance rather than short-term profits distributed to stockholders. This longer run perspective is a feature of Japanese business and is greatly helped by the existence of lead banks within affiliated groups that ensure access to loans even in periods when bank credit is restricted. (Eccleston, 1989: 31–33)

Long-term cooperative arrangements within stable networks of large, medium, and small enterprises in Japan have been further enhanced by the involvement of powerful trading companies—the *sogo shosha*—in the disposal of the outputs of the large enterprises that are engaged in such process-flow industries as steel, chemicals, petrochemicals, and synthetic fibers. In developing outlets for the ever-increasing output of these industries, the *sogo shosha* have built quasi-controlled networks of small- and medium-sized enterprises, to which they supply materials for downstream processing and distribution and to which they also extend financial, managerial, and marketing assistance. Like the "upstream" networks controlled by large manufacturers, these "downstream" networks controlled by large trading companies combine the market and financial power of a large enterprise with the flexibility, specific knowledge, and lower wages of small- and medium-sized enterprises (Yoshino & Lifson, 1986: 29).

④ Closely related to the above, a fourth feature of the Japanese multilayered subcontracting system has been its superior ability to take advantage of and reproduce wage differentials between different segments and layers of the domestic and world labor force. In Japan, as elsewhere, wages tend to increase with the size of the employing enterprise. Thus, in 1983, wages in large Japanese enterprises (300 or more employees) were on average 38 percent higher than in enterprises with 100 to 299 employees, 60 percent higher than in enterprises with 20 to 99 employees, 71 percent higher than in enterprises with 10 to 19 employees, and 106 percent higher than in enterprises with four to nine employees (Agency of Small/Medium Size Corporations, 1990: 11).

Actual differences in the rewards for effort are even greater than suggested by the above figures because of the far more generous fringe benefits and bonuses paid by the larger corporations and because of the greater duration and intensity of work in the smaller enterprises. Thus, while small firms operate a scheduled working week that is 10 percent longer than in larger firms, employees in large firms throughout the 1970s received a bonus payment equivalent to five or six months of basic pay, compared to a bonus equivalent to less than three months' pay in small firms. As for fringe benefits, a 1983 survey found that the costs incurred in providing company housing or housing loans, medical, nursery, or recreation facilities were at least twice as high in large firms (Eccleston, 1989: 58–59).

However large these differentials may seem, they pale in comparison with the differentials that separate small enterprises from workers in the bottom layer of the subcontracting system—the female home piece-workers. The hourly wages received by these piece-workers are only a fraction of the wage rates in the smallest enterprises—about one-fourth those of full-time male workers and about one-half those of full-time female workers in companies with five to 29 employees (Keizai Henshebu, 1990: 129). And, of course, at the household level, there are no bonuses ✳ or fringe benefits.

It is hard to tell whether and to what extent differentials in rewards for effort between large and small enterprises have been greater in Japan than in other core locations. Wage data, let alone data on bonuses, fringe benefits, and working hours as collected in different states are seldom comparable. Nevertheless, Bernard Eccleston has given a rough estimate for 1985 of the contrast between manufacturing firms with over 1,000 and those with fewer than 100 employees. According to this estimate, Japanese workers in small manufacturing firms earned 55 percent of what workers in large firms earned; the comparable figure was 75 percent in West Germany, 73 percent in the United Kingdom, 70 percent in France and Italy, and 66 percent in the United States. "When we take longer working hours into account the differential widens still further as wages per productive hour in small Japanese firms is only 46 percent of the sum paid in large firms" (Eccleston, 1989: 60).

But whether or not the differentials in question have been greater in Japan than in other core locations, what really matters is this: A system of interenterprise relations that assigns a greater, better articulated, and more stable role to the smaller enterprises in productive activities is better suited than less well-structured subcontracting practices to exploit and keep in place a patterned inequality of rewards for effort so as to minimize overall production costs. Japanese management has always been very conscious of the importance of taking full advantage of and keeping in place this patterned inequality—far more conscious than management in North America and Western Europe. From this point of view, the Japanese multilayered subcontracting system is but one aspect of a more general managerial strategy of interenterprise cooperation aimed at minimizing competition between large and small enterprises in the labor market. Another aspect of this general strategy has been the practice of the large corporations that occupy the "commanding heights" of the multilayered subcontracting system to recruit most of their workforce among people who have just graduated from school and only rarely to bid employees away from other companies. Even more important has been the practice of discriminating against the employment of women in the top layers of the subcontracting system. This practice has been instrumental in reproducing a large pool of female workers who are available for the superexploitation typical of the lower two or so layers of the system.

Both practices—particularly the latter—are of course pursued to varying extents by the management of North American and Western European core enterprises as well. But nowhere in other core locations have these practices been pursued as coherently and systematically as in Japan, where it is almost a rule that "the higher up the value-added chain, the bigger the firm, the larger the business profits, the more privileged the conditions of work and pay, and the more male dominated the workforce" (Hill, 1989: 466). What is more, as we move down the value-added chain, it is not just rewards for effort that decrease but security of income as well. As one official at the Tokyo Chamber of Commerce and Industry remarked, primary and secondary subcontractors have managed to keep afloat "because, like the big firms at the top, they too can pass the buck to their own subcontractors. Eventually the little guy at the bottom, often a housewife or a retired worker, is the one who 'gets the ax' " (Okimoto & Rohlen, 1988: 84).

⑤   This brings us to the fifth and, for our purposes, most important characteristic of the Japanese multilayered subcontracting system—its symbiotic relationship with the wider East Asian economic environment. The development of this symbiotic relationship since the middle 1960s is the subject matter of the next section of this chapter. Here, we shall limit ourselves to a few preliminary remarks concerning the connection between the domestic stability and world competitiveness of the Japanese multilayered subcontracting system, on the one side, and its tendency to expand regionally into East Asia, on the other side.

Japan has clearly accumulated capital at a remarkable rate over the last 30 years, probably due to this tendency. It is hardly conceivable that it could have done so, however, without undermining and eventually disrupting these patterns of cooperative arrangements, both between large and small enterprises and among the large enterprises themselves, on which the domestic viability and world competitiveness of the Japanese multilayered subcontracting system rests. The reason is that the reinvestment of an ever-growing mass of profits in the expansion of trade and in production facilities within any given economic space inevitably tends to drive the agencies of accumulation into one another's market niches in their attempts to counter downward pressures in sale prices and/or upward pressures on purchase prices in their own lines of business. The higher the rate of expansion, the stronger this tendency and the greater the chances that individual enterprises or groups of enterprises will get in one another's way, thereby engaging in fierce competitive struggles over sources of inputs or outlets for outputs.

Indeed, a tendency of this latter kind was evident in Japan in the middle 1960s, in the form of a revival of what was popularly called "excessive competition." This revival was associated with serious and growing shortages of primary inputs— land and labor—whose prices (particularly the wages of young factory workers) began to rise both absolutely and relative to the selling prices of the industrial groups engaged in the competition. Initially, the decline in profit margins was more than compensated by large and increasing productivity gains, but, by the end of the 1960s, productivity gains ceased to be large enough to counter the tendency of the rate of profit to fall (see Ozawa, 1979: 66–67).

Still, this intensification of competition and consequent crisis of profitability did not disrupt the cooperative arrangements on which the Japanese multilayered subcontracting system was based, nor did it end Japanese economic expansion. On the contrary, the Japanese multilayered subcontracting system continued to increase in scale and scope, and the economic ascent of Japan—as argued in the first section of this chapter—became the harbinger of a specifically East Asian economic miracle. The main reason for this outcome is that the accumulation crisis of the mid- to late 1960s marked the beginning of the transborder expansion of the Japanese subcontracting system. This transborder expansion, more than anything else, created the conditions not just for the continuing vitality of the multilayered subcontracting system at home but also for the spread of the miracle to select locations of East Asia.

THE TRANSBORDER EXPANSION OF THE JAPANESE MULTILAYERED SUBCONTRACTING SYSTEM AND THE EAST ASIAN ECONOMIC MIRACLE

In the first section we saw that the East Asian economic miracle has developed in three stages. It began in the 1960s as an exclusively Japanese phenomenon; it spread to select East Asian locations in the 1970s when, however, it was hardly distinguishable from a more general "catching-up" process that, to varying degrees, could be seen in almost all the low- and middle-income regions of the world-economy; and it emerged as a specifically East Asian miracle in the 1980s, when the general "catching-up" process of the 1970s collapsed almost everywhere—except in a handful of East Asian locations.

This evolution of the East Asian economic miracle has been integral to the changing pattern of the world-economic crisis that began in the late 1960s and, in ever-changing forms, has been with us ever since. Four aspects of this crisis bear directly on the subject matter of this chapter.

First, the intensification of interenterprise competition and rising wages that was faced by Japanese capital in the mid- to late 1960s was not an isolated phenomenon. Rather, it was a local form of a broad tendency that, in different ways and to different extents, showed itself throughout the world-economy. This more general tendency—toward an intensification of competitive pressures within and across national boundaries and toward rising labor costs in core locations— undermined the viability of the regime of fixed exchange rates pegged to a gold-dollar standard, which had been in place since the end of World War II and finally broke down in the summer of 1971. This breakdown, in turn, further exacerbated competitive pressures in the world-economy at large but particularly in those locations, such as Japan, that had relied heavily for their economic expansion on the competitive advantages afforded by an increasingly undervalued national currency.

Second, between 1968 and 1973—that is, before the first "oil shock" of late 1973—this general intensification of competitive pressures and rising labor costs in core locations was matched by a sudden acceleration in the transnational expansion of core capitalist enterprises. Thus, the annual outflow of direct foreign investment from all so-called developed market economies, which had increased by less than 50 percent between 1963 and 1968, more than doubled between 1968 and 1973 (see Hood & Vahlne, 1988: Fig. 3.1). Much if not most of this sudden acceleration can be traced to a widespread attempt on the part of core capitalist enterprises to escape, through a spatial diversification of their activities, the curtailment of profit margins that had been brought about by intensifying competition and rising wages in core locations. This tendency was particularly noticeable in the case of Japanese and West German enterprises that had till then been conspicuous by their absence in the development of transnational production networks but were now driven to move rapidly in this direction by labor shortages and, after 1971, by rapidly appreciating national currencies (cf. Fröbel, Heinrichs & Kreye, 1980).

Third, the relocation of production processes from high- to low- and, above all, to middle-income regions and jurisdictions, which had been brought on by the above acceleration in the transnational expansion of production networks, was in itself a factor in the general "catching-up" process of the 1970s. Nevertheless, between the end of 1973 and the end of 1979—that is, from the first to the second "oil shock"—this factor was supplemented and partly superseded by a massive increase in the supply of cheap credit and monetary instruments that was provided by North American and Western European financial institutions to numerous middle-income and select low-income countries. What seems to have happened is that the inflation of "oil rents" boosted the already overabundant liquidity of these financial institutions; these began outcompeting one another in the recycling of the liquidity to sustain the "catching-up" efforts of lower-income countries. And as these latter countries (or at least many of them) came to enjoy a practically unlimited supply of hard currencies and cheap credit, their efforts suddenly seemed to be succeeding. It was at this time that the Brazilian economic miracle outshone the East Asian performance and that the income gap between wealthy and comparatively poor countries seemed, with few exceptions, to be narrowing.

Fourth and last, the boom in the supply of capital to low- and middle-income countries, in the form of direct foreign investment and cheap credit, collapsed in the early 1980s, bringing the general "catching-up" process of the 1970s to an abrupt end. The first to collapse was direct foreign investment. After peaking in 1973, the total outflow of such investment from "developed market economies" had declined somewhat but had remained high through 1977, when it began to climb again to reach a new historic high in 1979. Then, in 1980, the outflow from North America started to fall precipitously; in 1981, the outflow from Western Europe also fell drastically. As a result, the total outflow from "developed market economies" in 1982 and 1983 was less than half of what it had been in 1978 and 1979 (Hood & Vahlne, 1988: Fig. 3.1).

The collapse in the supply of cheap credit followed on the heels of the collapse in direct foreign investment. That collapse began in late 1979, when the U.S. Federal Reserve began bidding up interest rates in an attempt to attract world liquidity to finance the escalating U.S. national debt, and it culminated in 1982, when the Mexican default provoked a drastic curtailment of lending to lower-income countries. As these countries came to be deprived of the unlimited supplies of capital to which they had become addicted in the 1970s, the general "catching-up" process ended as abruptly as it had begun ten years earlier.

The rise of East Asia as a major center of capital accumulation has proceeded in step with the above evolution of the world-economic crisis. It was the outbreak of the crisis in the late 1960s that drove Japanese capital to expand transnationally so as to boost the vitality of the multilayered subcontracting system on which its distinctive competitive advantage in world markets was based. In the course of the general "catching-up" process of the 1970s, the peculiar character of this expansion enhanced the competitive advantages of East Asia as the "workshop of the world." And it was the combination of the competitiveness of the Japanese multilayered subcontracting system as a "mode of production" and of East Asia as a manufacturing location that more than anything else accounts for the fact that among the many countries that were "called" to participate in the great race of the 1970s, the few that in the 1980s were actually "chosen" to rise in the global hierarchy of wealth were mostly East Asian.

The close connection between the outbreak of the world-economic crisis and the "take-off" of the transnational expansion of Japanese capital is starkly shown in Figure 3.1, which depicts the annual rates of growth in accumulated value (in U.S. dollars) and in the accumulated number of cases of Japanese direct foreign investment. Both curves show rising rates of growth, that is, an accelerating expansion, in the late 1960s and then, after a pause that is more marked for the

Figure 3.1

Rate of Increase of Accumulated Japanese Direct Foreign Investment

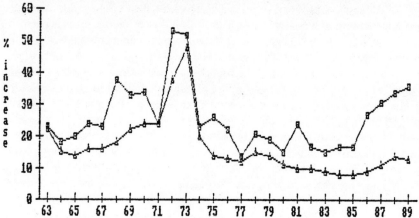

Note: squares-value in U.S. dollars; triangles-cases

Source: Calculated from Steven, 1990: 67 and Statistics Bureau Management and Coordination Agency, 1990.

"value" than for the "cases" curve, an explosive growth in the two-year period of 1972 and 1973. As a result of this explosive growth, the flow of direct foreign investment out of Japan, which in 1970 and 1971 still accounted for less than 3 percent of the total outflow from all "developed market economies," came to account for 5 percent of that total in 1972 and for more than 8 percent in 1973 and 1974 (calculated from United Nations Center on Transnational Corporations [UNCTC], 1983).

Some specific aspects of this great wave of Japanese direct foreign investment are as important as the numerical aspects. Three deserve note.

First, in expanding their operations abroad, Japanese enterprises have been far less insistent and reliant on majority ownership than U.S. and Western European enterprises. Thus, in 1971, minority ownerships and joint ventures accounted for about 80 percent of the foreign manufacturing subsidiaries of Japanese firms, as against 47 percent for French firms, 35 percent for Italian firms, about 30 percent for German and Belgian firms, and about 20 percent for firms of the United States, the United Kingdom, the Netherlands, Sweden, and Switzerland (Franko, 1976: 121). By a different count, four years later (in 1975), minority ownership accounted for 44 percent of Japanese overseas ventures, as against 8.3 percent for U.S. multinationals (Ozawa, 1979: 227).

It follows that data on direct foreign investment underestimate the actual extent and impact of the transnational expansion of Japanese production networks. Much of this expansion has not involved sinking Japanese capital into existing or new production facilities abroad and, therefore, does not show up in records of direct foreign investment. Still, in the course of the world-economic crisis, the significance of this unrecorded expansion in boosting the profitability of Japanese capital, the incomes of the receiving locations, or both became much greater than that of recorded investments made to acquire and retain majority ownership of production facilities.

Second, and closely related to the above, the great Japanese wave of transnational expansion of the late 1960s and the early 1970s consisted primarily of the transborder expansion of the subcontracting networks of trading companies and of the activities of small- and medium-sized subcontracting firms. As underscored by Terutomo Ozawa, the very success of Japanese large industrial enterprises in assimilating capital-intensive techniques of production had destroyed the location-specific advantages of early postwar Japan (an abundant labor supply and an undervalued yen), which, at the time, were essential to the prosperity or even survival of small- and medium-sized enterprises utilizing labor-intensive techniques in light-manufacturing industries. As labor tightness began to affect adversely the profitability of these enterprises in the mid-1960s, they relocated part of their activities to neighboring countries; by 1971, they already accounted for one-third of Japan's overseas manufacturing ventures. But it was the sharp rise of the yen in the early 1970s that rang the death knell for Japanese exports of light manufactures and that led to a major transplant of the lower value-added end of Japan's manufacturing activities to the soil of poorer neighboring countries. Thus, four major labor-intensive industries that had a large number of small- and medium-sized enterprises (textiles, metal products, electrical machinery, and sundries) together accounted for as much as 65.5 percent of the total number (and 55.4 percent of the total value) of the massive new overseas investments made during the two-year period 1972–73 (Ozawa, 1985: 166–167).

This massive transplanting of the lower value-added end of Japan's manufacturing apparatus could never have occurred without the leadership and assistance provided by the *sogo shosha*. As Jon Woronoff has observed, the small- and medium-sized enterprises that were involved in the transplanting would have been unable to move abroad on their own. That they moved as massively as they did is because they were assisted by the trading companies that were their suppliers, their customers, or both.

If the only way [for the smaller enterprise] to survive was by seeking cheaper labor abroad, the trading company knew how this could be done. It then helped find a local partner for a joint venture, since a small Japanese firm might not know how to operate alone in another country. It advanced some of the funds needed. And frequently the trading company took a small share of the equity since it hoped to act as agent for the purchase of raw materials or machinery and then later for the export of finished goods. (Woronoff, 1984: 56–58)

Throughout the late 1960s and early 1970s, the trading companies were the main leaders and organizers of the transborder expansion of the Japanese multilayered subcontracting system. But they were not the only ones. The large manufacturers that occupied the upper layers of upstream subcontracting networks also played a role, which became increasingly important from the mid-1970s onward. When these "parent" companies went abroad, they were followed by some members of their subcontracting "families," who knew that they "could count on considerable business from the outset plus a good deal of support" (Woronoff, 1984: 58).

Third and last, most of the transplanting of the lower value-added end of the Japanese manufacturing apparatus occurred within Asia, and, within Asia, the future Gang of Four received a disproportionate share. As we have seen, two-thirds of the total number of new overseas investments made during the two-year period of explosive expansion (1972–73) were accounted for by four major labor-intensive industries. To this, we can now add that most of the ventures by these industries were undertaken in Asia: 64.3 percent in textiles, 69.2 percent in metal products, 81.8 percent in electric machinery, and 75.4 percent in sundries (Ozawa, 1985: 167).

Asia's share was in fact the share of a small group of East and Southeast Asian countries among which the Gang of Four figured most prominently. Thus, data provided by Rob Steven show that the Gang of Four received 54 percent of all cases of Japanese direct foreign investment made in Asia in textiles between 1951 and 1974 and that most of the rest (42 percent) went to another four countries— Thailand, Malaysia, the Philippines, and Indonesia. The concentration was even greater for direct foreign investment in electrical machinery, the corresponding figures being 80 percent in the Gang of Four nations and 15 percent for the other four Southeast Asian countries listed above (calculated from Steven, 1990: Table III.3).

As a result of this spatial and jurisdictional concentration of the transplanting of Japanese labor-intensive industries, the expansion of Japanese foreign direct investment within the territories of the Gang of Four in the late 1960s and early 1970s was far more explosive than anywhere else. Thus, according to the Japanese Ministry of Finance, which was then in charge of authorizing overseas investments by Japanese companies, only 54 investment projects destined to go to the Gang of Four were authorized up through 1964: 26 for Taiwan, 18 for Hong Kong, 10 for Singapore, and none for South Korea. But in the next ten-year period, and mostly in the early 1970s, more than 20 times that number of projects was authorized: 581 for South Korea, 400 for Taiwan, 111 for Singapore, and 79 for Hong Kong—a total of 1,171 projects (half in South Korea alone) for the four territories as a group (Yoshihara, 1978: 18).

In short, the transnational expansion of Japanese capital of the late 1960s and early 1970s was primarily a transborder expansion of the Japanese multilayered subcontracting system. As such, it did not require majority ownership of the foreign facilities that were incorporated into Japanese trade and production networks. On the contrary, minority ownerships or even looser commitments were particularly suited to combining the reach and flexibility of the *sogo shosha* with the specialized knowledge and capabilities of local and Japanese small- and medium-sized subcontractors. Likewise, the expansion did not need to spread itself thin in faraway locations to "internalize" either sources of specialized inputs or outlets of equally specialized outputs—as multinationalism, American-style typically did. What Japanese capital was seeking were locations close at hand with efficient, cheap, and flexible labor supplies and with as privileged an access to the United States and other core markets as possible. From this point of view, Japan's former colonies of South Korea and Taiwan, which had as privileged an access to the U.S. domestic market as did Japan, and the city-states of Singapore and Hong Kong were as good as any others and, for the time being, more than sufficient for the purpose.

Whether locationally "optimal" or not, the transborder expansion of the Japanese multilayered subcontracting system was in any case more than adequate to enable the system to develop new divisions of labor within and between its different layers of subcontractors (which came to include small- and medium-sized foreign enterprises in a subordinate position and to incorporate, in its lower layers, supplies of labor considerably cheaper than the cheapest labor in Japan. While the new divisions of labor enhanced the overall productivity of the system, the incorporation of cheaper labor boosted Japanese competitiveness and profitability, over and above that gained from the enhanced overall productivity.

We suggest that the competitiveness and profitability of the regionally expanded Japanese multilayered subcontracting system has constituted the main foundation of the East Asian economic miracle of the 1970s and 1980s. As early as the 1970s, Japan and the Gang of Four were narrowing the income gap that separated them from the organic core faster than any other country or region at comparable levels of GNP per capita. The general nature of the "catching up" process in this period, however, was concealing the true extent of the competitive advantages conferred on Japan (as an accumulation center) and on the Gang of Four (as manufacturing locations) by the transborder expansion.

Moreover, after 1973 and throughout the 1970s, the profitability and competitiveness of this expansion were outshone by the increasingly massive transnational expansion of North American and Western European capital. In this period, the Japanese share of the total outflow of direct foreign investment from "developed market economies," which, as we have seen, had jumped from less than 3 percent in 1970-71 to more than 8 percent in 1973-74, began to decline. It fell to 7.2 percent in 1975-76, to 6.5 percent in 1977-78, and to 5.9 percent in 1979-80 (calculated from UNCTC, 1983).

At the same time, the escalation of the prices of oil and other raw materials drew Japanese enterprises onto a new path of transnational expansion that was not as peculiar as that of the late 1960s and the early 1970s. The top priority of Japanese direct investment in the mid- to late 1970s became the securing of supplies of oil and other raw materials, and this priority necessarily involved a wider geographical scope of operations that had the earlier expansion of the multilayered subcontracting system. Moreover, in the competitive struggle to secure steady and competitive supplies of primary products in faraway places, the *sogo shosha* were often not as effective as vertically integrated enterprises (see Hill & Johns, 1985: 377–378).

Under these circumstances, the organizational and locational peculiarities of Japanese direct foreign investment appeared to be "weapons of the weak" rather than the source of a fundamental competitive advantage—as they would turn out to be at a later date. Thus, in his exemplary study of what he has called "multinationalism, Japanese style," Ozawa has pointed out how the majority of Japanese manufacturers who were investing overseas were "immature" by Western standards; how the outward expansion of Japanese enterprises was the result of necessity rather than of choice—that is, the result of a struggle to escape the trap of rapid industrialization within a narrow, domestic, economic space; and how the willingness of Japanese multinationals to work out compromises with the demands of host countries (such as accepting minority ownership) was, at least in part, due to a weak bargaining position both vis-à-vis host governments and relative to North American and Western European competitors (Ozawa, 1979: 225–229).

The tendencies of the mid- to late 1970s, however, were misleading in one fundamental respect. Neither the transnational expansion of core capital nor the generalized developmental efforts of low- and middle-income countries could be sustained for long. The more core capital expanded transnationally and the more low- and middle-income countries expanded their industrial apparatuses, the fiercer the competition over increasingly scarce world-economic resources became. Sooner or later, the superior capabilities of the enlarged Japanese multilayered subcontracting system to tap the cheap labor power of low-income countries would emerge as a decisive advantage in the competitive struggle.

The moment of truth came in the early 1980s. As we have seen in the first section of this chapter, Japan and the Gang of Four accounted for five of the only six locations world-wide where the general "catching-up" process of the 1970s did not collapse in the 1980s. To this we can now add that the transnational expansion of Japanese capital continued unabated in the midst of the general collapse of direct foreign investment of the early 1980s.

As can be seen from Figure 3.1, the "value" curve for the early 1980s shows rates of expansion of the same order as for the middle and late 1970s, and the "cases" curve shows only a steady but slight deceleration. Neither curve shows stagnation, let alone the kind of collapse that was experienced in these years by North American and Western European direct foreign investment. Thus, the Japanese share of total direct foreign investment—calculated this time as a percentage of the *world* total, instead of the total from "developed market economies"—jumped from 4.7 percent in 1979-80 to 12.7 percent in 1981-82 and continued to climb thereafter to 12.9 percent in 1983-84, 13.3 percent in 1985-86, and 18.2 percent in 1987-88. The U.S. share, in contrast, fell from 39.2 percent in 1979-80 to 9.0 percent in 1981-82, and back to 4.6 percent in 1983-84. Although the U.S. share bounced back to 29.3 percent in 1985-86, it fell again to 21.2 percent in 1987-88 (calculated from Okumura, 1988: 276; International Monetary Fund [IMF], 1989: 68).

Partly related to the steadiness of the expansion of Japanese direct foreign investment at this time of general collapse and partly related to the global competitiveness gained by their firms' early and massive incorporation into the networks of the Japanese multilayered subcontracting system, the Gang of Four rose like a phoenix from the ashes of the general collapse of the developmental efforts of the 1970s. They have also come to enjoy an abundance of capital without parallel in countries at the same or even at a much higher level income.

South Korea—the only one of the Gang of Four to become indebted in the 1970s—has continued to enjoy plenty of credit in the 1980s and has even experienced an explosive growth in the inflow of direct foreign investment, from a yearly average of about $100 million in the 1970s, to $170 million in 1984, and to $625 million in 1987 (Ogle, 1990: 37). Moreover, like Singapore, South Korea has itself become one of the largest direct foreign investors among middle-income countries (IMF, 1989: 68). While Hong Kong has turned into one of the world's main financial centers, Taiwan has accumulated $74 billion in official foreign exchange reserves—more than any other country in the world except Japan (*New York Times*, Feb. 13, 1991: A12).

THE LIMITS OF THE EAST ASIAN ECONOMIC MIRACLE

Our contention has been threefold: that the sudden and exceptional prosperity experienced by Japan and the Gang of Four in the 1980s is the result of a single economic miracle; that the proximate origin of this miracle lies in the transborder expansion of the Japanese multilayered subcontracting system in the late 1960s and early 1970s; and that the miracle is an integral aspect of the world-economic crisis that prompted this transborder expansion and eventually made it triumph over alternative and competing forms of transnational capitalist expansion. An important aspect of this triumph has been a major new revaluation of the yen—a revaluation that began in September 1985 and that within two years raised the value of the yen relative to the U.S. dollar by 64 percent (calculated from Steven, 1990: Table I.4). Like the revaluation that occurred between 1971 and 1973, this new revaluation prompted a sudden acceleration in the rate of overseas expansion of Japanese capital (see Figure 3.1).

Can we expect this new spurt in Japanese direct foreign investment, supplemented as it is by the outflow of capital from the Gang of Four itself, to have developmental effects of the same order as the spurt in the late 1960s and early 1970s? Since this new spurt has also shown a strong preference for low-income Asian locations (Southeast locations in particular), we cannot rule out the possibility that, in the next decade or two, we shall witness a replica of the East Asian economic miracle of the 1970s and 1980s. There are good reasons, however, for being skeptical about the chances that this possibility will actually materialize.

For one thing, the agency of Japanese direct foreign investment no longer consists, as it did in the early 1970s, of predominantly small and medium-sized corporations that are driven to expand their operations in a limited number of neighboring territories as a matter of economic survival. Rather, it consists of large and powerful corporations that are endowed with the capability of taking the whole world as the relevant domain of their investment decisions and of actually organizing production processes over a wide range and variety of territories and political jurisdictions. To these corporations, investment in any particular location or region of the world-economy is a matter of choice rather than of necessity, and this fact alone puts them in a bargaining position vis-à-vis the business and governmental institutions of host countries that is incomparably stronger than the position in which Japanese overseas investors found themselves in the early 1970s.

Moreover, the systemic circumstances under which the current wave of direct foreign investment has been unfolding are altogether different from the systemic circumstances of the wave of the early 1970s. As we saw in the third section of this chapter, the collapse of the flow of capital from North America and Western Europe to low- and middle-income countries in the early 1980s has created a world-wide shortage of liquidity in hard currencies. This shortage, in turn, has provided the capitalist enterprises that have come to control world liquidity (among which Japanese enterprises figure most prominently) with unique opportunities to obtain production facilities and supplies at bargain prices from almost any location on the periphery and semiperiphery of the world-economy.

The wider geographical scale and scope of the current wave of Japanese direct foreign investment, together with the stronger bargaining position of its agents vis-à-vis the business and governmental institutions of host countries, is creating a pattern of direct foreign investment in Southeast Asia that is quite different from the pattern created in East Asia in the 1970s. Instead of multiple partnerships between small- and medium-sized Japanese firms and local corporations under the leadership of trading companies—a pattern that was crucial to the enhancement of the income-generating capabilities of South Korea and Taiwan—the intense Japanese investment activities in Southeast Asia during the last five years have brought into being a highly centralized industrial structure, "a de facto trade grouping, in which different Southeast Asian nations specialize in technologies that will feed Japan's biggest industrial giants." Southeast Asia thus seems to be well on its way toward becoming "Japan's manufacturing backyard" (*New York Times*, March 6, 1991: A1, D6).

In contrast to many U.S. competitors, Japanese companies are still noted for their willingness to tread lightly, for not insisting on majority ownership, for being less fazed by occasional political instability. "In most cases," the above article in the *New York Times* reported, "they exert careful control by placing Japanese in the top management posts and carefully doling out technology." These strategies, however, are no longer "the weapons of the weak" as they were in the 1970s. Rather, they are an expression of the changed conjuncture in the world-economy and of the newly acquired commanding position that Japanese corporations hold in global processes of capital accumulation. More specifically, they are an expression of a predisposition and a capability on the part of Japanese capital to keep its hands as free as possible in the exploitation of profitable investment opportunities as they open up in one location and wither in another. "As Thai and Malaysian labor costs rise, Japanese businesses are scrambling for access to

Indochina, especially poverty-stricken countries like Vietnam . . . desperate for hard currency'' (*New York Times*, March 6, 1991: D6).

Under these circumstances, host countries industrialize very rapidly, but the income gap that separates them from core countries does not narrow because, as soon as it begins to do so, the expansion of production capacity is shifted to yet-unexploited, low-income locations, of which there is an ample and growing "reserve." It is not surprising, therefore, that the new wave of Japanese direct foreign investment in Southeast Asia has brought about massive industrialization but practically no "catching up." Thus, in the 1980s, the rates of growth of manufacturing in Southeast Asia have been among the highest in the world—the annual rate of growth between 1980 and 1988 being 6.8 percent in Thailand, 7.3 percent in Malaysia, and 13.1 percent in Indonesia, as against an annual rate of growth of 3.8 percent for all countries reporting to the World Bank and of 3.2 percent for all high-income countries (World Bank, 1990: 180–181). Yet, in that same period, all three of those countries lost ground relative to the organic core (let alone to Japan and the Gang of Four) insofar as per capita incomes are concerned—the ratio of their GNP per capita to the GNP per capita of the organic core showing a *decrease* of 7 percent in the case of Thailand, of 23 percent in the case of Malaysia, and of 34 percent in the case of Indonesia (calculated from Table 3.1).

As we have seen in the first section of this chapter, contractions of this order among low- and middle-income countries have not been unusual in the 1980s, and, in a longer term perspective, Thailand, Malaysia, and Indonesia have lost less ground relative to the organic core than most other countries at comparable levels of per capita income. But to designate this comparatively less disastrous performance as economic success is to stretch the meaning of the expression a bit too far. The Asian economic miracle of the 1970s and 1980s has been confined strictly to Japan and the Gang of Four. If a wider miracle is in the making, its signs are still hard to detect.

NOTE

We would like to thank Terence Hopkins, Ravi Palat, and Beverly Silver for helpful comments on an earlier draft.

4

INTERNATIONAL SUBCONTRACTING AND GLOBAL CAPITALISM: RESHAPING THE PACIFIC RIM

Gary Gereffi

Most efforts to define the region known variously as the Pacific Rim, Pacific Basin, Asia/Pacific, and so on have been quite unsatisfactory. There is an inherent geographical bias in all these definitions, since they tend to view the region as a geographical given, despite the difficulties of "delineating the boundaries of the region, determining its center(s), and deciding whom of all the people who inhabit the region to include within it as serious participants in its activities" (Dirlik, 1991: 1). "Pacific Rim," one of the most commonly used terms, has the drawback of focusing too exclusively on the edges of the region, leaving out of the picture all that is inside it. "Pacific Basin" has the opposite problem, since it suggests that the center of the region is somewhere in the ocean. "Asia/Pacific" has the advantage of referring not just to the region's location, but also to one of its principal human components, although the Asian peoples are so diverse that the term negates any social specificity in the notion. Finally, the term "Asian-American Pacific" might be preferred as descriptively more comprehensive, including the peoples on both sides of the Pacific, but this apparent egalitarian inclusiveness is misleading. It glosses over the historical problem of changes in the scope and structure of competing interests in the constitution of Asia and the Americas.

The purpose of my paper is neither to defend any of these definitions of the region nor to add a new one. The Pacific Rim is not just a geographical region nor is it solely the by-product of elite-centered, Euro-American, "hegemonic ideologies" of expansion into the Pacific hinterland, although geopolitical factors undoubtedly have been important in shaping the internal dynamics of the region as well as its insertion into the world-economy. Rather, I prefer to take a more inductive or grounded approach that sees the Pacific Rim as a geographical arena that is tied together by a variety of economic and social networks. My empirical focus will be a comparison of three global industries: garments, automobiles, and personal computers. During the post-World War II period, the trade, investment, and migration patterns associated with these industries have linked East Asian and Latin American nations with the United States in ways that have both consolidated and reshaped the Asian-American Pacific region. Furthermore, one of the important consequences of these transnational production networks has been a weakening of the role of individual governments in formulating national development policies and in determining how these regions will be linked to the global political economy.

The chapter is divided into three parts. The first shows how the contemporary global manufacturing system has led to an increase in the importance of international subcontracting in the world-economy. A typology of export roles is presented that shows how the Pacific Rim countries are linked with one another and with the world-economy. Particular emphasis is given to the changes in these roles over time and to the main development objectives they serve.

The second part focuses on how the global sourcing of production through international subcontracting relationships is organized in several contemporary export-oriented manufacturing industries. Evidence from the garment, automobile, and personal computer industries indicates the evolution of a new pattern, whereby the "national segmentation" that characterized the import-substituting industries of the past is being replaced by a new logic of "transnational integration," based on geographical specialization and tightly linked international supply networks. In other words, the shift from import-substituting industrialization (ISI) to export-oriented industrialization (EOI) in many Pacific Rim nations has ushered in a new international division of labor in the world-economy.

The third part of this chapter considers the impact of these trends toward international subcontracting on the regional dynamics in East Asia and North America. Trans-Pacific trade, investment, and migration flows are leading to a simultaneous consolidation and multilateralization of these regional blocs, with important consequences not only for the development strategies of the export-oriented nations of East Asia, the Caribbean, Mexico, and Canada, but also for the process of industrialization being carried out in the United States.

INTERNATIONAL SUBCONTRACTING IN THE WORLD-ECONOMY: A TYPOLOGY OF EXPORT ROLES

Industrialization today is the result of an integrated system of global production and trade, buttressed by new forms of investment and financing, promoted by specific government policies, and entailing distinctive patterns of spatial and social organization. International trade has allowed nations to specialize in different branches of manufacturing and even in different stages of production within a specific industry. This situation has led to the emergence of a global manufacturing system in which production capacity has been dispersed to an unprecedented number of developing as well as industrialized countries (Gereffi, 1989a, 1989b).

In the contemporary global manufacturing system, the production of a single good commonly spans several countries and regions, with each nation performing tasks in which it has a cost advantage. This is true for traditional manufactures, such as garments, as well as for modern products, like automobiles and computers. "International subcontracting" refers to the strategy whereby transnational corporations (TNCs) assign the most labor-intensive phases of production of a shirt, a car, or a semiconductor to countries where the labor costs are lowest. Technology-intensive production processes tend to be located in the manufacturing plants of highly industrialized nations as well as in technically more advanced Third World sites such as the newly industrializing countries (NICs) of East Asia and Latin America. Typically, the research and development activities are retained in the home countries of the TNCs (the United States, Japan, or Western Europe) where corporate control functions are concentrated.

The Latin American and East Asian NICs have shifted from inward- to outward-oriented paths of industrialization in the world-economy (Gereffi & Wyman, 1990; Gereffi, 1990a). This transition has resulted in several kinds of international subcontracting arrangements: (1) export-processing zones; (2) component-supply production; and (3) commercial subcontracting. Foreign firms in these cases usually look for a contractor—either an individual agent or another firm—to do a part or all of the production process. The contractor may then subcontract the job to other agents or firms, who in turn may farm parts of the job out to still other subcontractors, until the production is completed. Thus, international subcontracting involves complex production networks that may contain many levels or tiers of transactions.

Not all exports involve subcontracting relationships. There are open-market exports between unrelated parties, in which the exporting firm may be owned locally or by a foreign enterprise. These independent exports thus constitute a fourth export role in the world-economy (see Table 4.1).

These export roles are not mutually exclusive. A given country may simultaneously occupy several roles, and the relative importance of these roles may change substantially over time. While each of these export roles has advantages and disadvantages in terms of a nation's development objectives, these roles should be seen as interactive sets that jointly determine a country's ability to benefit from its involvement in transnational productive networks.

The *export-processing role* refers to those nations that have foreign-owned, labor-intensive assembly of manufactured goods in export-processing zones. These zones offer special incentives to foreign capital and tend to attract firms in a common set of industries: garments, footwear, and basic electronics. Virtually all of the East Asian and Latin American NICs have engaged in this form of labor-intensive production, although the significance of export processing wanes as wage rates rise and countries become more developed.

In Taiwan and South Korea, export-processing zones have been on the decline during the past 10 to 15 years, largely because labor costs have been rapidly rising. These nations have upgraded their mix of export activities by moving toward more

Table 4.1
Industrial Export Roles in the World-Economy (Selected Examples from Latin America and East Asia)

Economic Role	Country/Industry	Production Process	Trends
Export Processing	Garments, footwear, and electronics assembly in a wide range of East Asian, Latin American, and Caribbean nations (U.S. imports: 806/807 tariff items before 1989)	Labor-intensive	Declining in importance in Taiwan and South Korea; resurgent in Latin America (e.g., Mexico's *maquiladora* industry)
Component Supplier	Mexico and Brazil: motor vehicles, computers, pharmaceuticals East Asian NICs: computers, TVs, electrical appliances, motor vehicles, sporting goods, etc.	Technology-intensive and Capital-intensive	Original-equipment manufacturer (OEM) production divided between "captive" and "merchant" producers
Commercial Subcontracting	A diverse array of finished consumer goods exports, mainly from Hong Kong, Taiwan and South Korea	Labor-intensive and Technology-intensive	Tendency for East Asian NICs to move to higher value-added items to avoid protectionist measures in core markets
Independent Exports	Diverse manufactured goods ranging from food, clothing and electronics items to construction and natural-resource based materials (e.g., cement, plywood and chemicals)	Mixed	Unlike the industrial and commercial subcontracting roles, independent export networks and marketing ties need to be established between the manufacturer and the distributor or retailer

skill- and technology-intensive products. The export-processing role in Asia is now being occupied by low-wage countries like China, the Philippines, Thailand, Indonesia, and Malaysia.

In Latin America, by contrast, export-processing industries are on the upswing because wage levels in most countries of the region are considerably below those of the East Asian NICs, and recent currency devaluations in the Latin American NICs make the price of their exports more competitive internationally. The export platforms in Latin America also have the advantage of geographical proximity to the most important industrial markets (North America and Europe), compared with the more distant Asian export-processing zones. Mexico's *maquiladora* industry is probably the largest and most dynamic of these export areas (see Gereffi, 1991). There are similar zones in Brazil, Colombia, Central America, and the Caribbean. Core country firms control the production, export, and marketing stages of the production networks for these consumer goods. The main contribution of peripheral nations is cheap labor.

The *component-supplier role* refers to the production of component parts in capital- and technology-intensive industries in the NICs for export and usually for final assembly in the developed countries. This type of international industrial subcontracting has two main subcategories: (1) "capacity" subcontracting, in which both the parent firm and the subcontractor engage in the fabrication of similar products in order to handle overflow or cyclical demand; and (2) "specialization" subcontracting, in which parts produced by the subcontractor are not made in-house by the parent firm. Whereas "capacity" subcontracting involves a horizontal disintegration of production, "specialization" subcontracting is a vertical disintegration of production (see Holmes, 1986: 86).

Component supply has been a key niche for the Latin American NICs' manufactured exports during the past two decades. Brazil and Mexico are important production sites for vertically integrated exports by TNCs to developed country markets, especially the United States, since the late 1960s. This is most notable in certain industries like motor vehicles, computers, and pharmaceuticals (see Newfarmer, 1985). American, European, and Japanese automotive TNCs, for example, have advanced manufacturing facilities in Mexico and Brazil for the production of engines, auto parts, and even completed vehicles for the U.S. and European markets (Gereffi, 1990b; Shaiken, 1987).

In Latin America, the manufacturing stage of component-supplier production is typically owned and run by foreign capital, sometimes in conjunction with a local partner. The export, distribution, and marketing of the manufactured items are handled by the TNC. This production arrangement is the one most likely to result in a significant transfer of technology from the developed countries to their supplier nations.

In East Asia, there are two variants of the component-supplier role. The first is similar to the Latin American arrangement in which *foreign subsidiaries* manufacture parts or subunits in East Asia for products like television sets, radios, sporting goods, and consumer appliances that are assembled and marketed in the country of destination (most often, the United States). The firms that engage in this form of specialization subcontracting can be considered as "captive" companies that supply the bulk of their production (usually in excess of 75 percent) to their parent corporation.

The second variant of the component-supplier role in East Asia involves the production of components by *local firms* for sale to diversified buyers on the world market. These "merchant" producers, in contrast to the "captive" companies mentioned above, sell virtually all of their output on the open market. The importance of "merchant" producers is illustrated in the semiconductor industry. South Korean electronics companies have specialized in the mass production of powerful memory chips, the single largest segment of the semiconductor industry, which are sold as inputs to a wide range of domestic and international manufacturers of electronic equipment. Taiwan, on the other hand, has targeted the highest value-added segment of the semiconductor market: tailor-made "designer chips" that perform special tasks in toys, video games, and other machines. Taiwan now has 40 chip-design houses that specialize in finding export niches and then developing products for them ("Sizzling Hot Chips," 1988). While the South Korean companies are engaging in a form of "capacity" subcontracting, the Taiwanese producers of specialty semiconductor chips represent a variant on "specialization" subcontracting.

The *commercial-subcontracting role* refers to the production of finished consumer goods by locally owned firms, whereby the output is distributed and marketed by large retail chains and their agents (Holmes, 1986: 85). This is one of the major niches filled by the East Asian NICs in the contemporary world-economy. In 1980, three of the East Asian NICs (Hong Kong, Taiwan, and South Korea) accounted for 72 percent of all finished consumer goods exported by the Third World to the member-states of the Organization for Economic Cooperation and Development (OECD); other Asian countries supplied another 19 percent, while just 7 percent came from Latin America and the Caribbean. The United States was the leading market for these products, with 46 percent of the total (Keesing, 1983: 338–339). In East Asia, domestic firms control the production stage of the finished-consumer-goods commodity chains, while foreign capital tends to control the more profitable export, distribution, and retail marketing stages. While the international subcontracting of finished consumer goods is growing in Latin America, it tends to be subordinated to the export-processing and component-supplier forms of production.

The latter two forms of international subcontracting, component-supply and commercial subcontracting, can be steppingstones to more autonomous levels of industrial development if the manufacturing countries introduce new products and gain some degree of control over the marketing of the goods that they make. Taiwan, with its technological prowess, is acquiring the flexibility to move into the high value-added field of product innovation. Without their own internationally recognized company brand names, a substantial advertising budget, and appropriate marketing and retail networks, however, Taiwan's indigenous producers will find it difficult to break free of the commercial-subcontracting role. South Korea probably has more potential to enter developed country markets successfully because its large, vertically integrated industrial conglomerates (*chaebols*) have the capital and technology to set up overseas production facilities and marketing networks. Thus, South Korea's leading auto manufacturer, Hyundai Motor Company, has become one of the top importers into both Canada and the United States since the mid-1980s (see Gereffi, 1990b).

The final role in this typology is the *independent-exporter role*. This refers to those export industries in which there is no subcontracting relationship between the manufacturer and the distributor or retailer of the product. These goods can range from construction materials (like cement, lumber, and standard chemicals) to a wide variety of food, clothing, and electronic items (such as beer, watches, jewelry, radios, etc.). Independent party transactions are most common for resource-based or mature products in which the logic of the comparative advantage paradigm still works to a degree. Transport and energy costs, exchange rates, wages, interest rates, and low-priced, resource-based inputs all play a determining role in the growth of these exports.

This typology of the different roles that the Latin American and East Asian NICs play in the world-economy shows that the standard development literature has presented an oversimplified picture of the semiperiphery. The East Asian NICs have been most successful in the areas of commercial subcontracting and component supply, with secondary and declining importance given to the export-processing role that is emphasized in "the new international division of labor" literature (Fröbel, Heinrichs & Kreye, 1980). The Latin American NICs, on the other hand, have a different kind of relationship to the world-economy. They are prominent in the commodity-export, export-platform, and component-supplier forms of production, but they lag far behind the East Asian NICs in the commercial-subcontracting type of manufactured exports.

Although each of these roles has certain advantages and disadvantages in terms of mobility in the world-system, the prospects for the NICs can be understood only by looking at the interacting sets of roles in which these nations are enmeshed. The Latin American nations tend to be far more economically diverse than the East Asian NICs. Many of the former possess a wide range of natural resources, abundant labor, and relatively large domestic markets. This allows Latin American nations to pursue a variety of export roles simultaneously, including raw material exports. The objective should be to create *competitive* advantage by maximizing the economic and technological benefits that can be attained from this industrial diversity, rather than to rely exclusively on the region's current *comparative* advantage in cheap labor and proximity to the U.S. market.

GLOBAL SOURCING: DIVERSE PATTERNS IN THREE INDUSTRIES

The three kinds of international subcontracting discussed in the preceding section are all used to promote the global sourcing of production, but their relative importance varies across industries. *Export-processing* production involves the labor-intensive assembly of manufactured goods, often in officially designated industrial zones that offer special incentives to foreign investors. This form of global sourcing has been significant in certain phases of all three of the industries considered below, since garments, certain auto parts (e.g., wiring harnesses), and the manufacture of semiconductors for use in personal computers all have labor-intensive assembly phases in the production process where major savings can be achieved in low-wage countries. *Component-supply subcontracting* refers to the manufacture of technologically sophisticated component parts for export to original-equipment manufacturers in the developed countries. This is an increasingly important feature of the automobile, computer, and household appliance industries. *Commercial subcontracting* of finished goods is based on specification buying by large-volume retailers, who market the goods under private labels or in their own retail outlets. This is particularly common in the garment industry, but it is also of growing significance in the personal computer, replacement auto parts, and footwear industries (see Gereffi & Korzeniewicz, 1990, regarding footwear). Finally, there are the *independent exporters*, who do not utilize subcontracting relationships in order to sell their goods abroad. They must assume the responsibility not only for production but also for overseas marketing that utilizes their brand names, as exemplified by auto producers in South Korea (Hyundai) and personal computer companies in Taiwan (Acer) and South Korea (Leading Edge).

These various types of global sourcing entail different sets of preconditions for the exporting countries. Export-processing production is based on abundant cheap labor, political stability, and often a battery of official investment incentives. This is the easiest of the export roles for a developing country to adopt, but it is also inherently unstable as wage levels and political conditions change. The component-supplier role requires more highly skilled labor and investors who are willing to set up capital- and technology-intensive plants in the NICs. A nation's proximity to core-country markets is an advantage for both the export-processing and component-supplier forms of global sourcing, since this decreases transport costs and increases the speed of delivery for seasonal industries like garments and footwear. Commercial subcontracting requires a local entrepreneurial class that has the capital and technological ability to supply large-volume, original-equipment-manufacturer (OEM) contracts for developed country markets. The size of firms is not as important as the ability to shift output flexibly in response to the buyers' needs. Finally, successful independent exporters must control export and distribution networks in global commodity chains, in addition to attaining a high degree of productive efficiency. Large vertically integrated firms have a major advantage here, as do those with distinctive or technologically innovative products. So far, among the NICs, South Korea has made the biggest strides in this direction because the *chaebols* have the financial, technological, and marketing resources needed to become fully internationalized.

Garments

The garment industry was one of the first sectors in which developing nations achieved a rapid growth of manufactured exports to the industrialized economies. The Third World share in international trade in this sector nearly doubled, from 22 percent to 41 percent, between 1970 and 1981. In the mid-1980s, clothing accounted for 21 percent of all Third World manufactured exports, with Hong Kong, South Korea, and Taiwan being by far the largest clothes exporters (Hoffman, 1985: 371). Together, the East Asian NICs accounted for 60 percent of all clothing imports to the United States in 1988 ($13.6 billion), while the total share for Latin American nations was just under 10 percent ($2.2 billion). As we can see in Table 4.2, although the East Asian share of U.S. clothing imports declined by 14 percentage points (from 73.5 percent to 59.6 percent) between 1980 and 1988, the Latin American nations (excluding Central America and the Caribbean) increased their share of the U.S. market by only 1 percentage point (from 8.6 percent to 9.8 percent) during this same period.

The manufacture of apparel has traditionally been a highly labor-intensive activity with low capital and technical requirements. The industry relies on a combination of dextrous, low-paid, and predominantly female workers, and sturdy, flexible, and relatively inexpensive sewing machines as the basic units of production.

Table 4.2
U.S. Imports of Textile and Clothing Products, 1980 and 1985–1988
(millions of U.S. Dollars, customs value)

Year		Total	Latin America[1]	Percent of total US imports	East Asia	Percent of total US imports
1980	Textiles	$2,676	$239	8.9	$929	34.7
	Clothing	6,848	586	8.6	5,035	73.5
1985	Textiles	5,274	389	7.4	1,985	37.6
	Clothing	16,056	1,070	6.7	10,727	66.8
1986	Textiles	5,768	446	7.7	2,177	37.7
	Clothing	17,288	1,216	7.0	10,814	62.5
1987	Textiles	6,511	543	8.3	2,268	34.8
	Clothing	20,490	1,627	7.9	12,606	61.5
1988	Textiles	6,748	567	8.4	2,225	33.0
	Clothing	22,877	2,231	9.8	13,642	59.6

[1]Excluding Central America and the Caribbean.
Source: U.S. Department of Commerce, *Highlights of U.S. Export and Import Trade*, various years.

Clothing manufacturing is a sequential, multistage activity that can be divided into three phases: (1) preassembly (the inspection, grading, marking, and cutting of the cloth); (2) assembly, which involves up to 100 sequential sewing operations; and (3) finishing, which basically entails pressing and packaging the completed garment (Hoffman, 1985: 375–376). Since the assembly of clothes from soft, limp fabrics requires considerable manual manipulation of the materials by machine operators at all stages of production, the industry has been highly resistant to automation.

The international organization of garment production is basically a response to three kinds of factors: (1) manufacturing costs, (2) national protective barriers, and (3) industrial flexibility. Materials and labor are the two primary manufacturing costs in garment production. Material costs are roughly the same for all producers. Labor costs, by contrast, vary considerably from region to region and are thus the main determinant of international competitive advantage in the apparel industry. The hourly wage for textile workers in 1982, for example, was $5.20 in the United States, $1.80 in Hong Kong, $1.50 in Taiwan, $1.00 in South Korea, $0.40 in the Philippines, and $0.20 in mainland China (Mody & Wheeler, 1986: 29). Since labor costs are at least four times greater in the United States than in the Asian NICs and China, firms operating in the United States are at a considerable cost disadvantage. The large savings in labor costs thus has led U.S. apparel producers to invest heavily in offshore production.

Protective trade legislation (voluntary and involuntary export quotas, import tariffs, and other trade restrictions) continues to have a dramatic effect upon global sourcing in the garment industry. The consequences of tariffs are generally more straight-forward than quotas because they directly increase the overall cost of imported products. Price-sensitive retailers tend to source their garments from firms in nations with low tariffs imposed on them because it lowers total costs. The effect of the U.S. export quota system on international sourcing is much more convoluted than that of tariffs, largely because the U.S. system itself is so complex. For example, the United States uses 75 narrow product categories for garment quotas, with many U.S. quotas based upon the quantity (or number) rather than on the value of exports. To evade these quotas, exporting nations commonly switch their production to items or materials not yet subject to quotas. In the late 1970s, Hong Kong apparel producers began to export garments composed largely of ramie, a rough linenlike fiber that was not included in U.S. quotas at the time. Similarly, in the early 1980s, some Hong Kong manufacturers started making jackets with zip-on sleeves, since the quota on jackets was tight, but there were no quotas on vests or sleeves (Dertouzos, Lester, & Solow, 1989: 292; Lardner, 1988: 60, 62–65).

Industrial flexibility refers to the ability of the industry to produce what buyers demand. In recent years, U.S. firms have started to become more responsive to retailers' demands in order to meet the challenge from foreign companies in a wide range of industries ranging from apparel to autos. Liz Claiborne, a major U.S. fashion company, began to source abroad less as a matter of price than because of the difficulty in finding capable domestic suppliers who were willing to give Claiborne the variety of fabrics and the careful tailoring the firm wanted (Lardner, 1988).

Technological innovations in the garment industry have begun to change the logic of global sourcing, however. Sophisticated computer-aided design (CAD) and computer-aided manufacturing (CAM) systems are now available to carry out the design, grading, and marking activities in the preassembly stage of production. In the assembly and finishing stages as well, numerical control and microcomputer-based sewing machines, robotic handling devices, and automated transfer systems are becoming more commonplace (Hoffman, 1985). Garment producers in the United States can thus keep tariff duties to a minimum by performing the technology-intensive and high value-added preassembly stage of apparel production in the United States, while the more labor-intensive assembly stage is still sourced offshore to low-wage nations. In addition, U.S. quotas that are based on quantity (rather than on value) of exports have led some of the major East Asian garment-producing nations to make higher value-added clothes in order to increase the profitability of their fixed supply of exports. This strategy of climbing the value-added ladder has been hindered by the marked currency appreciations that have affected East Asian nations like Taiwan and South Korea.

Automobiles

The international motor vehicle industry underwent a profound change in the 1970s and 1980s. The oil price rises of 1973 and 1979, coupled with the rapid growth of the Japanese automotive industry since the 1960s and the declining demand for motor vehicles in the main producing countries, significantly advanced the internationalization of capital and fostered the creation of a truly global industry. The three regional blocs of North America, Europe, and East Asia are becoming much more closely linked in trade, cross-investments, and joint production arrangements (Jenkins, 1987).

The leading automotive TNCs have transformed their global sourcing arrangements in two novel ways. First, the industry is integrating its production process on a global scale by the international sourcing of standard parts and engineering resources needed to design and build "world cars." In this way, certain countries have emerged as the key suppliers for basic components or even entire vehicles. Second, automotive TNCs are producing more complex components with advanced technologies in developing countries. This "world component-supply strategy" entails a higher degree of technological sophistication and country specialization than the complementary "world car strategy," which emphasizes broadly based and sometimes regional production schemes of a more labor-intensive nature.

The trend toward regional integration within the global strategies of car makers is well illustrated by Toyota's recent agreement with members of the Association of Southeast Asian Nations (ASEAN) to begin a component-parts exchange program (Smith, 1989). Diesel engines from Thailand, gasoline engines from Indonesia, steering gears from Malaysia, and transmissions from the Philippines are to be made in and shipped between participating countries for assembly onto cars that will eventually be sent back to Japan for export to overseas markets. Such an arrangement would help Japan to minimize tariffs within the ASEAN bloc and also avoid U.S. export quotas, since component supplies from the other Asian nations would not be counted as Japanese domestic content.

Mexico provides a good example of specialized component assembly for the U.S. market. Lured by low wages, a favorable currency exchange rate, close proximity to the United States, and favorable Mexican legislation, world automakers and parts suppliers have increased their exports from plants in Mexico (Gereffi, 1990b). Automobile engines are being manufactured by United States-based TNCs in high volume for incorporation into cars built in their U.S. plants. Mexican engine production is the epitome of global integration, combining "U.S. managers, European technology, Japanese manufacturing systems, and Mexican workers" (Shaiken, 1987: 2).

The common pressures toward internationalization in both production and trade have produced distinct results in the Latin American and East Asian NICs (Gereffi, 1990b: 106). Although South Korea and Brazil have both stressed the export of *finished vehicles*, their results stem from different kinds of corporate strategies and structures. The large integrated domestic auto companies in South Korea have been able to fund long-term investment and product development both at home and overseas, leading to the establishment of Korean automobile subsidiaries in major external markets like the United States and Canada. Brazil's exports of finished vehicles, on the other hand, reflect the desire of American, Japanese, and European TNCs to use Brazil as a regional base to serve their customers in neighboring Latin American and other Third World countries.

Taiwan and Mexico have tended to emphasize the production of *auto parts* in the global motor vehicle industry, with close ties to the U.S. market. Whereas Mexico has implemented this component-supplier strategy through the intrafirm networks of automotive TNCs, Taiwan has relied heavily on the efforts of 2,000 domestic auto parts companies, the majority of which are family businesses that are able to respond quickly to shifting consumer demand but less able to invest in the research and expensive production machinery needed to improve their design capability and technological sophistication. While Taiwan's auto assembly industry provided around 10,000 jobs in the mid-1980s, its parts industry employed 50,000 people. Nearly 60 percent of Taiwan's auto exports are sent to the United States. These are add-on accessories or spare parts sold for cars already in use; relatively few of Taiwan's auto parts exporters have major OEM contracts for new cars (Tank, 1986: 29–31).

In summary, these differences in the mode of incorporation of each of the NICs into the global motor vehicle industry are caused by national variations in industrial structure, the competitive strategies of the leading auto manufacturers world-wide, and the distinctive role of automobiles in advanced phases of ISI and EOI.

Personal Computers

The production of personal computers consists of four different stages that can be separated in time and space: knowledge-based research and design, advanced manufacturing, unskilled assembly work, and final product testing (Henderson, 1989; Castells, 1989). Each stage has distinct labor requirements, which has led to the spatial segmentation of the global industry. Research and design activities require ready access to highly trained scientists and engineers, which is facilitated by proximity to universities and research institutes such as those found in the innovative centers of the United States, Europe, and Japan. Advanced manufacturing and testing functions require skilled manual workers, technicians, and quality control supervision. This phase of production has been dispersed to semiperipheral locations in East Asia and Latin America in recent years; these locations contain, at a minimum, isolated pools of skilled labor and an adequate industrial infrastructure. Increased automation in the advanced manufacturing and testing areas of production, however, has led to a gradual return of some of these jobs to the more developed countries. Finally, assembly activities continue to draw mainly on unskilled labor, and they are overwhelmingly located in the low-wage areas of East Asia, Latin America, and the Caribbean.

Three primary patterns of global sourcing are evident within the personal computer industry (see O'Connor, 1985; Henderson, 1989). First, much like the garment and footwear industries, the personal computer industry depends to a considerable degree on the sourcing of semi-skilled, labor-intensive production operations from low-wage locations offshore. Second, the global sourcing of components and "peripherals" is common in the personal computer industry because developing nations are able to manufacture components without necessarily having the technological capability to make complete computer systems. South Korean and Taiwanese producers have specialized in producing computer hardware on an OEM basis for computer TNCs (Evans & Tigre, 1989). Third, the sourcing of finished personal computers from the Third World into the United States is a relatively limited phenomenon, since most developing nations lack the internal market that would be needed to allow them to become efficient broad-line producers of completed personal computers. Mexico has an arrangement with IBM, however, to export finished computers to the U.S. market, and similar arrangements are being considered in other NICs.

REGIONAL DIVISIONS OF LABOR AND THE RESHAPING OF THE PACIFIC RIM

The trend toward global sourcing arrangements and international subcontracting in the world-economy has profoundly affected the regional dynamics in East Asia and North America. While the internal division of labor *within* each region has become more complex, the economic and social linkages *between* the two regions have also increased. This has produced a simultaneous consolidation and multilateralization of these regional blocs.

From a regional perspective, East Asia has developed a very distinctive international division of labor. Japan is the technologically advanced core country of the East Asian region, with the East Asian NICs (South Korea, Taiwan, Hong

Kong, and Singapore) playing the role of a semiperiphery whose continuous industrial upgrading is pushing them toward more technology-intensive, high value-added exports. Taiwan and South Korea have also taken in some of the energy-intensive and heavy-polluting industries that are no longer encouraged to remain in Japan (such as chemicals, fertilizers, and mineral-smelting operations). The periphery in East Asia consists of the resource-rich, lower-wage countries, such as the Philippines, Malaysia, Thailand, Indonesia, and China, that not only supply the region with raw material exports but also specialize in the labor-intensive manufacturing industries that had been the export success stories of the East Asian NICs in the first stage of their EOI in the 1960s (see Cumings, 1987; Henderson, 1989).

A very similar regional division of labor is emerging in North America. The United States is the core country in North America, both as a production center and as a market. It has established tight transnational linkages with Canada and now with Mexico as well in a range of capital-intensive, high-technology industries such as automobiles and machinery, both electrical and nonelectrical. Unlike the East Asian situation, however, all three of the main economies in North America also are rich in natural resources. Although Mexico has traditionally been the site for labor-intensive exports from its "old" *maquiladora* plants, many of these same export-oriented assembly operations are now springing up in a number of Caribbean nations, which may become the favored locales for these peripheral economic activities. One additional element in the North American situation is the growing importance of Asian investments in the region, with Japanese firms concentrating on the "new" technology-intensive export industries and with Korean and Taiwanese companies investing in the "old" labor-intensive assembly operations (Gereffi, 1991).

Neither the proposed free trade agreement between the United States and Mexico nor a broader North American Free Trade Agreement (NAFTA) that would include Canada and perhaps the Caribbean as well is likely to diminish the substantial transnational integration that has already been established in the region. While NAFTA explicitly focuses on trade, the ongoing globalization of production in the world-economy has produced a "silent integration" in North America that makes the strategic investment decisions by TNCs the prime determinant of new intraregional and interregional trading patterns.

In a formal sense, *maquiladora* industries will cease to exist in Mexico as a legal category if a zero-tariff NAFTA is put into place. Historically, the main reason that *maquiladoras* were set up was to take advantage of the U.S. tariff provisions (806/807) that allowed participating firms to receive duty-free inputs from the United States and thereby to pay tax only on the value added in Mexico. With no tariffs, *maquiladora* plants would be an anachronism.

In reality, however, labor-intensive assembly industries tend to be established wherever low wages, adequate infrastructure, and political stability are to be found. Mexico remains a very attractive site for these investments, although there is also likely to be a sharp growth of "old"-style *maquiladoras* in the Caribbean and

Central America where labor costs are as low as in Mexico and where the "rules of origin" restrictions of a NAFTA may not apply. If Mexico follows the example of the East Asian NICs, it will try to promote the "new" *maquiladoras*, because of their added contributions to national development objectives, and to allow many of the "old" *maquiladoras* to migrate to other sites in the region (Gereffi, 1991).

It is important to note in this context, however, that there has been a proliferation of labor-intensive subcontracting plants on the U.S. side of the border as well. Industries like garments and electronics are burgeoning in large cities such as Los Angeles, Miami, and New York City, which can draw on vast pools of low-wage and, in many cases, undocumented immigrant workers from Mexico, Central America, the Caribbean, and Asia. Many of these plants have been set up by East Asian entrepreneurs to avoid U.S. trade barriers and to exploit low-cost labor, with the added advantage of direct access to the design and marketing centers in the United States. Thus, there are new social and economic networks that connect investment, trade, and migration flows between the countries at all levels of development in North America, with "reverse investments" from East Asian exporters into the region as well.

The trends toward North American integration indicate that the very concept of "national development" is being redefined. Indeed, it may already be outmoded. Countries are trying to create dynamic sources of competitive advantage that allow for both increased productivity and a higher standard of living for their citizenry. These goals are particularly difficult to attain in a region like North America, where nations are at such different levels of development and where the strength of transnational capital is so pronounced. The challenge for development studies is to discover how to promote an enhanced quality of life, participatory institutions, and a strong sense of cultural identity while national borders are becoming ever more porous.

If development theory is to be relevant for the 1990s, it will have to be flexible enough to incorporate both increased specialization at the product and geographical levels, along with new forms of integration that link the core, semiperipheral, and peripheral nations of the Pacific Rim in novel ways. The production and export networks of the garment, automobile, and personal computer industries illustrate the various modes of incorporation of the NICs in the world-economy and the continuing geographical realignment of the location of core and peripheral economic activities in today's global commodity chains.

5

STRATEGIES OF ECONOMIC ASCENDANTS FOR ACCESS TO RAW MATERIALS: A COMPARISON OF THE UNITED STATES AND JAPAN

Stephen G. Bunker and Denis O'Hearn

Raw materials prices determine the organic composition of capital and therefore of rates of profit and of capital accumulation. Disruptions of access to raw materials destabilize economies by provoking unemployment, causing inflation, creating bottlenecks, and threatening financial institutions with defaults and bankruptcies. Both capital and the state in industrialized nations therefore act strategically to assure continuous flows of raw materials, particularly of those that supply sectors of the national economy where there are opportunities for surplus profits or that are vital for the national defense.

Economic ascendants in the world-system elaborate especially aggressive strategies for access to raw materials. Their ascent often begins during periods of global expansion when demand approaches or surpasses existing capacity, which raises prices and limits accumulation. The rate of increase of their demand for expanded supply exceeds the global average, but previous ascendants have already captured most sources and may still dominate extractive and transport technologies. Furthermore, established core firms may be reluctant or unable to invest sufficient capital to assure the extra supplies that are needed by the new ascendant. Sustained ascent therefore requires that ascendants exploit weaknesses in the established political and economic relations that govern raw materials extraction and export in order to assure both independence of access and adequacy of supply. Their attempts to do so exacerbate the instability, subordination, dependency, and internal disarticulation of regional economies that depend on raw materials exports.

In this chapter, we examine the strategies of two rising economic powers to gain favorable access to raw materials. The first is the United States, which faced the task of displacing European imperial control of vast reserves. The United States did so by exploiting the weaknesses of the colonial powers—externally, in terms of colonial control, and internally, in terms of economic crisis and reconstruction.

In turn, Japan has exploited subsequent U.S. weaknesses in terms of peripheral economic control and industrial crisis.

RAW MATERIALS AND PACE OF INDUSTRIALIZATION: SOME INITIAL DIFFERENCES

The association of shifts in the core of world-system hierarchies with the acceleration in the expansion of industrial production has profound implications for resource extractive peripheries. Expanded industrial production generally requires expanded resource extraction. Both expansions require the investment of capital accumulated in the previous circulation of capital. Earlier cycles have often reduced or depleted the resource deposits located closest or most conveniently to the sites of industrial transformation. As technological and investment scales have generally increased during and between expansive cycles, so larger deposits are required at each subsequent cycle. The depletion of convenient sources and the increasing scale combine to drive the locus of extraction further from the geographical centers of world industry—in other words, further from the established infrastructure and beyond the spatial limits of the existing institutions of private property, credit, wage relations, and labor discipline that have evolved along with capitalist industry. Thus, the technological and infrastructural requirements imposed on seekers of raw materials in successive cycles become ever more complex.

Strategies of access vary over time and with specific raw materials according to the condition and structure of world financial and commodity markets, technological change, changes in the scale and organic composition of extraction and processing, number of economically viable sources of the raw material, and their location in space and topography. The economic, political, and technological strength of ascendants, relative to the requirements of attaining new sources of materials, may vary, however, with their level of industrialization at the time that they challenge the control of previous hegemons. Raw materials became a "problem" for U.S. industry after industrial capitalism was well developed, while Japan was forced to seek access to foreign raw materials relatively early.

The conditions under which the United States and Japan sought to expand their control of foreign raw materials were also different. The United States expanded its global access after World War II when the former hegemonic power, Britain, was practically spent. British colonial control was still in place, although it was under attack from within the colonies, which aspired to independence and to industrial modernization. The United States presented itself as disposed and able to invest dollars without demanding direct political control. British colonial administration of areas that contained vast reserves of raw materials was replaced by private investment in those resources, within a liberal international trading order policed by the United States. This solved the twin problems of security of access and adequacy of supply.

Japan started its ascent toward hegemony in the late 1960s, in a very different world. The United States was still a dominant political, military, and economic power. During the intervening 25 years, the enormous growth in the demand for raw materials in international commerce allowed major savings through the increased scale of transport. Both the expanded demand and economies in transport started to break down the regional trading blocs that U.S.-led direct foreign investment (DFI) had created. At the same time, U.S. private investments in peripheral minerals were threatened by burgeoning resource nationalism (see Girvan, 1980).

The industrial nations' demands for cheap and reliable sources of raw materials were satisfied in three central ways by each subsequent expanding power. Britain sought access through colonial control, imposing the conditions of extraction and the prices of resources through state power. The United States sought monopoly control, based on varying combinations of patent control and exclusive contracts with exporting states and of production-regulating agreements among a small number of large firms. Japan has sought (and seeks) to diversity sources in competitive markets. Each choice of strategy reflects the relations between the core nations and the means available to them to subordinate peripheral nations at economically viable costs. Both the second and third strategies may involve the creation of excess capacity, but excess capacity appears in distinct forms. Monopolies and oligopolies strive to capture reserves (potential capacity) by buying up or contracting for mineral deposits or potential energy-generating sites at low agricultural, rather than high mineral, rents, in order to freeze new entrants out of the market (see O'Hearn, 1990, on Jamaica; and Barham, 1990, on Canada). Diversification strategies, on the other hand, require the actual building of capacity rather than simply holding onto reserves, and thus require far more capital investment. The willingness of host countries to share in the costs of investment is therefore critical. Host countries, however, do not have access to market information, and so they may contribute directly to excess supply, driving prices below those required for them to repay the debts incurred in their share of investment. Furthermore, they are not likely to benefit from the consumption advantages which offset the effects of low resource prices to the international investors.

THE U.S. CASE: OLIGOPOLISTIC CONTROL WITHIN THE "GRAND AREA"

The immediate stimuli to the post-World War II drive for U.S. hegemony were the problems of access to industrial materials and of opening peripheral markets to industrial exports. The large-scale transfer of manufacturing operations to the periphery was only a vague possibility in the minds of more farsighted capitalists and academics. Materials and markets were needed "here and now."

While small miners, farmers, ranchers, and some industries favored a protected U.S. market, the postwar depression amply proved to large industrial and finance capital that accumulation at an expanding rate required access to foreign materials and markets. A series of studies undertaken by the Council on Foreign Relations

(CFR) set out a blueprint for a postwar world economic order, including an international monetary system, an international development bank, and agreements on international trade and the exploitation of minerals (Council on Foreign Relations, 1946). CFR members dominated executive agencies and postwar reconstruction bodies, which enabled the implementation of these programs (Shoup & Minter, 1977; Hogan, 1987; Wexler, 1983; Block, 1977).

The basis of postwar U.S. hegemony was the creation of a trading bloc or "grand area," in the interests of U.S. industrial capital. Shifting trade patterns—from primary to manufactured exports and from manufactured to private imports—created problems for U.S. producers. Peripheral exports of raw materials to the United States were not rising as rapidly as their imports of finished goods from the United States (Upgren, 1940c; 1940e). This imbalance created inflationary pressures, threatening U.S. industrial expansion (Upgren, 1940a). It was therefore necessary to increase U.S. access to peripheral resources at a greater rate than that at which markets for U.S. industrial goods were expanding. The "grand area" would solve the problems of raw materials supply and international demand simultaneously. U.S. capital exports would finance and organize peripheral raw materials production. The capital exports would be paid for by peripheral exports of raw materials (Upgren, 1940b). This system of trade would be regulated by DFI: While free trade opened the door to U.S. capital exports and materials imports, direct control of peripheral mineral reserves by private firms would ensure that such trade would increase over time.

The "grand area" would integrate Asia and the British empire into the existing United States-Western Hemisphere bloc (Upgren, 1940c: 18). The British empire contained most of the raw materials needed by U.S. industry, while Britain was a massive importer of surplus western grain, meat, and dairy products. The bloc's remarkable self-sufficiency, especially if other European empires were added (Upgren, 1940b, 1940d) would ensure both rapid accumulation and stability. Members would remain in the grand area if they were left with neither surplus exports nor unmet import demands (Upgren, 1941b).

Raw materials problems, Eugene Staley has emphasized, were political problems. Materials existed in abundance throughout the world, if only they could be acquired. They could be acquired by altering political boundaries, but raw materials requirements were so great that this would require the transfer of whole continents or empires, which was impractical. Thus, Staley asserted, "what a country really needs is raw materials within its trading area, not necessarily within its political boundaries" (1937: 58). Free access was possible by changing the meaning of political boundaries, by implementing an open door to U.S. investment, and by trade throughout the colonial empires. Giant integrated extracting-processing-fabricating firms could then step through the open door to obtain cheap and assured access to materials.

Stability of access to materials during periods of threats to trade within the "grand area" could be ensured by combining the concepts of the "strategic interests" of the U.S. state with the "critical interests" of U.S. industry. By establishing a state minerals policy with mechanisms to counteract threats to access, the state could become an "international maritime police" (in the words of Joseph Schumpeter) to enforce free trade. A major policy instrument for this purpose, apart from encouraging U.S. DFI, was the creation of stockpiles of "critical" materials.

European requirements for postwar reconstruction aid brought the opportunity to consolidate the grand area. CFR experts insisted that the British were so dependent on U.S. aid that they would take American direction on economic matters. Within an "Anglo-American condominium," U.S. capital would enter the empire under the same terms as that of British traders and investors. In time, other European empires would also be drawn into the scheme (Upgren, 1940c, 1940d, 1940e; 1941a, 1941b). A CFR study concluded that the "status of dependent areas is no longer the concern of individual possessing powers. On the contrary, both the native people and the world at large must be recognized as having a prior interest in the post-war settlement of this problem" (Sharp, 1942:2).

The establishment of the grand area required that British control of colonial investments and resources be broken down. Trade restrictions, land tenure regulations, the vesting of mineral rights in the crown, the control of foreign exchange, and investment regulations were strong barriers to U.S. DFI. The Colonial Office opposed U.S. involvement in the empire, on the grounds that U.S. aid administrators would become "American outposts working inside our Colonial Development schemes," that private economic power would be followed by state political power, and that foreign ownership might impede British access to colonial raw materials (CO 852/877/1 #11; CO 852/877/1 #15 comment; CO 852/877/1 #39). British industrial capital also opposed U.S. colonial investments as a threat to its control of protected colonial markets.

The British Treasury, however, favored bringing dollars into the colonies, regardless of threats to British political control. Since British capital was unable to extract colonial raw materials and get them onto foreign markets to earn dollars, argued the Treasury, then U.S. capital should do the job. Imperial power was also restricted by nationalist movements in the colonies and by general obligations and declarations in the Atlantic Charter and the United Nations Charter.

The strongest pressures to open the colonies to U.S. capital came from the Economic Cooperation Administration (ECA), the administrative organ of the Marshall Plan. U.S. officials made it clear to the European colonial powers that the United States wanted to trade aid for raw materials within their empires (CO 852/877/1 #4). The European nations could never achieve a balance of trade with the United States, they argued, and so the shortfall should be made up with Asian and African raw materials (CO 852/877/1 #16). This arrangement satisfied the British Treasury, because dollars would reconstruct Britain while the colonies would provide the raw materials that constituted the "quid of the quo" (FO 371/71822).

Events in the colonies also favored U.S. investments. Colonial uprisings, and the fear of such uprisings, had forced the British government to introduce limited welfare reforms and infrastructural development programs in the late 1930s. After the war, moderate nationalists in the colonies pressed hard for industrialization, and U.S. capital was the obvious source for new industry (CO 852/877/1 #15). These nationalists contended that British policies on taxes, exchange control, and profit repatriation discouraged prospective foreign investors, and they agitated for more local discretion over internal industrial policies (CO 852/1418 #25).

U.S. alliances with the moderate nationalists were supported by offers of aid and investment, leading to ironic British charges of "imperializm [sic] in the efforts made by the Americans to assert their ascendancy in international organizations such as the [World] Bank and the [International Monetary] Fund" (FO 371/82937). Throughout the empire, groups within the nationalist movements allied with the United States, in the hope that American investments would bring the "industrialization" that British colonialism had restricted. Little distinction was made between manufacturing and extractive investments—all were "industry." Of course, the 1960s and 1970s would show that even "moderate" nationalist movements could experience a learning process that would diminish their early enthusiasm for U.S. investments.

When the United States demanded that the European colonial powers open their colonies in return for reconstruction aid, the Europeans generally relented. England reduced colonial taxes, subsidies, and restrictions on trade and denationalized colonial mineral reserves (CO 852/1366 #104). Even where U.S. extractors did not actually invest, access for American buyers on equal terms with empire purchasers was a significant achievement. U.S. industrial consumers, who were accustomed to purchasing materials from relatively expensive domestic sources, could outbid imperial buyers.

The grand area was thus made feasible by U.S. hegemony, but it was not enough to open the door. Capital had to enter. Apart from creating the general environment for the entry of private capital, the U.S. state facilitated DFI in two particularly important ways. First, it established programs to identify sources of materials. Second, it directly financed private capital investments through its aid and stockpile programs.

The central goal of direct oligopolistic control of reserves is to create a competitive advantage for both industrial purchasers and integrated downstream users by keeping the costs of extracting materials substantially below their world market prices. Within such a strategy, comprehensive intelligence about peripheral minerals allows oligopolists to corner the most advantageous reserves. This was the purpose of the technical missions set up under Harry Truman's Point Four program.

The major innovation of Point Four was the placement of scores of technical missions in the European colonies. Teams surveyed existing mines and searched for new reserves. The surveys were supplemented by an ECA-administered "serialization" (detailed listing) of colonial reserves, mines, and smelters. In 1951, the ECA informed colonial mining firms that it was serializing colonial mines and smelters. Serialization forms required detailed information on production and reserves. Colonial governments and mining firms were told that failure to return the forms might jeopardize their future aid from the ECA and that priority in allocations of equipment and supplies would be given to projects that were detailed in the returns. Serialization was quite successful because the ECA directly approached colonial mines and authorities, who were susceptible to threats of withdrawals of aid. Through its technical programs, the U.S. state gained direct access to the colonies against the wishes of the British state.

Very few direct investments were initiated under Point Four, leading the British to conclude that the U.S. investment plans for the colonies were largely hot air (CO 852/1258/4). This was a misunderstanding of the significance of Point Four, however, which lay in liberalization agreements, hundreds of technical missions, and thousands of colonial surveys that were carried out under the program. These paved the way for subsequent direct investments.

The flow of U.S. DFI into peripheral extraction during the 1950s and 1960s was high. The real book value of U.S. multinational corporation (MNC) assets in peripheral mining and smelting more than doubled between 1950 and 1968 (Mikesell, 1987: 41). The numbers or levels of new investments, however, are not the most significant indicators of U.S. success in opening up the periphery. A few large productive investments by a few oligopolistic firms, along with the acquisition of a greater number of reserves, is more important. The central players included huge iron and steel companies (Bethlehem and U.S. Steel), the aluminum giants (Kaiser, Reynolds, and Alcoa), the copper giants (Kennecott, Anaconda, and Phelps-Dodge), the nickel giant (INCO), and multimetal firms (AMAX and Freeport).

One general effect of U.S. hegemony was to encourage the large materials processors to increase their backward integration into peripheral mining. This was particularly true in steel (including alloy minerals) and aluminum, which along with petroleum dominate industrial raw materials. Investments by Bethlehem Steel and U.S. Steel, for example, aimed at gaining direct control of reserves of the metals that are necessary for making alloys. This control gave them immediate advantages and protected them from shortages of world supply. At the same time, it also reduced their ability to react swiftly and creatively to rapidly changing market conditions and left them particularly vulnerable to markets characterized by excess supply and low prices. In addition, it left them vulnerable to peripheral minerals nationalism in the 1960s and 1970s.

Several massive mining projects, and some smaller ones as well, were financed by Marshall Aid. The largest and most important of these were the Jamaican bauxite projects. Among all critical materials, postwar industry most increased its use of aluminum in terms of bulk and value. The metal's lightness and strength and the possibility of its amalgamation with a wide range of other metals made it particularly apt for incorporation into the technologies that defined leading industrial sectors after the war. It competed strongly with copper and tin for the rapidly expanding markets that those older metals would have dominated. Yet aluminum also presented great problems of access to U.S. industry. Virtually all bauxite was imported, and bauxite reserves were limited. The existing reserves were controlled by a handful of producers that also exerted vertical control over the manufacture of alumina, aluminum, and many aluminum fabricates. No major producers were based in the United States. Pressures from the U.S. state, culminating in the Marshall Plan, changed this.

During the war, vast new reserves of bauxite were discovered in Jamaica. While there was intense conflict over access to the reserves among Alcan, Reynolds, and the Dutch firm Billiton, the British Colonial Office hoped to keep the reserves "within the empire" by declaring them property of the crown and by giving sole mining concessions to Alcan. The U.S. State Department favored Reynolds' access to the reserves, on the basis of the company's assertions that an empire monopoly in Jamaica would allow the British to dominate international aluminum markets for "perhaps a hundred years" (Post, 1981: 472–473). The future of Reynolds was thus tied directly to U.S. "national interests."

With the help of strong pressure on Britain by the State Department, Reynolds obtained options on substantial Jamaican bauxite lands. Still, its ability to mine the lands and the conditions of mining remained in doubt until the United States used reconstruction aid as a trading chip for bauxite. In 1948, the ECA joined Reynolds in its negotiations with the British state about terms of access to Jamaican bauxite. The ECA insisted that Reynolds be given full mining rights on the lands for which it had options; that the Jamaican government grant concessions to Reynolds, including exemptions from import duties, and low, fixed royalties; that Reynolds' subsidiary remain incorporated in the United States; that Reynolds be free to import capital inputs from dollar sources; that the bauxite be shipped in U.S. carriers; and that the United States receive repayment for financing the mines in aluminum delivered to its strategic stockpile. The British state adamantly objected to each of these points but was eventually forced to concede when the United States threatened the withdrawal of reconstruction aid to Britain. As one British official put it, the British state would not want to "force a potential clash with the E.C.A." (CO 852/942/3 #28).

The ECA/Reynolds' victory over the British state had broad implications for U.S. access to colonial raw materials. It improved the conditions of access, because it established the principle that U.S. extractors would be free to import capital inputs from the United States. British attempts to force extractors to buy their fixed and circulating capital from British sources would have placed a burden on U.S. investors. Moreover, they would have removed part of the rationale for the grand area: access to colonial markets for U.S. capital goods. The entry of U.S. capital goods into the periphery increased the technical dependence of those areas on core industry. In addition, by negotiating directly with the colonial government, however titular it might have been, the United States undercut imperial control, gave new legitimacy to moderate national elites, and increased the illusion of U.S. "anti-imperialism." The terms won by Reynolds were repeated in other Jamaican bauxite concessions and became a model for U.S. negotiations with other peripheral states.

Bauxite was the most important but not the only material affected by the Marshall Plan. The United States also negotiated increased supplies of a long list of other critical materials, including manganese, nickel, chromium, and others. The ECA, for example, financed manganese extraction by a subsidiary of Union Carbide in the Gold Coast, while the United States traded capital equipment for manganese in India, against British opposition (FO 371/71944). The ECA also financed supplies of many other important materials from the colonies of Britain, France, Holland, and Belgium.

Many ECA-financed colonial projects became the basis of U.S. "strategic" stockpiles. In theory, stockpiles were meant to insure supplies during wars or economic difficulty. From the grand area point of view, stockpiling provided finance for new or expanding DFI while ensuring the availability of materials to industry. In practice, stockpile funds were often diverted to high-price domestic purchases, often of unusable minerals, in return for congressional support (Bidwell, 1958).

The stockpiles became quite large, particularly in materials critical to industry but consumed on a small scale (e.g., alloy metals such as manganese, nickel, chrome, tungsten, and cobalt). Stockpiles of tin, rubber, copper, lead, and zinc were also significant. European colonies were particularly important suppliers of manganese, chrome, cobalt, tin, and rubber. Increased foreign production of these materials was financed through Marshall Aid and the Export-Import Bank, primarily to mining firms with a U.S. interest and typically tied to long-term supply contracts (Bidwell, 1958).

Stockpiles of tungsten were of a different nature. Between 1951 and 1956, the U.S. government offered to buy a quantity of tungsten over 15 times the average annual output of U.S. mines at a guaranteed above-market price. In 1957, a group of senators from Western states, arguing for continuation of stockpiling, asserted that the domestic tungsten industry would collapse within three months if stockpiling were stopped. This turned out to be true, and domestic production practically stopped by the end of the year, but the withdrawal of U.S. government purchases also helped reduce the price of the metal from foreign sources to its lowest level since 1950 (Bidwell, 1958).

With regard to raw materials strategies, and particularly to stockpiles, the strength of the United States was also a weakness. For many years, its near self-sufficiency in a series of basic materials created substantial domestic mining interests. Materials strategies were often sidetracked by domestic minerals lobbies. The intervention of anti-expansionist domestic class factions had an ironic effect on U.S. raw materials policy, however, when put into the context of world markets. To U.S. industry, which had grown up using high-priced, protected, domestic materials, the stockpile purchases of domestic materials freed them to purchase cheaper foreign materials. In copper, smaller local suppliers with political clout beyond their market power were kept quiet through stockpile purchases, while the largest producers and purchasers developed parallel foreign operations, using state aid and subsidies that would have faced fiercer opposition by domestic miners in the absence of the stockpiles.

A final important effect of stockpiles was their use to control markets for materials that were not controlled by oligopolies. Tin sales by the U.S. stockpilers stabilized world market prices between 1956 and 1974 (Smith & Schink, 1976). The stockpilers avoided dumping large quantities of minerals on world markets, but they were willing to use stockpiles to veto precipitous price increases by minerals cartels (Smith & Schink, 1976: 721). Fears of stockpile dumping created stability of supply and prices until the 1970s. Finally, because the stockpiles had been formed during the early postwar years, only sales subsequently affected prices, and only in a downward direction. Gordon W. Smith and George R. Schink (1976: 721) have estimated that tin prices were depressed by 5.3 percent between 1956 and 1967 due to sales of stockpiles.

The ideal degree of price suppression for a given commodity, however, depended on its market characteristics. The direct control of reserves by large forward-integrated producers—and competition around the capture of reserves—created a parallel market structure in certain minerals. A proportion of the mineral (the critical proportion supplying U.S. industry) was traded within firms at internal transfer prices, while the remainder of the material was traded on the open market at a price determined by supply and demand. The relative importance of stockpiles across materials thus depended on the degree to which market prices, as opposed to internal cost-plus prices, were faced by industrial consumers. In tin, where the market was clearly dominant, stockpiles kept a crucial cap on prices. Bauxite, however, was predominantly traded within the firm, so that relatively high open-market prices created a cost advantage for oligopolistic extractors/consumers.

U.S. strategies for acquiring access to raw materials can be summarized as the following. The door was opened to access through the creation of the grand area, with liberal schemes of trade and finance dominated by the United States. The preferred means of access was the direct capture of reserves, productive capacity, and market shares by oligopolistic self-financed extractors. These producers were often subsidized by U.S. aid and, increasingly, by externally financed infrastructure. U.S. industrial competitive advantage depended on a parallel "market" structure, where integrated oligopolistic firms gained cheap access to materials at imputed internal transfer prices that were consistently lower than world market prices for the same materials. As a result, costs of materials were lower both for the integrated producers and for their industrial consumers than they were for those consumers who depended on world market sources. This competitive advantage was maintained so long as world market supply remained limited; therefore, market prices for the materials remained high relative to the oligopolists' costs of obtaining the same materials.

Minerals that were not dominated by U.S. capital through direct control of reserves were controlled through the market, often by using stockpiles to manage supplies and prices. Even where stockpiles were ineffective, U.S. industrial consumers may have dominated peripheral markets as oligopsonists who were willing to pay prices that were slightly higher than the prevailing market price but lower than domestic alternatives.

These arrangements were limited, however, by the learning process of peripheral states. Direct access that was negotiated during the early postwar era was advantageous to the buyer/extractor and provided a small return for the host country. Over time, peripheral states began to demand a better deal for their materials, leading to nationalization of resources and to pressures for new terms of trade between exporters of primary commodities and exporters of manufactured goods. Oligopolistic control of reserves and of markets became a less successful strategy, and new strategies based on indirect market control became advantageous. National pressures for the control of resources and the subsequent internationalization of markets, combined with rising technological costs and market instability, led to a transition from DFI under oligopolistic control to new forms of investment, particularly joint ventures with diversified sourcing of materials (Oman, 1984, 1989; Bomsel, Marques, Ndiaye & de Sa, 1990). These new forms of investment eliminated U.S. competitive advantages by creating excess capacities in basic minerals, and driving market prices below the costs of extraction and processing for integrated oligopolists. The Japanese have been particularly aggressive in seeking out joint ventures, and the Japanese government has actively coordinated the minerals investment strategies of national firms.

THE JAPANESE CASE: CREATING AND EXPLOITING UNCOORDINATED EXCESS CAPACITIES

U.S. strategies to secure access to minerals during its rise to industrial and military preeminence responded to the colonial structure of the early and middle twentieth century. The United States manipulated the nationalist aspirations in the colonies of European states to secure access to monopolized reserves. It used Europe's desperate need for capital to coerce access through the threat of withholding Marshall Aid and established institutions to reinforce a liberal international trading and investment regime. U.S. firms competed successfully for control of reserves of raw materials. In the present postcolonial, multipolar world-economy, the Japanese have taken advantage of the increased scale of the extraction and processing technology, of large surpluses of finance capital, of aspirations for national development in resource-rich nations, and of peripheral nations' defiance of direct economic control to exploit new forms of investment—in particular joint ventures with poor and indebted states willing to assume even greater levels of debt to achieve sovereign and technical control over their own resources and to construct downstream linkages around extractive revenues and infrastructure.

Like the Americans before them, the Japanese have played to the aspirations of peripheral nations to expand participation in and benefit from raw materials extraction. The Japanese, however, have substituted new forms of subordination, based on competition between multiple indebted suppliers in a market destabilized by uncoordinated excess capacity, for earlier forms, which were based on DFI in mineral extraction and oligopolistic control of world minerals markets. This has greatly weakened the established oligopolists engaged in fully owned, self-financed, primary extraction by moving the locus of surplus profit forward in the commodity chain, allowing for upward pressures on the costs of new mining projects and downward pressure on the prices of basic metals (Oman, 1984: 43, 45, 46, 67, 68).

Both access to debt-funded capital participation by diverse host countries and freedom from having capital sunk in obsolete mines and processing plants allow the Japanese much greater freedom to play the game that they themselves are promoting. They are free to allow excess capacity to drive prices down, below average or even marginal costs, because low Japanese equity participation means that the flow of profits lost as prices fall is smaller than the subsequent profits gained due to the corresponding reduced costs of downstream production. The older minerals firms have been forced to play the same game, but with far less freedom of action than the Japanese. They follow Japanese participation in joint ventures with their own participation, out of fear of losing more of their already crumbling market position. Yet this increases excess capacity even further, creating further downward pressure on prices. In the meantime, sunk capital forces the older firms to continue producing in their older projects, even though this production may be at a loss if accounted at prevailing market prices. The older companies are thus forced to exacerbate the conditions leading to their own loss of control and to add to the uncoordinated excess capacity that drives prices down. The Japanese have proportionately less exposure in their individual joint ventures than do the U.S. companies, thus diminishing their risk and increasing their leverage (Bomsel et al., 1990). They can take full advantage of their market access as consumers at lower prices, without the burden of continuing large fully owned projects at a loss. This puts the Japanese firm at a distinct competitive advantage relative to the older firms.

Multilateral and commercial banks have strengthened the tendency toward excess capacity. Conditions in the early 1970s drove banks to pursue new opportunities for lending. Marian Radetzki (1980) has maintained that outside financing for mineral projects grew from no more than 20 percent of the total before the 1960s to levels between 60 and 80 percent (cited in Bomsel et al., 1990: 44). "Whereas some 80 to 90 percent of investment funds in developing countries' mining projects came in the form of equity capital up till about 1960, during the 1970s the proportion was only about a third" (Oman, 1984: 46). As mining companies reacted to resource nationalism by threatening to reduce investments, the World Bank sought to expand its loans to developing nations, making ample credit available for host countries and firms to assume major equity in mining and processing projects. The belief in price stability and in the growth in minerals markets played into the World Bank's excessive optimism about the promise of large mineral projects. Bomsel et al. have perceived the World Bank as deliberately expanding mining capacity internationally.

The World Bank services responsible for monitoring the mineral raw materials markets in fact produced the most exaggeratedly "optimistic" medium-term demand forecasts in the 1970s, not so much in our opinion because of scientific blindness as because of the conviction that it was the duty of the Bank to promote the development of capacity in this sector. (1990: 44)

The Bank's interest in promoting capacity to protect industrial expansion and international accumulation was justified at the local level by the popular old notion that underdeveloped nations could capture capital for repaying their debts through subsequent raw materials exports (Bosson & Varon, 1977). Bomsel et al. (1990) have suggested that consuming firms and nations also put pressure on both commercial and multilateral banks to finance joint ventures in raw materials in order to prevent shortages when multinational corporations started to show reluctance to invest their own equity capital in direct ownership. Charles Oman (1984: 68) has specifically cautioned that the complaint that national ownership and control of mineral resources in developing countries would produce overcapacity and therefore limit willingness to invest is an argument that can be used by established oligopolists in hopes of discouraging a further diversification of supply.

One of the major effects of the growing participation of international finance capital in mining projects was to further the separation of investment in infrastructure from the investment in mines or processing. The United States had previously attempted to impose such a division of financial responsibilities on Britain, but with limited success. Many of the projects financed by Marshall Aid and the World Bank in the 1950s and 1960s further separated the cost of infrastructure from the cost of mining. In the 1970s and 1980s, the development banks strongly pushed loans to nations for the construction of dams, roads, ports, and railroads as development projects in their own right, with the attractive promise that major portions of their costs would be offset by mineral revenues. Mineral enterprises have thus been freed of a major portion of the capital risk, while the state and the development banks have invoked linkage theories to justify the expense of the infrastructure (see Bunker, 1989). National firms and the state in the host country rely on the promise of upstream revenues, while the multinational firms that hold minority equity can benefit from greater access to markets, enhanced capacity to profit from the sale of technology and licensing, continued access to insider information about local mineral policy, and the political leverage that their association with national elites offers them. The involvement of international banks also protects them from disadvantageous changes in contracts and concessions, as well as from the threat of expropriation, to which they were far more vulnerable as self-financing, wholly owning foreign direct investors (Girvan, 1980; Oman, 1984). Sharing in a joint venture thus increases host country exposure to risk and to debt while reducing state capacity for adversarial regulation of the foreign investor.

This outcome is particularly significant in light of claims that joint ventures became attractive to multinational mining companies and that financing them became attractive to international banks in response to the perceived threat of nationalization or disadvantageous regulation that emerged from the more interventionist measures of mining states during the 1960s and 1970s (Mikesell, 1979; Bosson & Varon, 1977; Oman, 1984: 71–74). Resource nationalism was indeed threatening to the old oligopolistic system of control, but the beneficiaries of the resulting changes have been the ascending economies at the industrial core rather than the peripheral mineral exporters. The reasons for this lie both in the nature of mineral extractive enterprises (Bunker, 1989) and in the greater flexibility of the core economies to exploit competition between less developed trading partners and to manipulate terms of trade, points of profit, and access to credits and foreign exchange. The early optimism of Theodore Moran (1974), R. Bosson and B. Varon (1977), Norman Girvan (1980), and David Becker (1983) about the capacity of host governments to increase their bargaining power over time has been belied by the facility with which firms and states in the core, particularly those less encumbered by the earlier forms of dominance, have turned the threat of local control into an advantageous means of spreading risk. Dominance in the minerals industry has shifted, but the exporting nations have borne the cost of the shift without receiving many of its benefits.

The resultant peripheral debt has moved indebted countries back toward using raw materials exports as a means of capturing foreign revenues and attracting direct foreign investment and loans. The optimistic resource nationalism of the 1970s and its emphasis on capturing linkages and using revenues to drive import substitution industrialization (ISI) further upstream have been replaced with the direct export of raw materials. In the process, economic planning has been subordinated to short-term, economically indefensible strategies based on the manipulation of interest and exchange rates. This often involves a public commitment to huge infrastructural projects, whose debt service and maintenance costs endure in the long term. The state thus sacrifices its autonomy and administrative coherence to the easy but in the long-term ineffective bargain for debt relief. In the process, the state's bargaining position with MNCs and foreign governments is progressively weakened. The sharp decline of minerals markets in the early 1980s and the aggressive policies of the Japanese in fostering competing joint ventures in the same minerals have greatly exacerbated this loss of sovereign control and coherent policy (Bunker, 1989).

The shift in Japanese strategy, from direct investment to diversified excess capacity, is exemplified by its aluminum policy, which may be compared with the U.S. capture of Jamaican bauxite in the 1940s. Costs and prices of aluminum soared after 1973, but the urgency to substitute light for heavy metals as oil prices rose increased demand even more rapidly. The oil shocks of 1973 and 1979 had profound effects on finance, energy, markets, ownership, and spatial distribution in the industry. Rising production costs, new economies of scale that vastly increased investment per plant, price instability, expanded demand, and the surging resource nationalism of many mineral-rich poor nations reduced the capacity and willingness of the six major producers, all based in Europe and North America, to continue dominating sources, regulating supplies, and leading markets. The high price of oil favored the relocation of smelters to areas with large hydroelectric potential. Many such places that existed in the core nations were already developed, and increasing popular resistance to industrial pollution also threatened to raise the cost of new installations in the developed countries.

Most of the sufficiently large remaining bauxite deposits were located in the tropics. Many tropical nations were enthusiastic to develop industry that was linked backward to their minerals. This, combined with the conventional equation of electrical energy with forward linkages into technologically advanced industry, hydroelectricity's dependence on ample and reliable rainfall into large drainage basins, and the vast supply of surplus revenue that the oil-exporting nations had deposited in the core nations' banking systems, created a break in the established structure of the global industry that the Japanese could exploit. Their consumption of aluminum was growing more rapidly than that of any other nation, and they had been startled by several threatened shortages of key raw materials. The eagerness of various peripheral countries to control and process their own raw materials challenged the hegemony of the traditionally dominant firms. The availability of easy credits allowed these countries to share in the huge investments required for energy and transport infrastructure and for refineries and smelters. Peripheral states consequently allowed core participants in joint ventures to reduce their equity participation, along with their risk exposure, enabling the introduction of the strategy of creating excess aluminum capacity, with the lion's share of costs (in terms of lower resource prices) being shifted to the periphery.

This process is amply demonstrated by the current mineral extraction projects in the Brazilian Amazon. Major deposits of iron ore and bauxite were discovered in the Amazonian state of Para in the 1960s. The different ways that these deposits were developed reflects in part the very different strategies of old oligopolists and emerging hegemons. In the case of iron, U.S. Steel was a partner in an enterprise located close to the mouth of the mine. There was considerable conflict between U.S. Steel and its Brazilian partner, a state company, over the size of the undertaking and the best means to export iron. U.S. Steel wanted a relatively small rate of extraction and the use of a relatively cheap river transport system to the Amazonian port of Belem. CVRD, the Brazilian company, wanted to build a railroad to Sao Luis, a deep-water ocean port that would allow shipment in ships large enough to compete for the Japanese market. U.S. Steel was aiming at the regional oligopolistic control that it had used so well in the past, with a moderate amount of controlled excess capacity, while the Brazilians were aiming at the Japanese market. CVRD had developed close relations with the Japanese during the 1960s, selling iron to them under long-term contracts mediated by Japanese trading companies, and the Japanese were actively participating in CVRD's diversification into large-scale mineral shipping.

The bauxite reserves discovered at about the same time had a different history. Alcan went into a joint venture with CVRD and a number of other international investors to extract bauxite, but the Japanese also initiated a combined alumina-aluminum plant to be fueled by a large dam built on the Tocantins River. The initial joint venture proposed between a consortium of Japanese smelters and other users, banks, and trading companies was for a smelter with a capacity of 800 thousand tons per year, with the joint venture contributing $800 million (U.S.) to the construction of the dam. From the beginning, the dam was justified by the alternative uses available for the energy generated, including the forward processing of aluminum.

In 1976 and 1977, the Brazilian government undertook major initiatives to speed the development of the Carajas iron mine and to promote the processing of alumina and aluminum from the Trombetas bauxite mine, an undertaking that required far more capital than the mine itself. U.S. Steel, a partner in the Carajas venture, was bought out, and the state-controlled CVRD started a search for other sources of capital. Complex negotiations with private and public holders of capital in Japan resulted in joint ventures to develop an alumina refinery and an aluminum plant. Forward contracts with Japanese and German buyers, tied to public and private loans, were finally crucial in bringing Carajas on line. The Carajas mine is the largest in the world that produces such high grade ore, and the aluminum-alumina complex as originally planned would have been the largest in the world. Japanese and German participation in these projects anticipated that they would have major long-term effects on both the supply and price of minerals. U.S. Steel and other U.S. mining interests' opposition to the Carajas project, which included pressure from the state government of Minnesota to prevent a World Bank loan, demonstrate the interests of the older oligopolists whose major equity capital was concentrated upstream.

The joint ventures in alumina and aluminum, like the Carajas mining project, began as Brazil's strategies to achieve national self-sufficiency in nonferrous metals, but they ultimately responded far more to Brazil's external financial crisis and to the regime's internal legitimacy crisis than to business rationality. A coherent program to achieve self-sufficiency in an expansive nonferrous metals industry was displaced by policies aimed at maintaining legitimacy and at capturing foreign exchange in order to maintain short-term stability during a time of economic crisis. The Brazilian bargaining position was directly conditioned by its parlous fiscal situation, its technological dependence on Japan, and its general need for both foreign capital and the legitimacy conferred by massive projects. Most important, the falling terms of trade for all minerals made the export-dependent, crisis-ridden, Third World exporters disastrously competitive with each other.

The Japanese took advantage of this resource competition by aggressively pursuing joint ventures in aluminum smelting with Indonesia, Australia, Venezuela, and Canada. They played the different host countries off against each other, creating excess capacity in the world-economy, reducing their own investments, and increasing those of the host countries. This game was particularly costly to the host countries because so much of the cost of aluminum is in the development of hydroelectric power. The Japanese exploited the resource nationalism of bauxite-rich countries with hydroelectric potential by promising that the availability of cheap electricity would attract other industries. Thus, national states were persuaded not simply to provide the energy and transport infrastructure for aluminum smelters but also to do so with forward contracts on energy prices that were viable only under the assumption of multiple associated industrial users.

In the Brazilian case, the joint venture, ALBRAS, which was composed of CVRD and a Japanese holding company, was expected to contribute substantially toward the building of the dam that would supply the smelter's electricity. In 1974, the Japanese announced that the smelter project would not be viable for them if they invested in the dam. Not only did they pull back from investing in the dam, but they also demanded, and got, a price ceiling for electricity tied to the price of aluminum, a publicly financed city for laborers, and a publicly built port. Even though the Ministries of Finance and Planning and the key officials of CVRD felt that the project was no longer viable, the government could not withdraw without losing credibility. The Geisel government simply proceeded with a project that its Planning Minister knew was economically irrational as early as 1976.

The Japanese later insisted on downsizing the ALBRAS plant to less than half of its original planned capacity. They stopped the development of the associated alumina plant, alleging that it was more economical to import alumina from Surinam and Venezuela than it was to refine Trombetas bauxite. Thus, a major justification for the huge public infrastructural expenditures—the integration within the nation of the mining and processing of Trombetas bauxite—simply did not occur. Clearly, the Japanese had no interest in processing bauxite or alumina. Their interests were in primary aluminum. They manipulated Brazilian aspirations for forward integration from the mine but were not committed to this development.

Alcoa felt obligated to follow the Japanese lead in its negotiations over aluminum smelting in the Amazon, even though the company was concerned about the resulting overcapacity (author's interview, Pittsburgh, June 1990). In both aluminum and iron, major public investments aimed at integrating mineral extraction and processing with national industrial development in the 1960s and early 1970s were transformed into campaigns to capture foreign currencies, even at the cost of long-term debt, diminution of national control, and questionable business decisions. This transformation responded to the strategies of the ascendant economic powers—Japan and Germany—to exploit the weaknesses of oligopolistic control and the developmentalist commitments and economic difficulties confronting Brazil.

The Japanese played variations on this strategy in Indonesia and Venezuela, adapting their tactics to local political conditions and aspirations. Then they played each host nation off against the other as they demanded and got more local government equity participation and debt assumption, lower power rates, and a far greater share of the total investment assumed by the state and defined as public than in the original proposal. These host governments thus participated directly in creating the excess capacity that lowered the price of their own exports and also justified scaling back the projects from the size that had been used to justify huge public expense in the first place. The local and national states assumed huge public and social costs for a far smaller return than was originally proposed and have remained highly susceptible to new offers to expand capacity because they are so desperate to pay for this infrastructure. This is the new form of excess capacity, and it has been very cheaply achieved by the Japanese.

NEW FORMS OF INVESTMENT IN THE SHIFTING HIERARCHY OF THE WORLD ECONOMY

Oman (1984, 1989) has written persuasively that "new forms of investment" (NFI), defined as international investments in which foreign investors do not hold a controlling interest via equity participation, has played an increasingly important role in the relations between developed and underdeveloped economies since the early 1970s (1984: 12). Oman has broadly depicted NFI as "the set of methods by which a foreign company has been able to undertake, and even in certain cases to stimulate the creation of production capacity in a host country without having to rely on equity ownership to assert partial or total control over the investment project. In the mining industry, NFI became substantially dominant during the 1970s" (Bomsel et al., 1990: 11). Two-thirds of the major base metal projects (iron, copper, and aluminum) undertaken since 1970 have relied on NFI (Oman, 1989; Bomsel et al., 1990: 17). Oman and his associates have perceived NFI as the result of changing market and financial conditions, together with the increased involvement of national states in the periphery. They have acknowledged that NFI have had a far greater impact proportionately in the extractive sector than in other sectors. They have limited their perspective, however, to factors that reflect the conjuncture of market demand and capital costs while ignoring the changing structure of the world-economy and the particular structural position of extractive economies within it. Hence, they have considered the difficulties confronting raw materials exporters to be conjunctural rather than structural.

We argue instead that natural resource extraction subjects regional economies to disadvantages that emerge from locational rigidities, dependence on external markets and technologies, and the imperative for industrial capital to reduce the costs of raw materials. NFI is simply the most recent of a series of historically conditioned strategies by which capitalist firms and industrial nations have assured themselves of cheap, reliable access to raw materials. These strategies have varied with technical, political, and financial conditions in the world-economy, but because they follow the initiatives of industrialized countries, they have tended to redound to the disadvantage of the resource-exporting countries, though the degree of disadvantage has varied with time and with the commodity itself. NFI, like DFI before it, is best seen as a reflection of competition within the core, both between firms and between national economies. DFI was the result of U.S. strategies to exploit contradictions in the world-economy, particularly as its industry expanded following World War II. NFI was implemented by the Japanese to exploit a different set of contradictions as they began their ascent to industrial hegemony.

U.S. and Japanese strategies alike were responsive to both structure and conjuncture in the world-economy. They reacted to the changes in the minerals sector and in world financial markets in ways that changed those sectors and markets. U.S. attempts to gain access to raw materials through DFI, within a liberal grand area policed by the United States, reflected both the declining control of the colonial powers over peripheral raw materials and the new opportunities for entry created by the desire of emerging nations for rapid industrialization. Those opportunities were magnified by the discovery of new reserves (or new technologies for exploiting previously unprofitable reserves) and by market conditions that favored access through backward integration. By exploiting these new opportunities through direct investments, however, the U.S. strategy encouraged the emergence of new contradictions, including the resource nationalism that addressed the failed hopes of earlier U.S.-peripheral alliances. Furthermore, although a stable grand area depended on the reconstruction of Europe and Japan, their reemergence as industrial powers created new conflicts of hegemony and a new competition for sources of raw materials. The stability of the grand area was maintained for a time, with Japan obtaining its industrial raw materials through long-term contracts with external suppliers. Contradictions within the grand area strategy and Japan's need for better terms of access due to its rapidly expanding accumulation, eventually created the conditions that favored NFI over DFI.

Japanese attempts to gain access to raw materials did not necessarily aim to create excess capacity but they inevitably did so. The Japanese did not foster resource nationalism and aspirations for forward linkage, but they did manipulate these effectively in ways that allowed the creation of excess capability while sharing minimally in the risks involved. The predisposition of host countries to share in investment costs and to assume most or all of the infrastructural costs created a condition that the Japanese could exploit but that other nations and firms then felt they also had to exploit in order not to lose market share. Once the Japanese strategies became operational, other firms were forced to use NFI, even if they had far more reason to fear the effects of excess capacity on the profitability of their existing operations. In this way, the minerals oligopolies were forced to accelerate the demise of their old system of market control.

The Japanese had a number of advantages in playing the system that they were stimulating. By creating excess capacity at little risk to the foreign investor, NFI effectively lowers the cost of raw materials. This favors those companies with the least upstream integration and the least financial exposure in the primary goods themselves, because consumption gains from low prices are not counteracted by upstream losses from the same phenomenon. The companies that dominated the older forms of DFI with full or majority ownership were thus far less able to use NFI to their own advantage, since they were far more liable to lose from the lower prices of raw materials. NFI stimulated a move toward downstream profit taking, while companies with upstream integration were far less able to make these shifts.

Japanese agility was also heightened by deliberate coordination between private sectors and the state. Tensions and contradictions are inevitable in strategies that depend on collaborative action by multiple firms and banks, whose major profits emerge at different points in the production chain. Joint ventures leading to excess capacity necessarily reduce or eliminate profits from the upstream investment. Oman (1984: 83) has cited Terutomo Ozawa's (1979) claim that 80 percent of Japan's overseas investments in the extractive industries that they operate with majority equity are unprofitable as individual ventures. The primary goal is to secure sources of supply. Oman has opined that the Japanese willingness to use NFI in extractive industries depends on the relation between the private and public sectors to provide "the foundation for firms to undertake ventures where such social benefits as securing access to raw materials for the home economy transcend the private benefits of individual investment projects or even of individual investors." Even though he has cited Ozawa (1979: 34–35) on the importance of government subsidies to Japanese firms in mineral joint ventures, Oman has not fully taken into account the extent to which the state, via direct loans and credits, has adjusted its own contribution to joint ventures such as ALBRAS and Asahan in order to sustain the incentives that these ventures have provided for private investors.

Japan's resource poverty and dependence have prevented small or obsolete primary industries from demanding or obtaining the kinds of costly protection that distorted U.S. stockpiling strategies. Close coordination of state and private capital in pursuing the "national interest," defined as stable access to cheap raw materials, is therefore easier to achieve. The close articulation of consumers and producers in Japan, both through MITI and through the Keidanren (a private association of large Japanese companies), meant that consumers could make demands on mining companies more effectively than they could in the United States. Nonetheless, in both cases, there were pressures from consumers to provide credits and technologies that would allow host countries to participate in the costs of the minerals projects. As the more dynamic companies moved their profits downstream, greater benefits could be gained by increasing the costs of these technologies to the host partners in joint ventures, a factor exacerbating the rising costs of developing new projects and further heightening the tendency to NFI. As capital costs rose and raw materials prices fell, the pressure on the members of the crumbling oligopoly to follow NFI rather than DFI strategies increased as did the likelihood of increased debt and diminished returns to the host countries.

6

AGRO-FOOD RESTRUCTURING IN THE PACIFIC RIM: A COMPARATIVE-INTERNATIONAL PERSPECTIVE ON JAPAN, SOUTH KOREA, THE UNITED STATES, AUSTRALIA, AND THAILAND

Philip McMichael

INTRODUCTION

Analysis of the current restructuring of world capitalism invariably focuses on industrial dynamics, in particular the consequences of the recent process of decentralization of industry to the high-income periphery. Often ignored is the related, but inverse, process of agricultural centralization in metropolitan states. Nowhere is this clearer than in the Pacific Rim, where East Asian (e.g., Japanese and South Korean) agro-food markets provide the most significant growth potential for agricultural exporters like the United States and Australia. This division of world labor in agriculture is not quite so centralized, however, as some peripheral countries such as Thailand have adopted industrial agriculture and rival the United States as agro-food exporters.[1]

More significant than a reconfiguration of international trade is the broader question of the "internationalization" of agriculture and its relationship to international political economy. Thailand's successful agro-export substitution strategies (high-value food products for traditional tropical commodities) are one example of the internationalization of Third World economies (Raynolds, Myhre, McMichael, Carro-Figueroa, & Buttel, 1991). The recent expansion in the periphery of agro-industrial production and of so-called "nontraditional exports" has exacerbated tensions in the state system and reflects an intensification of global capital mobility. In turn, an aggressive U.S. agricultural export policy is symptomatic of U.S. hegemonic decline and industrial decentralization. This shift in the international division of labor has fueled considerable, neomercantilist, GATT-style pressure on East Asian states to liberalize their farm sectors and expand agro-food imports.[2] The change thus exemplifies heightened international and national tensions in the world-economy, as well as the U.S.'s need to mobilize international enforcement mechanisms to maintain competitive advantage in an increasingly competitive world-economy. The goal of this chapter is to outline the contours and political economy of the Pacific Rim agro-food system and to address the issue of restructuring as it affects and integrates the agricultural sector of the United States, Japan, South Korea, Australia, and Thailand, respectively.

THE DIVISION OF LABOR BETWEEN THE UNITED STATES AND EAST ASIA

By 1980, after a decade of the intensive internationalization of the U.S. agriculture, about 30 percent of the value of U.S. agricultural output was exported, notably to Japan. In the same year, in a report entitled the *United States-Japan Trade Report*, the Committee on Ways and Means of the U.S. House of Representatives observed: "We are as a developing nation supplying a more advanced nation—we are Japan's plantation: haulers of wood and growers of crops, in exchange for high technology, value-added products. . . . This relationship is not acceptable" (quoted in Hillman & Rothenberg, 1988: 62–63). Current U.S. policy that calls for a Japanese liberalization of agricultural imports would arguably intensify this division of labor, however. There was a perceptible shift to agriculture as a key export industry during the 1980s—most notably in the Reagan administration's articulation of a universal liberalization of agriculture to be institutionalized through the GATT.[3]

Much is made of the industrialization of East Asia and of its contribution to the decline of U.S. economic hegemony. But in order to understand that process fully, it is necessary to transcend trade relations and to examine the postwar restructuring of the region. There are two key points to make. First, East Asian agrarian regimes, especially that of Japan, were reconstructed in the form of the dominant metropolitan model of agricultural nationalization, whereby the agricultural and industrial sectors' commercial articulation fuels national economic growth (Friedmann & McMichael, 1989). This arrangement took a "statist" form (Moore, 1985), in which agriculture was subordinated to the needs of industry, initially in an import-substitution phase and then for export industrialization. During the latter phase (for Japan in the late 1950s and for Korea in the late 1960s), farmers successfully demanded protection (Anderson, 1983: 331–332), and agriculture obtained industrial inputs (Hayami, 1989: 44; Burmeister, 1988).

Second, the content of the East Asian developmental model was profoundly conditioned by U.S. policies concerning land reform and food aid. The "Bureaucratic-Authoritarian Industrializing Regime" (Cumings, 1987) depended upon the agrarian regimes established under American tutelage as well as on concessional PL 480 (largely surplus American food grains disposed of through food aid to feed urban proletariats) wage foods. Within a Cold War framework (in relation to Chinese and North Korean reforms), the United States reconstructed the farm sectors of Japan, South Korea and Taiwan as stable smallholding constituencies with legally limited land tenures. The relation between the state and the rural constituency was mediated by powerful agricultural cooperatives—ranging from the relatively democratic NOKYO in Japan to the thoroughly authoritarian

NONGHYUP in Korea. Land reform was a key to the reconstruction of agricultural cooperatives and to their integration, via traditional agro-bureaucracies, into the state. This parastatal phenomenon conditioned the developmental trajectories of East Asian states. First, land reform eliminated potential landed resistance to the subordination of the farm sectors to subsequent export-oriented industrialization. Second, the new landowners reimbursed the government for their land in crops, as wage foods for urban labor forces, over a 15-year period (McMichael & Kim, 1991).

The smallholding character of East Asian farming contradicts Japan's and Korea's industrial export strategies. On the one hand, within a context of expanding world grain markets, these farm sectors have become increasingly costly in fiscal terms as well as for domestic consumers and food processors.[4] On the other hand, the national governments' dependence on the rural vote or the food question politicizes national (agricultural) policy. In Japan, even as the size of the farm sector has dwindled, rice self-sufficiency has remained a profound national security issue (in food, health, and political terms). In addition, NOKYO has politically unified the remaining but increasingly differentiated farm sector behind a protectionist policy supported by the consumer lobby umbrella organization Shodanren (Weigand, 1988: 233). There are discernible trends towards rice liberalization, however, led by Keidanren (Federation of Economic Organizations) and by the Japan Federation of Employers' Association (Gordon, 1990; Higashi & Lauter, 1987: 129). In Korea, polarization between economic nationalists, who oppose the perceived U.S. influence over the Korean government (following import concessions to U.S. tobacco and beef in 1988), and economic liberals, who advocate agricultural "structural adjustment," is fracturing both the state bureaucracy and civil society. Because of this politicization of the agricultural issue, the farm vote is currently "up for grabs" (Burmeister, 1990: 717–719; and see Lee, Hadwiger, & Lee, 1990: 422).

These tensions have been focused on the bilateral relations between the United States, and Japan and Korea, respectively, because of the significance of these East Asian markets for U.S. agricultural exports.[5] While Japan is the largest consumer of U.S. agricultural exports, South Korea is the second largest market. Japan is in fact the world's largest food importer (Hillman & Rothenberg, 1988: 38). In 1989, Japan imported from the United States 84 percent of its corn, 71 percent of its sorghum, 75 percent of its soybeans, 55 percent of its wheat, 43 percent of its beef and veal, 38 percent of its poultry meat, 99 percent of its citrus, and 43 percent of its cotton; Korean imports from the United States were in the following proportions: 77 percent of its wheat, 87 percent of its corn, 86 percent of its soybeans, 19 percent of its beef, and 61 percent of its cotton (USDA, 1990: 72, 76). East Asia overtook Europe in 1983 as the largest regional market for U.S. agricultural products (Coyle, 1989: 47). In turn, Japan and the East Asian NICs depend on the U.S. market for outlets for their manufactures, such that, in the past five years, the Asian NICs have run large trade surpluses with the United States that have exceeded their trade surpluses with the rest of the world (USDA, 1990: 3).

AGRO-FOOD RESTRUCTURING

The Internationalization of East Asian Consumption and Production Relations

In a very real sense, the tension arising from this relationship is a legacy of U.S. hegemony. This had two aspects: the food aid program and the internationalization of the U.S. agro-industrial model. Both integrated East Asian agriculture into international capital circuits, particularly those organized around U.S. exports of agricultural commodities and agribusiness inputs. Food aid linked U.S. disposal of surplus agricultural goods with industrialization policies in client states like Japan and in newly independent Third World states like Korea (Friedmann, 1982a). For Korea, which ranked third behind India and Pakistan in food aid receipts from 1954 to 1974 (USDA, 1977), cheap concessional food kept wages low and underwrote labor-intensive manufacturing for export. Food aid reinforced the Korean government policy of low domestic grain prices, contributing to a rural depopulation on the order of more than 12 million people between 1957 and 1982 (Lee & Yamazawa, 1990: 143; Moore, 1985: 105). In fact, Korean domestic wheat production fell by 86 percent between 1966 and 1977, while wheat imports increased fourfold (Wessel, 1983: 173). For Japan, complementing a rice-growing policy with cheap U.S. grains translated into competitive exports. This relation began in 1954, with the Mutual Security Act, whereby U.S. surplus farm products were sold locally; the proceeds went to finance military infrastructure first and agribusiness infrastructure second. In the same year, the Japanese state budget allocations to agriculture decreased markedly (Ohno, 1988: 17).

The PL 480 scheme conditioned the reconstruction of East Asian diets, despite a continuing commitment to rice as the staple food of cultural preference. Counterpart funds from food aid, assisted by the governments, financed the local promotion of bread substitutes for rice and the establishment of local agro-industrial operations[6] (Wessel, 1983: 173-174; Shinohara, 1964). When concessional sales to Japan and Korea ended in the 1970s, commercial wheat imports continued to grow. This was the first stage in a complex process of the internationalization of consumption as proletarianization extended markets for American grains (Friedmann, 1990).

Once the process of industrial class formation was proceeding within this international relationship, however, the second element of the food regime entered the equation. With import liberalization, the focus shifted from wheat to other commodities. Most notably, corn and soybean imports marked the internationalization of production, as a stage beyond the initial internationalization of consumption via wheat imports. While Japan and Korea have maintained self-sufficiency in rice, other grain and soybean self-sufficiency has declined significantly over the period (Wessel, 1983: 172). In addition, there has been a gradual decline in rice consumption and a growing replacement of rice with flour-based products and animal protein. Japanese rice consumption has been decreasing by about 2 percent annually (Ohno, 1988: 15). We can trace the emergence of an industrial class system in the parallel shift from an essentially starchy diet (rice and other grains) to more diversified class diets that include the increasing consumption of animal protein, fat, vegetables, and fruit. For Japan, "per capita consumption of chicken increased 32-fold during 1955–86, red meat 8-fold, dairy products 6-fold, and eggs 5-fold" (Taha, 1989: 9). Between 1950 and 1985, livestock production increased from 7 percent to 27 percent of the value of Japanese agricultural output, while that of rice declined from 49 percent to 33 percent (Riethmuller, Wallace, & Tie, 1988: 154).

Between 1961 and 1987, the value of East Asian farm imports increased at twice the rate of world imports (Huang & Coyle, 1989: 42). The greater part of this trade expansion can be attributed to the transnational development of the intensive livestock complex. There are two sides to this process: the expansion of the animal protein subsector in East Asia and the expanding imports of (primarily U.S.) feedstuffs.

Expansion of the animal protein subsector in Japan and Korea was linked in each case to the upgrading, or rationalization, of the farm sectors to raise rural living standards toward urban-rural parity. Japan's Basic Agricultural Law (1961) was geared to improving the international competitiveness of Japanese agriculture via mechanization and enhanced irrigation, to liberalizing food imports other than rice, and to encouraging selective diversification: from rice into cattle and fruit (Ohno, 1988: 20). The expectation was that, by liberalizing food imports, Japanese manufactures would gain greater access to metropolitan markets.

In terms of the structure of Japanese agriculture, there were two particular consequences: On the one hand, high government rice supports sustained a growing specialization in paddy farming, which, once mechanized, was sufficiently profitable as a small-scale monocrop to allow farmers to seek off-farm work (Hemmi, 1987: 28, part-time rice farming is now on the order of about 90 percent); on the other hand, government subsidies to shift farmers into other specializations has indirectly raised the level of Japanese agricultural protection (Hillman & Rothenberg, 1988: 24–27), except for imported feedstuffs. In fact, the steady expansion and concentration of the Japanese intensive animal protein subsector (Japanese Statistical Yearbook, 1989: 164) is complemented by free access to imported feeds, which "has increased the effective protection conferred by price-support policies" (Hillman & Rothenberg, 1988: 50). Between 1960 and 1984, while Japanese agricultural production grew annually at the rate of 1.5 percent, agricultural imports grew at 7.9 percent—such that the area devoted to U.S. feed grains for Japanese livestock exceeds that on which the Japanese grow their staple rice (Hillman & Rothenberg, 1988: 38, 43).

The legacy of Japan's rice self-sufficiency policy has been a rapid rural depopulation and urban proletarianization, on the one hand, and the internationalization of an expanding intensive meat complex, on the other. Sourcing this combined process, food and feed imports increased from 3.6 to 18.6 million metric tons during 1960–73, 70 percent of which was accounted for simply by increased domestic consumption (Hemmi, 1987: 26, 27). Over the longer period from 1960 to 1987, imports of major feed grains, corn, and sorghum increased 15-fold, soybeans more than fourfold, and wheat twofold (Ohno, 1988: 20).

An analogous development occurred in Korea in the early 1970s when the government mobilized the farm sector via the Saemaul Undong (New Village Movement), centered in the agricultural cooperative, NONGHYUP, to adopt green revolution techniques to upgrade agricultural productivity in the service of rice self-sufficiency (Burmeister, 1988). With industrialization and the rapid rise in real incomes on the order of an 83 percent increase per capita during 1975–88, class diets changed and animal protein production expanded. The animal protein subsector was a joint venture between the Korean government and U.S. counterpart funds from food aid sales; in 1975, Cargill and two other U.S. grain corporations set up poultry and animal feed processing plants (Wessel, 1983: 174). During the 1970s, the Korean government subsidized beef cattle raising (40-fold growth between 1960 and 1977), parallel to an expanding dairy cattle business. The beef cattle industry came under closer government regulation in the early 1980s as part of a plan for diversified farming and a producer price stabilization policy. Concentration in the beef cattle industry began in the 1980s (Lee et al., 1990: 431–432). A substantial rise in the compound feeds consumed by beef cattle from 1975 to 1987 indicates the specialization and internationalization of this agro-food subsector (Harris & Dickson, 1989: 297–299).

Internationalization of U.S. Agriculture

This internationalization of consumption and production relations in East Asia complemented the dramatic internationalization of U.S. agriculture in the 1970s. This process was rooted in the demise of the stable world food order that had been constructed, via American food aid, during the preceding postwar decades. It took the form of a policy shift, from national agricultural commodity supply management (via the food aid program, which was organized around direct aid to farmers and production quotas) to a demand management policy. The latter policy is geared to commercial exports and provides export incentives to farmers. It pursues international trade liberalization both to maximize U.S. "comparative advantage" and to reduce production costs, such as petroleum inputs (Tubiana, 1989: 38; Revel & Riboud, 1986: 91–98). In general, internationalization produced a rise in monocultural export cropping in the United States, accompanied by a significant concentration of landholdings. Henceforth, U.S. agricultural fortunes would depend profoundly on the world market.

The consolidation of U.S. export agriculture was a symptom of declining U.S. hegemony (for a cause and effect argument, see Revel & Riboud, 1986: 58). In the late 1960s, with the rising costs of empire and a severe trade deficit, the U.S. government established the Williams Commission, which investigated the possibility of mounting a "green power" program (Wessel, 1983: 162–163). The

1971 report recommended that the United States specialize in high technology, capital equipment, armaments, and computers, and in agricultural export commodities, such as food and feed grains. Interestingly enough, the Williams Report also expressed leniency toward Japanese agricultural protection (Hemmi, 1987: 27).[7] As a result, the U.S. government dismantled its regulatory structure (credit and price supports), shifting from food aid to commercial exports. President Richard Nixon devalued the dollar, and an export push occurred, reinforced by the massive U.S.-Soviet grain deal of 1972. U.S. wheat exports increased 90 percent in the first four years of the 1970s, and grain prices rose by 400 percent (Wessel, 1983: 163). In conjunction with the growing food dependency of the Third World, particularly of those middle-income states that anchored world-economic growth in the 1970s, these changes in U.S. policies fueled a 60 percent expansion of the world grain trade from 1974 to 1980, of which the U.S. share was 80 percent.

The internationalization of U.S. agriculture is evident in the relative expansion of markets: from 1960 to 1980 export markets rose by 150 percent, while domestic markets rose by only 25 percent. Indeed, since 1970, U.S. farm exports have increased by 425 percent (Krebs, 1988: 19), and now one acre in three is for export production of three primary low-value products (LVPs: wheat, corn, and soybeans). Accompanying and reinforcing the export focus, there has been a shift in the productive base of American agriculture, from mixed livestock and cropping toward specialized corn and soybean production, in addition to wheat farming. During the 1970s, the proportion of farm land committed to export production expanded from one-half to two-thirds. Associated with this orientation has been the social polarization of the U.S. farm sector, including a rising incidence of hired labor, which increased from 25 percent to 50 percent of farm labor in the 1970s (Strange, 1988: 40–41). In addition, in the context of the international farm crisis of the 1980s and the greater price instability associated with unstable international trade, there has been further land concentration, aided in part by government subsidies.[8]

New Internationalization Trends

Current trends in the process of internationalization express a profound national/international tension, reverberating in international regulatory fora such as the GATT as well as in the recent "structural adjustments" of domestic farm sectors as national governments negotiate world market position. The relatively stable postwar food regime, expressed in the low and stable prices of metropolitan agricultural exports from 1956 to 1972 (Tubiana, 1989: 29), has unraveled over the past 15 years as the world-economy has entered into a long crisis of organization. The current world food order is marked by intensified competition, price instability, and an unregulated international trade in agricultural commodities.

A proximate cause is the spread of the U.S. model, which created national competitors in two guises: countries that successfully adopted the green revolution as a form of food import substitution (e.g., Argentina, India, Pakistan, Indonesia, Turkey) and thereby contracted markets for U.S. commodities, and countries that have emerged as rival exporters of agricultural commodities (the European Community, Brazil, Argentina, Thailand, Taiwan, China, and even India). Unstable competition also stems from floating exchange rates, which varies effective protection (Hathaway, 1987: 14), and from the asymmetry between publicly subsidized metropolitan farm sectors and (nationally) unregulated, frequently disaggregated, but still cost-competitive, Third World farm sectors (McMichael, 1992).

Thus, the principle of trade complementarity, which had characterized the period of U.S. hegemony, has yielded to heightened competition in world markets for commodities (including agricultural ones), capital, and foreign exchange. In *formal* terms,[9] the stable geopolitical hierarchy has unraveled with the rise of rival industrial and agro-food producers. The 1980s ushered in an era of "permanent surpluses" (Insel, 1985), such that the United States has lost its ability to regulate international agricultural trade, becoming instead the "residual supplier" of world grains (in 1974, the United States held 24 percent of world stocks, which had increased to 45 percent by 1984). It is now compelled to resort to the GATT to maintain its competitive advantage in sluggish world agro-food markets.[10] In *substantive* terms, the United States currently retains its dominance as global production and consumption relations increasingly correspond to the U.S. agro-food model, providing markets for agro-inputs such as feed grains and technologies. In the 1980s, the United States became the world's "restauranteur" rather than its breadbasket (Wessel, 1983: 4), more than two-thirds of its exports being feedstuffs.

Nevertheless, current U.S. pressures on East Asian states to liberalize their imports reveal a need to expand markets for high-value products (HVPs), especially in light of potential competition from lower-cost producers of specialized feed grain and soybeans elsewhere in Latin America and Southeast Asia. Since the Japanese government's report, *Basic Directions of Agricultural Policy in the 1980s*, diversification of feedstuff sources has intensified—in corn in Thailand and Indonesia, in soy beans in Brazil, and in coarse grains in South Africa, China, Argentina, and Australia—all through joint public-private ventures (Hillman & Rothenberg, 1988: 46–47).

There are two well-known responses to the limits of East Asian smallholding in the face of the internationalization pressures induced by the trade crisis, and each is transforming the agricultural sector. First, policy shifts in both Japan and South Korea involve structural reform—generating specialized paddy farming (supplemented by off-farm work), livestock farming, and horticulture, and encouraging trade liberalization (see Huang and Coyle, 1989). Perhaps related to the liberalization trend, the second response is an offshore move, by Japanese capital in particular, to source the Japanese market from lower-cost production locations— beef ranching and feedlots in the United States, Australia, and New Zealand, and poultry raising in Thailand, Indonesia, and Mexico (Coyle, 1990: 52). In fact, during the 1980s, Japanese meat imports rose continuously, while imports of feed grain slowed, leveling off in 1987: "on a grain equivalent basis, Japanese meat imports were about 12 percent of total grain imports in 1980, rising to 25 percent in 1989" (Coyle, 1990: 51).

These two responses to the limits of East Asian farming express, on the one hand, a significant rise in animal protein consumption as offshore supply supplements local supplies—one indicator in 1989 being a dramatic redirection of Australian and New Zealand beef exports from the United States to East Asia (USDA, 1990: 26). On the other hand, the expansion of offshore supply represents a significant reorganization of world animal protein production. Previous internationalization of production relations involved the transnational integration of regionally specialized subsectors of the animal protein complex (Friedmann, 1991). In this form, East Asian livestock industries were supplied with feedstuffs from the United States, as well as from other suppliers such as Brazil, Argentina, Thailand, and China. Alongside, and sometimes instead of, this international sourcing arrangement, a new form of internationalization has appeared, in which the animal protein production complex is recombined within feed supply regions under the aegis of large corporate processors. One indicator is the changing composition of Japanese imports, toward a greater proportion of HVPs (Evans, 1988), especially beef. Imports from competitive feed-supply regions reflect the Japanese policy of maintaining stable beef prices for consumers—a policy begun in 1975 (Dyck, 1988: 55) and now reinforced by the imminent removal of beef quotas following the agreement of 1988 (Coyle, 1990: 51). Rising poultry imports result from government regulation of local feed prices, disadvantaging local poultry producers vis-à-vis foreign producers (Coyle, 1990: 52).

The recombination of the animal protein complex in feed-supply zones of the Pacific Rim expresses both general and particular aspects of the process of internationalization in the Pacific Rim of the 1980s. Generally, a world market for animal protein is emerging, taking the form of standardized, class-differentiated global diets (Friedmann, 1991). Within this context, a common model of agribusiness operation is vertical integration (Watts, 1990). More particularly, given the peculiarities of East Asian political economy, expanding East Asian agro-food markets have become a metropole to surrounding agricultural supply zones. Just as Britain was supplied with foodstuffs from the New World more cheaply than from her own high-cost farm sector, so Japan (and, to some extent, its South Korean imitator) has a growing agricultural perimeter in the Pacific Rim. Thus, the animal protein complex is proliferating in neighboring feed-supply zones with the advantage of economies of scale: "The inescapable reality is that ruminants are efficient converters of low-grade roughage to high-grade protein: countries with plentiful supplies of roughage will have a competitive advantage over Japan" (Coyle, 1990: 52). But this is not all, because this is no mere matching of supply with demand. Rather it involves a reconstruction of regional agricultures, under the aegis of Japanese agribusinesses that are concerned with Japanese taste preferences.

Two cases in point will illustrate this development: Australia and Thailand. Australia is emerging as a significant site of grain-fed beef for the East Asian markets, especially since the new beef agreement signed by the governments of Japan, Australia, and the United States in 1988 (Gorman & Mori, 1990). By 1989, 80 percent of Australian grain-fed beef exports went to the Japanese and South Korean markets, reflecting the recent expansion of Japanese investment in Australian feedlots. Japanese investment concentrates in special long-grain-fed cattle, providing the marbled beef favored in Japan, and is undertaken mostly by "trading companies with meat divisions of major meat packers with import divisions" (Gorman & Mori, 1990: 44). Japanese investors identify the following advantages in Australia's beef cattle industry: Australia's ability to ship fresh chilled beef and its lower costs for producing grain-fed beef; its providing an alternative supply zone to the United States; and the opportunity for Japanese firms to influence the organization of production and processing. In fact, Australia's share of Japanese markets for chilled beef grew from less than 10 percent in 1986 to more than 50 percent in 1989 (Gorman & Mori, 1990: 42, 46). The framework for this development has been the drastic deregulation of Australian agriculture over the past decade (Lawrence, 1987), one result being that nation's exposure to steadily declining world wool and wheat prices, such that "many farmers are abandoning wheat and wool for beef." This sector is rapidly being reorganized by Japanese capital, in particular by the substitution of large, specialized, and integrated corporate feedlots for more traditional cattle pasturing (Lawrence & Campbell, 1991: 105).

Thai agricultural reorganization has shifted from its traditional role in the international division of labor as an exporter of primary products (rice, sugar, pineapple, and rubber) to exporting cassava (feed grain), (canned) tuna, shrimp, poultry, processed meats, and fresh and processed fruits and vegetables. Former exports, such as corn and sorghum, are now mostly consumed domestically in the intensive livestock sector. Targeted as "Asia's supermarket," Thailand's food processing industry has expanded rapidly on a foundation of rural smallholders under contract to agro-food processors—in 1988, investment increased 43 percent, and exports of processed foods increased in the realm of 20 percent. Food companies "from Japan, Taiwan, the US and Europe see Thailand as the most promising base for export-oriented production, especially in comparison with competitors like Indonesia, the Philippines, or Taiwan" (Goldstein, 1988: 48). In the 1970s, Japan began investing in Thai agriculture to expand feed (soybeans and corn) and aquaculture supply zones for Japanese markets (Suthy & Kongsak, 1986: 193), and, in the 1980s, Japanese direct investment in Thai agriculture grew from 1.6 million baht in 1979, to 42.2 million baht in 1984 (Surachai, 1986: 99). Typically, Japanese food companies enter into joint ventures with Thai agribusinesses, providing high-technology production facilities and market access abroad (Suehiro, 1989: 270).

Thai poultry production is organized around growers contracting with vertically integrated firms. The Thai government has supported this development, making tax and other concessions available to large firms (Chesley, 1985: 69–70) and underwriting the distribution of land to landless farmers for crops and livestock farming via the Bangkok Bank's Agricultural Credit Department (Rainat, 1988). Thailand's mature feed supply industry, coupled with low-cost labor, gives its poultry producers an edge of about 28 percent in cost competition with their U.S. counterparts (Schwartz & Brooks, 1990: 13), especially in the Japanese market, which is primarily (80 percent) for deboned chicken. Thus, the Thai share of Japan's broiler imports almost doubled, to 41 percent between 1980 and 1987, to overtake U.S. exports, which fell from 59 percent to 40 percent (Bishop, Christensen, Mercier, & Witucki, 1990: 23). This specialized relation is reinforced by Japanese investment in Thai poultry processing, which, like Japanese investment in the U.S. and Australian feedlot industry, allows the tailoring of livestock products for the Japanese consumer.

This growing displacement of Japanese and South Korean agriculture by proliferating supply zones is perhaps the third phase of the internationalization of Pacific Rim food systems. The initial phase involved the reconstruction of East Asian diets along Western lines. The second involved the reconstruction of East Asian agricultural production centered on the rise of the livestock industry supplied by U.S. and other feedstuffs. The third movement involves the reconstruction of supply zones such as the United States, Australia, and Thailand—especially in the development of integrated animal protein complexes sponsored by Japanese capital.

The significance of the current movement is that it is configuring a new food regime, in the aftermath of the food regime associated with the era of the Bretton Woods system (McMichael, 1992). The so-called "second food regime" of the postwar era was anchored in a U.S. state-sponsored intensive accumulation process geared to (cheap) food consumption that was incorporated, Fordist style, into the accumulation process itself (Friedmann & McMichael, 1989). Agricultural industrialization accounted for the rise of durable foods, the input of which (e.g., fats, sweeteners) displaced tropical export commodities, and for food surpluses channeled to the Third World via U.S. food aid (Friedmann, 1982, 1990, 1991). Peripheral food dependency grew, and the terms of trade worsened, prefiguring the 1980s debt crisis. This crisis in turn became a vehicle for restructuring the Southern states and their agricultural sectors (McMichael & Myhre, 1991). The second food regime ended with the dismantling of the Bretton Woods system and the commercialization of U.S. export agriculture (in the context of rising agro-export competition from the European Community and some green revolution beneficiaries). This marked the end of a stable system of international food prices that had been anchored in a nationally regulated U.S. farm sector. It also represented a turning point in the history of other (national) farm sectors, which were now under pressure to deregulate—whether political pressure exerted through fora such as the GATT or the economic pressure of an increasingly competitive world market.

CONCLUSION

The crisis of East Asian agriculture must be situated in relation to these pressures. Its predicted demise (Hemmi, 1987; Ohno, 1988) is perhaps a logical outcome of the singular pursuit of industrial competitive advantage in the world-economy.[11] In geopolitical terms, the deregulation of East Asian farming is the *quid pro quo* for a development model premised on both the U.S. military umbrella and access to the U.S. market for industrial exports (McMichael, 1987). For Japan, the *quid pro quo* involves expanding agro-food imports. This must also be seen, however, as a condition for obtaining leverage in international negotiations to extend foreign markets for Japanese manufactures and capital (Raghavan, 1990: 71). For the United States, the *quid pro quo* helps to offset the U.S. trade deficit, but the internationalization of Japanese capital raises the competitive stakes as rival supply zones emerge.

We are in the midst of an intense maneuvering for advantage in the world-economy, with agro-food restructuring as simply one component of the larger matrix of forces. The present juncture is a transitional one—between the previous (second) food regime that was anchored in the Pax Americana and an emerging world order that threatens to be organized through the GATT, institutionalizing a neomercantilist international trading system for the benefit of the core states, and in particular its TNCs.[12] The food component is increasingly centered on HVPs, elevating agribusiness beyond the family farmer to plantation or estate and to contract farming organized by food companies or their equivalent. A world market for agro-food products has emerged, both as inputs—especially the current trend of grain substitutes and generic inputs—and as processed foods. Agricultural trade is potentially less a matter of state-to-state exchanges and more a matter of world exchanges dominated and organized by TNCs,[13] the strongest supporters of the GATT-style liberalization measures (Wysham, 1990; Weissman, 1991). These forces for liberalization have already gained a strong foothold within the political economy of the East Asian states, as industrialists, food processors, and exporters challenge agro-food protectionism and encourage the importation of HVPs. With sluggish grain markets, HVP growth directly challenges the content of U.S. "green power" in LVPs. For Japan, especially, there is an elemental tension between a national rice policy, which structures land use and the farm sector, and the growing importation of HVPs, many of which are produced by Japanese offshore capital. Here the conflict between national and international forces is expressed in the ongoing realignment of political forces around the "food question."

Thus, the attempt to expand agro-food markets in East Asia reveals the profound contradiction between the process of internationalization and the salience of the nation-state in this period of restructuring. National (commercial) agricultures arose within the context of the world-economy and inter-state system. As the content of the world-economy changes and as states shed their national foundations to accommodate themselves to the internationalization of capital (McMichael, 1991), the contingency of national farm sectors is revealed, notably in the restructuring of family farm systems on the Pacific Rim.

NOTES

I wish to thank Chul-Kyoo Kim, Research Assistant, Cornell University, for his assistance in the preparation of this paper, as well as Larry Burmeister and Harriet Friedmann who commented constructively on the draft. I also acknowledge the financial assistance of Hatch Grant #6404 undertaken at the Cornell University Agricultural Experiment Station.

1. Rivalry is relative, as countries like Brazil, Argentina, Thailand, and even China constitute alternative supply zones for certain agricultural commodities. However, none match the sheer volume of exports of the United States, and its ability to influence world market prices and to protect its farm sector (c.f., Charvet, 1990: 179).

2. The *Economist* has suggested that the General Agreement on Tariffs and Trade (GATT) "has a fundamentally mercantilist character. It embodies the idea that domestic producers have a prior claim to domestic markets, that exports are "good" and imports "bad," and that unilateral protection creates national economic advantage. . . . In the 1990s [if America pursues the route of "fair trade" on its own terms—that is, exercising its muscle with super-301, threatening higher U.S. trade barriers] the interests of exporters will no longer be aligned with the true national interest—which is to lower barriers to imports. Instead, they will be aligned with demands for higher barriers, as a way of putting pressure on foreigners" (December 15, 1990: 16).

3. It is worth noting that a precondition of this goal, as a serious goal, would be a restructuring of U.S. agriculture away from low-value bulk foods and raw materials, toward high-value products, which have become the locus of growth (and more stable markets) in world agricultural trade since 1980, accounting for the first time for more than 50 percent of the total value of world agricultural trade (Hillman & Rothenberg, 1988: 63).

4. Japanese rice producer prices exceed world prices by eight to ten times, and consumer prices are only slightly lower because of an expensive subsidy (Hathaway 1987: 29).

5. However, Chikara Higashi and G. Peter Lauter have written: "the impact of agricultural exports on the bilateral trade imbalances is minimal. In 1986, for instance, a study of the congressional research service of the Library of Congress concluded that the elimination of all Japanese agricultural import restraints could increase American sales by approximately $1 billion, but this would decrease the overall bilateral trade deficit by only 2 percent" (1987: 126).

6. In 1967, Western Wheat Associates arrived in Korea to spearhead an eat-wheat campaign, supported by agribusiness companies, encouraging a dietary shift to lunch-rolls and sandwiches. In 1972, the first automatic biscuit and cracker equipment was installed in three plants, and by 1979, more than 21,000 housewives in more than 100 cities attended special sandwich-making classes. In 1975, over 7,000 bakeries had appeared, and in 1978, Korea joined the "billion dollar club" of purchasers of imported farm goods from the United States (Wessel, 1983: 173).

7. The report said: "Japan is now by far our largest single customer; its imports of more than $1.2 billion in 1970 were two-and-one-half times those of a decade earlier. On the other hand, our market growth in Europe was less favourable. . . . The Commission recommends that the United States should immediately and vigorously assert its agricultural interests in bilateral discussion at the highest political level. . . . As Japanese products

flood international markets the slow pace of Japanese import liberalization efforts has come under increasing criticism. Nevertheless, by mid-1971 official Japanese residual quantitative import restrictions have narrowed to a number which is not much larger than those of most W. European Countries'' (quoted in Hemmi, 1987: 45).

8. ''In the US 4 percent of farms, operating 22 percent of the land, sell nearly half of all agricultural products. This last figure is expected to increase to three-quarters in the year 2000.'' ''[I]n 1984, 15% of farms producing three-quarters of the output obtained 70 percent of direct government payments'' (Commins, 1990: 59, 65).

9. Here I draw on Giovanni Arrighi's (1982) distinction between formal and substantive elements of hegemony.

10. As Jimmye Hillman and Robert Rothenberg have stated: ''Japan's restrictive trading practices are not a major factor in the current predicament of American agriculture. Their effects account for relatively little of the weakness in foreign demand from the United States. One of the major causes has been the strengthening of the dollar against other currencies (through late 1985). More important still, recent years have seen a deep recession among the industrial countries with which the United States conducts most of its farm trade. On the other hand, many of the customers of the United States are less developed countries whose purchasing power is constrained by insufficient foreign-exchange earnings and mushrooming debt-service obligations'' (1988: 70–71).

11. There is a perceptible unraveling of the agrarian coalitions in both Japan and Korea. For example, NOKYO has integrated itself into the agro-industrial complex, as a supplier of agro-inputs, exacerbating the cost-price squeeze for paddy farmers and specialized livestock producers alike (Ohno, 1987). In addition, some larger farmers are bypassing the cooperative system, in part because NOKYO's democratic foundations limit its ability to offer volume discounts (Smith, 1988: 32). With the concentration of the beef cattle industry in Korea, specialized producers are gaining representation through independent commodity organization (Lee et al., 1990), and there is a political realignment of the farm constituency (Burmeister, 1990).

12. As Chakravarthi Raghavan has written: ''Even now, the IMF and the World Bank . . . exercise an enormous influence on the economic policies of [the Third World] including in the area of trade policy. However, while the World Bank is able to hold out a carrot, it is unable to wield the stick, which the trading system and its retaliation provisions provide'' (1990: 60).

13. Joyce Kolko has written: ''For instance, six TNCs control the distribution of 60 percent of the world's coffee, three TNCs sell 75 percent of the bananas, fifteen control more than half of the world's sugar trade, two TNCs control half the wheat trade, and two companies produce more than half of the farm machinery'' (1988: 175).

PART III

POLITICS OF THE
INTERSTATE SYSTEM

7

TRANSITION IN THE ERA OF U.S. HEGEMONY: INDIAN STATE EXPANSION AND WORLD-SYSTEMS ANALYSIS

Sankaran Krishna

By any yardstick, the contemporary Indian state is economically all-pervasive. On the industrial front, the state runs 8 of the top 10 and 14 of the top 25 industrial firms (Bardhan, 1984: 103–104); state-run companies recently owned 77.62 percent of the total paid-up capital of all industry (*India Today*, 1989: 63); the state owns nearly 25 percent of the paid-up capital of the so-called private industrial sector, and employs two-thirds of the 23 million workers in the organized sector of the economy (Rudolph & Rudolph, 1987: 22). Through nationalized banks, insurance agencies, development banks, control over foreign exchange and institutions such as the Unit Trust of India, the state exercises further direct ownership over the main sources of credit for enterprises. Finally, the state, through its planning agencies and the myriad licenses and permits, "regulate(s) patterns of private investment down to industrial product level, choice of technology, extending to scale, location and import-content" (Bardhan, 1984: 38).

On the agricultural front, the state plays a preponderant role in subsidizing vital inputs such as fertilizers, electricity, pesticides, seeds, and irrigation (Chakravarty, 1987: 104–127). It influences prices through its purchases on the open market and the actions of the Prices Commission, serves as a major retail outlet through its vast network of "ration shops," and influences the legal form of property relations through its periodic (and largely unsuccessful) efforts at land reform. Finally, it has largely replaced the moneylender as the main source of rural credit. Together, the degree of economic penetration is impressive, although it has to be emphasized that economic pervasiveness is not tantamount to the state's autonomy from propertied classes.[1] In historical terms, however, the emergence of this state is very recent. Most analysts would date it to the decades immediately following independence from Britain, especially the period of the Second and Third Five-Year Plans (1956–66).

This chapter argues one interpretation of this transition. In terms of world-systems theory, one could argue that India moved from the periphery to the semiperiphery largely through a strategy of statist, mercantilist withdrawal from the world-economy.[2] The period of this transition coincided with the heyday of American hegemony, roughly 1945 to 1971. I argue that these two events (or processes)—Indian transition and American hegemony—are intimately related. Specifically, the emergence of the pervasive Indian state cannot be understood without examining the interaction between the state, domestic society, and the world-system. The ability of state élites to mediate between domestic society and the interstate system formed both the locus of their power and the limits to their autonomy. Thus, one of the paradoxes that has emerged is that the hegemonic power in the world-system, which was supposedly committed to open markets and the free flow of the factors of production across national boundaries, greatly assisted the Indian state in constructing a highly protectionist, statist, and self-reliant economy and thereby closed the doors of one of the world's largest markets, at least partially.

In detailing the interactions that underlay the Indian transition, this chapter will be in dialogue with the notions of hegemony and state, as they are found in most works within the world-systems perspective. My argument is that the Indian experience can be utilized to arrive at a richer, more open-ended, and dialectical understanding of these concepts, one that is sensitive to the socially articulated, contingent, often accidental, and nonteleological character of history. This effort is structured as follows: The first section examines the critical role played by international aid in general, and U.S. agricultural aid in particular, in the emergence of a pervasively statist, import-substituting economy in India; the second section highlights the paradoxical nature of U.S. hegemony and the mediatory character of state power in the world-system; and the third section concludes the chapter with some thoughts on the implications of this analysis for the world-systems perspective.

U.S. HEGEMONY AND INDIAN STATE EXPANSION

Indian state élites made explicit their overwhelming commitment to industrialization at any cost soon after independence (Nayar, 1972). A symptomatic quote from this period, from India's first prime minister, Jawaharlal Nehru, captures this desire concisely: "Now, India, we are bound to be industrialized, we are trying to be industrialized, we want to be industrialized, we must be industrialized" (quoted in Byres, 1982: 135). The nationalist struggle for independence had articulated a particular vision of development that would entail massive state intervention into the economy. In terms of this articulation, the independent state situated itself in a mediatory position between the "domestic" and the "foreign." The reversal of underdevelopment thus hinged on the ability of new state élites to mediate this relationship in ways that would not replicate historical patterns. The panacea for this was to be self-reliant, planned, heavy industrialization.[3]

The ambitious plans for state-led industrialization hinged, in turn, on two key assumptions: (a) that foreign aid and know-how would be available for what was, in essence, a highly protectionist, import-substituting industrialization strategy, and (b) that the agrarian sector could be neglected over the short term without a precipitous decline in the availability of food or a rapid inflation in wage goods. Both assumptions were dubious, to say the least.

Indian economic performance in the first decade after independence did little to warrant any optimism on these counts. Between 1947 and 1957, India's sterling balances (the leftover foreign exchange reserves after colonialism had ended) dropped from a healthy Rs 1,612 crores[4] to Rs 681 crores, much of the decline due to indiscriminate imports on private account. India's average import bills during the Second Plan period were a full 50 percent higher than during the First. By 1956, the ambitious Second Plan was already threatened by a dire shortage of foreign exchange (Bhagwati & Desai, 1970). On the agrarian front, the threat of famine compelled the importation of 10.56 million tons of food in the years 1949–51 (Bhatia, 1970: 44). If food imports in hard currency were continued, there would be little prospect of conserving enough foreign exchange to get the Second Plan off the ground.[5] Moreover, efforts to attract Western aid for Indian development in the early 1950s foundered (Merrill, 1990), and the Soviet bloc was likewise lukewarm to the idea (Clarkson, 1978).

The "solution" to the twin crises of foreign exchange and food shortages came about in ways that highlight the central argument of this chapter. A set of conjunctural circumstances in global geopolitics, in the political economy of American agriculture and aid, in post-Stalin Soviet foreign policy, and in Indian domestic class formation all interacted to produce a fleeting period within which the Indian state could substantially "pull off" the Second and Third five-year plans and, in the process, effect a transition from peripheral to semiperipheral status within the world-system.[6] The Second Plan began with a massive increase in public investment with the outlay for the public sector totaling Rs 3,650 crores, which represented an increase of Rs 2,100 crores over the First Plan (Bhagwati & Desai, 1970). Of this, Rs 1,200 crores were to be raised by deficit financing, and the domestic money supply increased by 33 percent over this period. Almost one-half of the large-scale public investments went into heavy industries with enormous capital concentrations, long gestation periods, and little prospect of an immediate reentry into the economy as goods or services (the latter expanding by only 18 percent in this period, as noted by Rath & Patvardhan, 1967).

Against this great expansion in public investment, there was a sharp cut in the relative share of agriculture, which dropped from 37 percent under the First Plan to 22 percent and 23 percent under the Second and Third Plans, respectively. Hence, despite increases in food production in 1954 and 1955 (Chopra, 1981: 288), the index number of wholesale grain prices kept rising. Food shortages could necessitate imports, thereby cutting into already precarious foreign exchange reserves that were earmarked for the industrialization drive. Such shortages could also result in political demands, especially from rural Congress politicians, for a reorientation of the heavy-industry bias of the Second and Third Plans. Inflation in the price of wage goods could render the entire industrialization drive much costlier. Finally, the only way to raise the necessary foreign exchange to pay for food imports might have been to compromise the extreme self-reliance strategy and invite foreign direct investment as the *quid pro quo* for further aid.

Perhaps the most important global circumstances that ensured that none of this came to pass were (a) the presence of vast food surpluses (especially wheat) in the United States, and (b) a sharp shift in Soviet foreign policy toward countries such as India after 1954. The former ensured that, at least for the decade from 1956 to 1966, India could be assured of large-scale food imports (indeed, the largest in all previously recorded history) on extraordinarily favorable terms. The latter resulted in a situation in which the United States (and its allies) and the Soviet Union were locked in a competition to curry the favor of nonaligned countries such as India. This conjuncture greatly favored the Indian state in terms of access to concessional credits and allowed that state to divert the received aid into state-run industries rather than into the private sector.

The problem of U.S. agricultural overproduction predated the Second World War, but that war, European reconstruction, and the Korean War kept the mounting surpluses in check. By 1954, however, the total stocks accumulated and stored in the United States amounted to an entire year's production (Friedmann, 1982b: 261–262) and cost the U.S. Treasury something on the order of $1 billion per year to maintain (Schnittker, 1968: 3). Further, these surpluses were not going to be temporary either: Owing to the complex history of U.S. electoral politics and the role of farm lobbies in putting together Franklin D. Roosevelt's New Deal coalition, legislation either to reduce subsidies to American farmers or to limit the acreage under food crops was unlikely to survive the passage on Capitol Hill (Peterson, 1979).

On the international front, U.S. food aid had already had a demonstrable effect in "securing the free world against Communism" in Western Europe, Korea, and Taiwan and in aiding regimes resisting the Soviet Union. It was against this backdrop that the Agricultural Trade Development and Assistance Act of 1954, better known as Public Law 480 or PL 480, emerged. The primary targets of PL 480 were poor Third World countries, which also happened to be the ones with little or no hard currency to pay for food imports. The U.S. Congress solved this problem by making the vast bulk of PL 480 exports payable in the nonconvertible domestic currencies of the importing countries. From July 1, 1954 (the day the program began) to December 31, 1971, 68.6 percent of all PL 480 exports worldwide were paid for in the recipient's currency (Shenoy, 1974: 1–3).

Between July 1956 and December 1971, India imported a total of $5.6 billion worth of commodities, mainly wheat. This comprised fully one-fourth of all PL 480 exports globally, making India the single largest recipient by far (Shenoy, 1974: 5). Of India's imports, 90 percent were paid for in rupees, representing no drain on foreign exchange. In the period as a whole, India imported a total of 76.54 million tons of food, and of these, PL 480 accounted for 57.95 million tons, in other words, 75.71 percent of all food imports were under this concessional scheme (Chopra, 1981).

Of the $5.6 billion worth of commodities sold to India (paid for in rupees and deposited in Indian banks on U.S. account), the U.S. Embassy in India, with the consultation of the Indian government, recycled $3.47 billion (again, in rupees) as developmental loans to the state. This represented 72 percent of the total proceeds. Further, of all the grants and loans that were recycled in this fashion, 41 percent was invested in industry and 24 percent in agriculture. Needless to add, even of the 41 percent that was invested in industry, the lion's share (85 percent) went to the state sector's heavy industries (Bhagwati & Desai, 1970).

Clearly, the Indian state had access to an enormous fund of food imports, that were lent on the most generous concessional terms possible. This circumstance meshed perfectly with the state's emphasis on heavy industry.[7] The benefits accrued not just in terms of cheap food, but also and more importantly in the amount of foreign exchange that the policy freed up to continue with the Second Plan strategy. Given the magnitude of the savings, it is quite legitimate to argue that access to concessional food imports in domestic currency may have saved the Second and Third Plans from either abortion or at least drastic modification.

In domestic politics, the imports insulated the state somewhat from the agrarian propertied classes that were increasingly restive with the strong focus on industrialization and the threatening rhetoric (if not the reality) of land reform (Brass, 1980a, 1980b; Nair, 1979).[8] A few figures immediately establish this. In the period from 1957 to 1967, food imports paid for in rupees amounted to 386.21 percent of the total internal procurement of domestically marketed surpluses by the state.[9] Even if one were to make the extreme assumption that the Indian state could have socialized the retail trade in food grains and cornered all commercially marketed surpluses for this period, these imports would still have represented 36.5 percent of the maximum possible commercial surplus. The PL 480 imports were distributed through a state-run network of ration shops located predominantly in urban areas, and the number of these shops increased from 37,600 to 142,800 over this period (Chopra, 1981). Thus, imports made it easier to contain inflation in the areas most affected by the tremendous increase in public spending, areas that also happened to be the most sensitive politically—the cities and towns.

Finally, in terms of the role that PL 480 commodity assistance played in the overall foreign aid to India, 38.1 percent of the total utilized aid in the Second Plan and 29.7 percent in the Third Plan came from this source (Bhagwati & Desai, 1970). The opportunity "benefits" of this untied aid and the saved foreign exchange are, of course, incalculable.

Not all of this was purely accidental. Indian planners were aware of the existence of the huge surpluses within the United States and of the American compulsion to dispose of them by any means possible. The Indian Foodgrains Enquiry Committee (Government of India, 1957) spelled out this realization quite unequivocally when it noted:

[T]he world supply position is relatively easy so far as wheat is concerned. . . . *We feel that it would be to our advantage to take fairly large quantities of wheat and some quantities of rice from the USA under PL 480. For imports under such concessional terms not only relieve us of our immediate foreign exchange commitments but also help us to build a rupee fund which can be utilized for development purposes. . . . In fact, assurance of continued imports of certain quantities of foodgrains will constitute the very basis of a successful food policy for years to come.* (Government of India, 1957: 93–95, emphasis added)

Upon closer examination, a more complex reality underlies the surface appearance of a coherent and unified state acting to utilize U.S. surpluses in this fashion. This chapter will briefly attempt to highlight the main components of this complexity. PL 480 imports, in many ways, represented a "minimax" resolution of the various viewpoints concerning the strategy of development to be followed. For example, the Finance Ministry, while hardly enamored of the huge deposits of Indian currency accruing to U.S. account in Indian banks, clearly had an interest in containing inflation and, especially, in conserving foreign exchange. The Food Ministry, though aware of the possibility that domestic wheat farmers were being adversely affected by the cheap imports, did not vehemently oppose them for different reasons (for evidence of such price repression of domestic products, see Shenoy, 1974; Nair, 1979). The Nehru period was marked by heavy rhetoric on radical land reforms and by support for community development and cooperative schemes. Although none of these programs did much to alter the social relations of production in the countryside radically, the conservative rural classes, which dominated Congress regimes in the various state governments, were preoccupied with taking the sting out of Nehruvian land reforms rather than actively opposing the strategy of development itself. Had food production continued to fall, the state might have been forced at least to attempt a more rigorous implementation of its land reforms. PL 480 imports alleviated the necessity for the various state governments and the Food Ministry to show results in land reform.

Thus, there emerged a constellation of interests within various parts of the state apparatus that united behind the PL 480 scheme and the windfall that it represented for industrialization. Each section of the government supported the scheme for its own reasons, but the overall image was of the Indian state behaving like a coherent and united actor and capitalizing on a particular conjuncture of global and domestic circumstances to implement its agenda of development.

At the same time, the question of food aid served to fragment U.S. hegemonic power. The different departments and branches of government disagreed on the aims of the program until the mid-1960s. Without excessive detail, the main faultlines fragmenting the U.S. government on this issue can be summarized as follows. The U.S. Department of Agriculture, which had primary jurisdiction over the disposal of the surpluses, was loath to connect them to concessions from the recipients in terms of either their foreign or their domestic economic policies. The Department of State's concerns that PL 480 exports not affect the export markets of U.S. allies in Europe or Latin America were not always shared to the same degree by the Department of Agriculture (Peterson, 1979: 37).

Linking food aid to foreign policy concessions on the part of India proved illusory (Merrill, 1990). Concessions in terms of reducing the strong statist and protectionist nature of Indian planning (and its relative neglect of agriculture) might have been attempted, however, and to a small degree they were. These had limited chances of success for a variety of important reasons.

India was hardly unique in terms of its attempts to "catch up" with the developed West through a partial withdrawal from the world-economy. The economic justification for this approach was strongly buttressed by the geopolitics of the Cold War at this time (Basu, 1985). In this context, support for aiding India's state sector came from diverse sources, including such unlikely candidates as Walt Rostow, who had just authored *Stages of Economic Growth* (Merrill, 1990: 155). It is perhaps worth noting that the world's hegemonic power, which was committed to the maintenance of a liberal foreign trade regime, was explicitly supporting the construction of a statist and protectionist economy. Furthermore, the justifications for doing so had to do with both geopolitics and some appreciation for the problems of "backward development," even from the archetypal neoclassical economists.

As far as tying PL 480 aid to Indian investment in agriculture, even though this was occasionally attempted, the prospects for success were bleak. First, it must be remembered that the dominant developmental ethos of the time equated development with rapid industrialization. The conceptual leap of the mid-1960s, which came to regard the Third World peasant as a rational animal capable of responding to price signals, was not yet a reality (Nair, 1979). Indeed, there is some evidence that certain sections within the United States government were quite explicit in discouraging any linkage between PL 480 and Indian investment in agriculture. Orville Freeman, the extremely influential Secretary of Agriculture under John F. Kennedy and Lyndon B. Johnson, recalled the years just preceding his tenure as follows:

There were provisions for investment in agriculture and for economic development, but they were largely ignored and no real pressure was put on them. Also, there was a great deal of concern that in the process of using food and developing agriculture in these countries, we would be creating competition for our own exports. . . . The thought of making internal agricultural development (in third world countries) a condition for Public Law 480, I don't recall ever, ever rising at all. (1969: 4–5)

Thus, in contrast to the picture of a somewhat unified and coherent state in India on this issue, the state in the United States emerges as an incoherent and vacillating entity, with agencies working at cross purposes. In terms of the relational basis of state power argued at the beginning of this chapter, this fragmentation in the United States clearly redounded to the advantage of Indian state elites.

Before turning to an analysis of these historical developments in terms of their implications for notions of the state and hegemony, I would like to complete the story of the transition, as it were. By the late 1960s, the geopolitics of the Cold

War had undergone a shift: Southeast Asia and the Vietnam War had come to center stage, and the salience of a country such as India declined. With Nehru's death in 1964 and an emerging class of domestic agrarian entrepreneurs (created partly as a result of landlord abolition and the way in which land reforms were implemented, that is, by eliminating absentee landlords and consolidating the power of rich farmers and large tenants), a shift in agrarian strategy toward a Green Revolution model seemed likely. The monsoon failures of 1966 and 1967, domestic pressure groups, and a very high degree of leverage exercised by the Johnson administration together encouraged this shift to an explicitly capitalist strategy of agricultural growth.[10]

Since the early 1970s, the relationship between the state and the new entrepreneurial agrarian classes has undergone a marked shift—the state has been unable to resist the demands of these classes for more remunerative prices, increasing subsidies, and higher Plan outlays. Agricultural incomes remain virtually untaxed, despite a sharp increase in income from land, especially in areas most affected by the Green Revolution.

This has led to the current situation, in which India is "self-sufficient" in food grains, with mounting "buffer stocks" in storage and even occasional instances of food exports; at the same time, large sectors of the population do not have enough to eat (Sen, 1982). The earlier period, in which U.S. surpluses insulated the state from the propertied agrarian classes, has given way to a contemporary reality: Agricultural subsidies (especially for fertilizers) now dominate public expenditure at unprecedented levels.

On the industrial front, as noted at the outset, the ambitions outlined at independence have been substantially achieved. Thus, a United Nations Conference on Trade and Development (UNCTAD) report of 1982 that assessed import substitution in developing countries ranked India second in terms of domestic production of capital goods (China and Brazil flanking India), with a degree of self-sufficiency between 75 and 90 percent (UNCTAD, 1982). Foreign aid, which had played such a key role in the Second and Third Plans, declined to 10.6 percent for the Sixth Plan (most of it from multilateral sources, especially the World Bank), and the inflow of foreign investment amounted to less than 6 percent of total investment (Rudolph & Rudolph, 1987: 10–11). One measure of the inward-looking orientation is the fact that India's share of world trade has declined from 2.4 percent in 1951–52 to 0.5 percent currently (Economist Intelligence Unit, 1990: 49).

Even as this degree of self-reliance has been achieved, global and domestic pressures in the years of declining U.S. hegemony are working to curtail sharply the degree of maneuverability available to the state. Rhetorical pretensions to the effect that the expansion of the state sector represented the entering wedge of socialism have been, by and large, jettisoned. Today, the prevailing view among important sectors of the state elites and within civil society is that the state has fulfilled its historical mission—providing the infrastructure for private capitalist development. Accordingly, formerly inviolable state agencies that are now at risk of privatization include nationalized banks, development banks, insurance corporation, lending organizations such as the Industrial Credit and Investment Corporation of India (ICICI) and even the "successful" (by the abysmal standards of India's public sector) oil and petroleum corporations. The domestic pressures forcing a retreat of the state are greatly augmented by international lending agencies, notably the World Bank and the International Monetary Fund. As sources of cheap aid with no strings have dried up and as the Cold War winds down, a whole new global conjuncture faces the Indian state in the 1990s. All these factors clearly point to an explicitly capitalist strategy of development with the state retreating in the face of these multiple pressures.

Thus, the heyday of American hegemony saw the construction of a highly protectionist and statist economy in India. Correspondingly, the waning decades of U.S. hegemony are seeing the increasingly capitalist character of development and a growing inability to resist the "logic" of the world capitalist system.

STATE AND HEGEMONY

Fundamentally, this chapter regards state power as emerging from and inhering in the ability of the state elites to articulate and maintain distinctions, boundaries, and margins between the "domestic" and the "foreign" or the "world-system." State élites legitimize themselves by the constant articulation and reproduction of these categories, which are thus seen not as the objective givens of a reality "out there," but as the contested results of social and political practices. One of the clearest expositions of such a view is found in the work of Robert Cox, wherein he has noted:

The world can be represented as a pattern of interacting social forces in which states play an intermediate though autonomous role between the global structure of social forces and local configurations of social forces within particular countries. . . . power is seen as emerging from social processes rather than taken as a given in the form of accumulated material capabilities, that is, as the result of these processes. (1984: 277–278)

Such a processual understanding of state power is somewhat alien to many works within the world-systems perspective. Given their explicit focus on capital accumulation on a world scale and on the evolving forms of a global division of labor, as well as their insistence that this is the only relevant level of analysis, questions of state formation and the mediatory character of state power are deemed epiphenomenal or, at any rate, derivative of the more fundamental levels of analysis. To cite a not atypical quote from Immanuel Wallerstein:

The development of the capitalist world-economy has involved the creation of all the major institutions of the modern world: classes, ethnic/national groups, households—and the "states." All of these structures postdate, not antedate, capitalism; all are consequence, not cause. (1984: 29; cited in Rupert, 1990: 430)

While it is true that one can cite other quotations that reveal an appreciation of precisely what is described here as a processual view of social power (see, for example, Wallerstein 1974: 9; 1984: 20; 1987: 322-323), the logic of analysis tends to the ahistorical and to derive every particular from a more abstract, generalized theoretical edifice (see Brenner, 1977; Gourevitch, 1978; Rupert, 1990, for incisive critiques on these grounds). The purpose of the macrohistorical narrative of state formation in the previous section was to highlight the socially contested and the open-ended nature of state power and of change in the world-system. The details reveal the fragile and almost accidental character of the choices made and the long-term impact of those choices. There is little in the narrative that suggests the working out of some essentialist grand design whereby core, peripheries, and semiperipheries emerge and stabilize an otherwise unstable and polarized world-system. Such explanations and imputations of grand design appear more plausible as *a posteriori* impositions of pattern on a complex process that could have evolved at various points in India, in very different directions from the ones that emerged in the end. Perhaps most importantly, the processual view of state power that is argued here allows for a more enabling variety of politics: The future trajectories of change are not determined by closed theoretical edifices but by the struggle constantly to articulate and reproduce the conditions of social reality itself.

As we turn to the question of hegemony, we see that the previous section highlights the very ambivalent effects of U.S. hegemony on Indian state formation. At one level, we noted the paradox of a power supposedly committed to the maintenance of global free trade and open markets assisting in the construction of a highly statist and protectionist economy. This realization of the ambivalent effects of U.S. hegemony is well documented in world-systems analyses. Thus, Bruce Cumings has noted with regard to American hegemony:

Its very breadth . . . made for a style . . . that was more open than previous imperialisms to competition from below . . . and particularly to disparities of attention . . . that give leverage and room to maneuver for dependencies. . . . this form of hegemony fused security and economic considerations so inextricably that the United States has never been sure whether economic competition from its allies is good or bad for grand area security. . . . American post-war hegemony grew less out of specific human design . . . than out of the longterm reaction of hegemonic interests to the flow of events. (1987: 49-50)

At a more fundamental level, however, hegemony is perhaps better conceptualized in terms of the globalization of a particular "social structure of accumulation" by the leading economic, social, and political power in the world. This focus moves the discussion away from merely observing patterned regularities in history—the sequencing of superiority in different productive sectors, the average time spans of hegemonic ascent, the length of wars that precede hegemonic rise, and the preponderance of material and military resources that underwrite hegemonic status (Wallerstein, 1984: 38-39). In contrast, this perspective focuses on the ability of a country to appear as the embodiment of the ideal society, as a vanguard in the process of production and accumulation, as having found the "solution" to the fundamental contradictions of capitalism as a system of production itself.

Such a notion of hegemony is exemplified in the work of Giovanni Arrighi, which notes:

In all three historical instances of world hegemony, the hegemon was also the leader in the organization of global processes of capital accumulation and, in this sense, it was the leading capitalist state of its epoch. But the three states were "leading capitalists" to different degrees and in different ways. If we focus on the representation of interests within the executive of the three states . . . then we reach the conclusion that each successive hegemonic state has been *less* capitalist than the previous one. However, while the hegemonic state has become less and less capitalist in this sense, the interstate system has become more and more capitalist in the sense that each and every one of its members has been subject more and more closely to the capitalist logic of power. (1990a: 405–406, emphasis in original)

Seen in this light, American hegemony, its role in the emergence of a pervasive state, and the current retreat of that state in India all become less paradoxical. Ultimately, notwithstanding the rhetoric of socialism, radical land reform, and so forth, Indian expansion in the postwar period has basically consolidated a capitalist society. It is a capitalist society in which the state has played (and continues to play) a predominant role, but it is a capitalist society all the same. In this sense, the hegemonic role of the United States has been reflected not so much in redirecting Indian development along a particular path but in enabling Indian state elites to accomplish a difficult transition from a peripheral to a semiperipheral country. It is quite conceivable that the nature of the political, economic, and social choices made in the 1950s and 1960s (and, consequently today) would have been vastly different were it not for the sheer magnitude of U.S. foreign (especially food) aid to India. This is not to suggest that these alternative choices or movements would necessarily have proceeded along lines that may be described as anticapitalist: probably not. There is no gainsaying the fact, however, that the hegemonic power's assistance facilitated the emergence of a heavily statist version of capitalism in India, even as it partially removed this area from the direct ambit of U.S. private capital.

These ideas resonate strongly with the notion that hegemony consists less in the direct exercise of power and more in the diffusion of a particular social structure of accumulation, in its direction of the choices made, and, ultimately, in the vision of the desired future that has been presented to the peripheral and semiperipheral countries of the world.

CONCLUSION

This brief discussion of state and hegemony in world-systems analysis suggests one of the more interesting aspects of this perspective in general. Broadly speaking, one discerns a certain critical antinomy or inconsistency in the approach as a whole. In essence, this antinomy reflects a basic tension between, on the one hand, a fundamentally positivistic, teleological, and closed view of historical change, social structures, and the world-system itself and, on the other hand, an open-ended, dialectical, and nonpositivistic view of social reality. One example of this is the fairly derivative view of social institutions (class, nation, etc.) within world-systems analysis that was revealed in the discussion of the state above, complemented by a nuanced and finely textured notion of historical change exemplified by the discussions of hegemony. This example is representative of similar tensions that run through many of the critical works within the perspective (prominent illustrations of this tension can be found in Hopkins et al., 1977: 126–127; Wallerstein, 1974: 7–9; 1984: 7–8, 35, 185; 1987: 322–323).

The macrohistorical narrative of Indian state formation emphasizes a paradox: The period of American hegemony coincided with the construction of a highly statist and protectionist version of development in India, while the waning decades of U.S. hegemony (1971 to the present) have witnessed the beginnings of a dismantling of this closed economy, the progressive inability of state elites to continue with their earlier strategy, and the increasing subjection of the Indian economy to the "logic" of the world capitalist system. The paradoxical character of this development, it is argued in this chapter, is mitigated if one reconceptualizes state power and hegemony in ways described above. In other words, a more compelling mode of analysis becomes available if one resolves the antinomy inherent in world-systems analysis in favor of an open-ended, dialectical, and nonpositivistic epistemology.

NOTES

I would like to express my thanks to Ravi Palat and Mark Rupert for helpful comments on earlier drafts of this paper.

1. For a discussion of how economic pervasiveness has not translated into genuine autonomy from social classes in India, see Atul Kohli (1987: 15–32, and 51–88). For a discussion of similar issues in a global context, see Peter Evans (1985).

2. The category of semiperiphery has given rise to much debate within world-systems analysis. Considerations of length prevent me from engaging this interesting literature. In this paper, semiperipheries are defined simply as areas that incorporate within themselves both core-like and peripheral production processes. For the discussions themselves, see Alvin So (1990: 198–200) and, especially, William G. Martin (1990).

3. The irony of "resisting" colonialism and achieving "independence" while trying to remake society in the image of the Western countries is obvious here. For perceptive analyses, see Ashis Nandy (1980) and Partha Chatterjee (1986).

4. 1 crore = 10 million.

5. The other, obvious option—generating foreign exchange through sustained exports to Western countries—was never seriously considered by the new regime. This long history of "export pessimism" in Indian development is detailed well in Jagdish Bhagwati and T. N. Srinivasan (1975).

6. For excellent analyses that focus on Cold War geopolitics as a major possibility condition for aid to India, see Sanjib Basu (1985) and Dennis Merrill (1990); for the reversal in Soviet attitudes toward Indian development after Stalin, see Stephen Clarkson (1978).

7. For details on the very favorable (from the perspective of the borrower) terms of PL 480 aid, see Mitchel Wallerstein (1980) and B. R. Shenoy (1974).

8. Also see Shenoy (1974) and Nilakanth Rath, and V. Patvardhan (1967). One should be careful not to exaggerate the degree to which agrarian producers in India were organized on a class basis at this time or the extent to which they actively opposed the statist industrializing strategy. As Sarvepalli Gopal (1979) has observed, the Second and Third plan strategies did have considerable domestic and international support at the time, notwithstanding later criticisms of their industrial bias.

9. For definitions and estimates of the marketed surplus and the commercially marketed surplus within India's food grain economy for these years, see Dharm Narain (1961) and T. J. Byres (1974).

10. For contrasting interpretations of this shift in agrarian strategies, see Francine Frankel (1978) and Kohli (1987).

8

ASCENT THROUGH NATIONAL INTEGRATION: THE CHINESE TRIANGLE OF MAINLAND-TAIWAN-HONG KONG

Hsin-Huang Michael Hsiao and Alvin Y. So

INTRODUCTION: MAINLAND CHINA, TAIWAN, AND HONG KONG BEFORE THE 1980s

Before China was incorporated into the capitalist world-economy by the mid-nineteenth century, there was only one Chinese state (So, 1984). The Qing Empire ruled over both Taiwan and Hong Kong. In the mid-nineteenth century, however, the Qing Empire lost the Opium War and was forced to give up sovereignty over Hong Kong to Great Britain. In the late nineteenth century, the Qing Empire lost another war and handed over Taiwan to Japan, which ruled the island until the end of World War II. In 1949, the Chinese Communist Party (CCP) captured the Chinese mainland and forced the rival Nationalist Party (Guomindang, or GMD) to retreat to Taiwan. With U.S. military backing, the GMD was able to survive and build up the Taiwan state. In short, the Chinese nation, after its incorporation into the world-economy, was divided into three separate states: the socialist state on the mainland (the People's Republic of China or PRC), the authoritarian state in Taiwan, and the colonial state in Hong Kong.

Between the 1950s and the 1970s, these three states pursued different developmental policies. On the mainland, the socialist-Leninist state endorsed Maoism as its ideology and mobilized poor peasants and workers as its supporters. Consequently, the socialist state collectivized agriculture, nationalized urban industry, put politics in command, and focused more on issues of equality than on economic growth. In addition, the socialist state pursued the goal of self-reliance, declaring that it needed no help from either the capitalist core states or the socialist semiperipheral states and adopting a closed-door policy for almost three decades (Blecher, 1986).

In Taiwan, the authoritarian capitalist state was highly committed to the promotion of economic development. Learning from its mistakes on the mainland, the GMD quickly launched a land reform in the early 1950s to redistribute land ownership to small farmers. With massive U.S. aid and with the United States willing to open its markets to Taiwanese products, the GMD was able to promote import-substitution industrialization (ISI) in the 1950s, export-processing zones and export-led industrialization in the 1960s, and industrial deepening in the 1970s (Gold, 1986; Hsiao, forthcoming).

In Hong Kong, the colonial capitalist state preferred not to get directly involved in promoting economic development. It adopted a more or less *laissez faire* policy of nonintervention, avoiding the responsibility of economic planning, export promotion, and home-market protection (So, 1986). The development of export-led industrialization in Hong Kong in the 1950s and 1960s, then was due mostly to the entrepreneurship of Chinese refugee capitalists (who had brought capital, international connections, and machinery from Shanghai to Hong Kong) and to the availability of cheap, docile, refugee laborers (who had fled to Hong Kong to avoid the turmoils of the Communist Revolution).

By the end of the 1970s, however, the PRC, Taiwan, and Hong Kong had run into various kinds of developmental problems. In the PRC, the socialist state experienced economic stagnation. Its economic productivity had reached a plateau and could not be raised any further through mass mobilization. Moreover, its industrial technology was outdated, its industrial bureaucracy ossified, and its state workers not motivated to work hard. There were also very serious unemployment problems, as the population had doubled from around 500 million in 1953 to 1,000 million in 1980 (Riskin, 1987).

The two newly industrializing economies of Taiwan and Hong Kong, by contrast, began to experience the limitations of export-led development. Internally, as a result of their economic successes, there were labor shortages, increasing numbers of labor disputes, escalating land prices, and the emergence of environmental protests—all of which served to raise the cost of production. Externally, Taiwan and Hong Kong faced stiff competition from Southeast Asian states and the PRC in exporting goods to the capitalist core, particularly due to the emergence of protectionism in the core since the 1970s. Furthermore, Taiwan was forced to increase the value of the Taiwan dollar, due to its huge foreign currency reserves, thus reducing its competitiveness in the world-economy (Gold, 1987; Chen, 1980).

Thus, the PRC, Taiwan, and Hong Kong had all reached a critical conjuncture in their developmental trajectories in the late 1970s. Their previous developmental policies—Maoist socialism, state-led and *laissez faire* export industrialization—had run into difficulties, and they needed to formulate new strategies to overcome their problems. What kind of developmental options were then available to them?

According to Immanuel Wallerstein (1979), there is a possibility of ascent through national integration. For Wallerstein, the key to a semiperipheral breakthrough is for a country to have a large enough market to justify an advanced technology, for which market it must produce at a lower cost than the existing producers. This market enlargement and cheapening of production can be achieved by expanding political boundaries and thereby promoting economic integration with its neighbors (So, 1990: 184).

Since most of the citizens of the PRC, Taiwan, and Hong Kong still look upon themselves as Chinese and identify their political entities as integral parts of a single Chinese nation, one more developmental strategy available to them is national integration. The aim of this chapter is to examine how socialist PRC, authoritarian Taiwan, and colonial Hong Kong have developed their specific strategies of national integration in order to achieve upward mobility in the world-economy. In particular, this paper will focus upon the actors who have formulated the integration strategy, the economic and political complexities of this national integration, and the profound impact of this integration strategy on the development of the PRC, Taiwan, and Hong Kong.

THE PEOPLE'S REPUBLIC OF CHINA'S STRATEGY IN THE 1980s

Open-Door Policy

The PRC's initial strategy for upward mobility was its reincorporation into the world-economy. Subsequently, in addition to calling for increasing privatization and deregulation, an open-door policy toward foreign investments developed. This open-door policy began with the establishment of 4 special economic zones (SEZs) in 1979, the opening of 14 coastal cities and Hainan Island in 1984, and the extension to 3 delta areas in 1985 (So, 1988).

This open-door policy was aimed to attract large-scale, high-tech capital investment from U.S. and Japanese transnational corporations (TNCs). The preferred form of operation was "joint-venture" projects between the PRC government and the TNCs, so that Chinese managers could acquire advanced technology, Western management know-how, and information about the world-market conditions from their foreign partners. It was hoped that these joint-venture projects would invigorate aging state enterprises, raise industrial production to levels comparable to those of core states, help Chinese industries to break into the world market, and earn the needed foreign currency through export-industrialization.

In order to attract foreign investment, the PRC tried hard to improve the investment climate. Over 200 pieces of joint-venture legislation were passed. The socialist state spent enormous amounts of capital in infrastructure construction, and special privileges, such as cheap factory sites, low rates of taxation, low wages, and tariff exemptions, were granted to the TNCs (Simon, 1990).

Nevertheless, these Chinese concessions failed to impress the TNCs. There were frequent complaints about unnecessary regulations and the numerous layers of required permits from the Chinese bureaucracy. Projects that had been formally approved at upper levels might not receive cooperation at lower levels. In addition, there were many complaints about operational problems (including labor laws that prevented TNCs from freely hiring and firing Chinese workers), difficulties in getting reliable supplies of high-quality raw materials, the lack of enterprise autonomy, and the inability to remit foreign currency profits out of China. Finally, the TNCs expressed concerns about the closed Chinese market. Even though TNCs had invested in the PRC, their products were still not allowed to enter the Chinese market. Since the TNCs could invest in other peripheral states that provided a better investment climate, they did not need to stick to the PRC. Thus, the TNCs generally tended to invest just enough to maintain footholds in the PRC (Battat, 1991). In this respect, the open-door policy failed to achieve its goal of attracting high-tech capital investment from the TNCs.

National Unification Drive

Side by side with the open-door policy was the drive toward national unification. The old generation of CCP leaders perceived national unification as a historical mission that they were duty-bound to accomplish in their lifetimes. As they were getting older and older, they expressed a sense of urgency and listed unification as one of the great tasks of the 1980s (Nathan, 1990).

The CCP used a two-step approach to promote national unification. This began with the strengthening of civil society contacts, such as family reunions, tourism, academic meetings, sports events, trade, and investments. Beginning in 1979, the CCP proposed the "three communication" (San Tung) policy, seeking to develop trade, postage, and transportation relationships between Mainland China and Taiwan. In the early 1980s, the CCP granted special favors to Chinese capitalists from Hong Kong. Whenever the big Hong Kong capitalists were in Beijing, they would be asked to hold highly publicized meetings with high-ranking CCP leaders (like vice-premier Deng Xiaoping and Party secretary Hu Yaobang), including "heart-to-heart" talks for a couple of hours, photo sessions, news conferences, and grand banquets. Those Hong Kong capitalists who had failed to receive patronage from the colonial government were especially impressed by the friendship of the CCP, feeling a sudden elevation in their social status and influence.

After civil society contacts, the next step was to push for unification talks. In the early 1980s, the CCP formulated a "One Nation, Two Systems" model for unification. According to this model, the capitalist economies and life-styles of Hong Kong and Taiwan would remain unchanged after national unification with the socialist PRC. As special administrative regions (SARs) of the PRC, the Hong Kong and Taiwan governments would have a high degree of autonomy, with self-governance in administrative, legislative, and judicial matters. For Taiwan the GMD would even be allowed to retain its military forces and conduct an independent foreign policy.

The national unification drive was highly successful. In the early 1980s, Great Britain was lured into unification talks with the PRC, which resulted in the signing of the Joint Declaration to return the sovereignty of Hong Kong to the PRC in 1997. The PRC also won numerous diplomatic battles with Taiwan, forcing most of the core states to sever ties with Taiwan in order to set up diplomatic linkages with the PRC (Gold, 1987).

In light of the success of the unification drive and the failure of the open-door policy, a new strategy of upward mobility was formulated by the CCP in the late 1980s. On the one hand, the TNCs kept on complaining about the PRC's investment climate, and they remained unwilling to bring in high-tech capital investment. On the other, Hong Kong capitalists developed a cordial relationship with the CCP, and their investments expanded very rapidly. Therefore, the CCP calculated that it was better to reorient its trade policies to favor capitalists from Hong Kong and Taiwan rather than the TNCs. The rationale was that increasing economic integration with Hong Kong and Taiwan would strengthen their dependence on the PRC's labor, natural resources, and markets, by which means a vested interest group within their civil societies could be developed that would push their states toward political unification.

Coastal-Development Strategy

In 1988, a 22-point regulation was approved by the CCP to encourage Taiwanese investment in production and land development in Hainan Island, Guangdong, Fujian, Zhejiang, and other coastal provinces. The regulation guaranteed that Taiwanese establishments would not be nationalized, that exported goods from Taiwanese investments would be free from export tariffs, that Taiwanese management would have complete autonomy in running their firms in Mainland China, and that Taiwanese investors would be granted multiple entry visas. The same privileges, of course, had already been granted to the Hong Kong investors (Hsiao, 1989a).

There were several crucial differences between this coastal-development strategy and the previous open-door policy. First, instead of appealing to American, European, and Japanese investors, the coastal-development strategy was targeted at investors from Taiwan and Hong Kong. Second, instead of aiming to attract large-scale investments from TNCs, the present strategy was targeted at small investment projects from small- and medium-sized firms in Taiwan and Hong Kong. Third, instead of demanding high-tech, capital-intensive investment and the utilization of local materials, the present strategy allowed investment in labor-intensive industries that relied solely on imported raw materials. Assembly-line industries would help to solve the serious unemployment problem, and foreign raw-materials imports would help to ease the shortage of raw materials in the PRC. Fourth, instead of getting approval from such central government agencies as the Ministry of International Economic Relations and Trade, the present strategy decentralized investment decision; municipal and county government officials were authorized to sign contracts with foreign investors. Finally, instead of encouraging joint-venture contracts, the present strategy preferred wholly owned foreign investment because of capital shortages (Battat, 1991; Nathan, 1990).

It seems that this coastal-development strategy has been successful in attracting direct foreign investment (DFI) from the capitalists of Hong Kong and Taiwan. By 1990, over 60 percent of all DFI in the PRC were from Hong Kong, which amounted to $10 billion (U.S.) out of a total of $16 billion (U.S.) of actual investment. The capitalists of Hong Kong also employed an estimated 2 million industrial workers in the PRC, about twice the number that they employed in Hong Kong (Lall, 1991: 3; Battat, 1991: 1). With respect to Taiwanese direct investment in the PRC, it increased from $100 million (U.S.) in 1987 to $1 billion (U.S.) in 1989, and to $2 billion (U.S.) in 1990. By 1990, Taiwan had become the number two investor in the PRC, surpassing even the United States and Japan (Lee, 1991a: 1).

What then explains the success of this coastal-development strategy? It seems that the CCP officials have been more comfortable in dealing with citizens of Hong Kong and Taiwan than with Americans and Japanese. This may be due to the fact that the people of the PRC, Taiwan, and Hong Kong are all "Chinese," sharing a common cultural tradition and used to a similar way of doing business (Battat, 1991). On the one hand, capitalists from Hong Kong and Taiwan frequently invoke their kinship and community ties (through generous donations to local schools and the sports arena, etc.) so as to strengthen their social bonds with the people of the PRC. On the other hand, CCP officials have been more flexible in enforcing labor practices, foreign currency policies, and tariffs toward their Hong Kong and Taiwanese compatriots because these favors can be legitimized through appeals to national unification. If the same favors were granted to Western businessmen, the officials would be condemned for betraying national interests! This differential treatment of Western businessmen and Taiwanese and Hong Kong compatriots helps to explain why the PRC has been able to attract investments from Taiwan and Hong Kong but has failed to do so for the Western TNCs.

Impact on the PRC's Development

This coastal-development strategy has had a significant impact on the PRC. First, it has led to peripheral industrialization of the coastal provinces. In the late 1980s, the coastal provinces turned into the peripheries of Taiwan and Hong Kong, providing the latter with a cheap and docile labor force, natural resources, and investment opportunities. Since the PRC is still politically strong and its socialist state still has the capacity for planning, this peripheralization has also served to trigger a new wave of industrialization in the coastal provinces, especially in the special economic zones and the Pearl River Delta in South China.

Second, the very success of peripheral industrialization in the coastal provinces has nevertheless led to crucial regional differentiations within the PRC. While the rest of the heartland provinces have remained relatively unaffected, the coastal provinces are rapidly moving toward capitalism. On the one hand, this situation has led to higher rates of economic growth, better standards of living, and democracy movements; on the other hand, it has also brought such social problems as prostitution, juvenile delinquency, and crimes (Hsiao, 1989a). Consequently, the coastal provinces are turning into the "core" of the PRC and are beginning to take advantage of their "peripheral" heartland provinces.

③ Third, these regional imbalances are manifested in the factional conflicts between "conservatives" and "reformers" inside the CCP. While the reformers have wanted more opening toward the world market and greater liberalization, the conservatives have remarked that there is already too much "spiritual pollution" and political instability. The height of this intraparty struggle, of course, was the purge of Party Secretary Zhao Ziyang and the events of Tiananmen Square in 1989.

Despite the CCP calls for a recentralization of the planned economy in the wake of Tiananmen Square, however, it seems that the reformers' coastal-development policy has remained intact as of the spring of 1991. Kuen Lee (1991b) has pointed out that the PRC recently opened the entire Shanghai and Pudong regions for foreign investment, instituted new foreign venture laws, and devalued the Chinese dollar (RMB) by 20 percent to boost exports. The continuation of the coastal-development policy in the 1990s will certainly intensify the factional conflicts inside the CCP.

TAIWAN'S STRATEGY IN THE 1980s

In the early 1980s, when the Taiwanese state was confronted with the developmental problems of rising production costs and world-wide protectionism, it did not pursue the policy of national integration. Instead, it adopted such policies as industrial restructuring (moving from labor-intensive to capital-intensive and high-tech industries), diversification of trade in the world market, and transferring some of its labor-intensive industries to the Southeast Asian region.

In addition, the Taiwanese state promoted democratic reforms from above. After Western core states severed their diplomatic ties with Taiwan and after the GMD was criticized by Amnesty International for human rights violations, the Taiwanese government went through a crisis of legitimacy in the early 1980s. In order to regain legitimacy in the interstate system, the GMD lifted martial law, legalized the formation of opposition parties, tolerated dissent, and allowed social movements to spread (Cheng, 1989). After winning elections and feeling less threatened by the PRC's unification drive, the GMD began to formulate a new strategy of upward mobility in the capitalist world-economy.

Beginning to Play the China Card

In 1985, the GMD announced the "Three Nos" policy: No direct trade, no contact with PRC officials and agencies, and no interference in indirect trade. Couched in obscure language, this policy actually suggested that the GMD, though still prohibiting citizens of Taiwan from having any "direct" contacts with the PRC, would permit "indirect" trade between the two countries through an intermediary like Hong Kong.

In November 1987, after the GMD won its first election against the newly established Democratic Progressive Party, it further liberalized its policy toward the PRC. The GMD announced that PRC-born Taiwan citizens would be permitted to visit the PRC for family reunions and that other Taiwan citizens would be allowed to visit the PRC for tourism and other civilian purposes (such as sports and academic conferences). These civil society contacts would help to accelerate the "unofficial" economic linkages between Taiwan and the PRC. In 1988, the Taiwanese business community was further attracted by the PRC's coastal-development strategy, which encouraged direct investment in Fujian and Guangdong provinces.

In the beginning, Taiwanese small capitalists were the first group to engage in "unofficial" trade and investment with the PRC. For their own survival in prolonging the life cycle of their sunset labor-intensive industries, they risked their property and the danger of punishment by the GMD to explore the PRC's labor market. Although the GMD legally prohibited such direct trade and investment in the PRC, it did not impose severe punishments on those firms that were found to be investing in the PRC, except for such minor harassments as restrictions on bank loans and closer scrutinies of tax returns. Since trade and investment in the PRC were so profitable, Taiwanese investment increased very rapidly in the late 1980s.

With respect to investment, Taiwanese capital ranked second to Hong Kong capital among all foreign investors in Fujian province. In the Hsia-men special economic zone, Taiwanese investment topped Hong Kong's as the largest outside capital source. Although two-thirds of Taiwanese investment was in manufacturing industries, the Taiwanese also invested in real estate, tourism, resource extraction, and chemical industries.

While Taiwan's indirect trade with the PRC (via Hong Kong) was only $1.47 billion (U.S.) during the five-year period from 1979 to 1983, it expanded to $2.61 billion (U.S.) during the three years from 1984 to 1986. After the Taiwan state declared that there would be no interference in indirect trade, the volume jumped to $7.72 billion (U.S.) during a three-year span from 1987 to 1989, almost twice the combined total of the previous two periods and an annual average of $2.54 billion (U.S.) (Li, 1991: 26). Industrial materials and parts, such as manmade fibers, clothes, machine equipment, electronic parts, and plastic raw materials, emerged as major export items to the PRC. Imported items from the PRC included traditional herb medicines, animal by-products, fish and sundry goods, leather, iron, and so forth. In sum, this rapid expansion of "unofficial" trade and investment set the stage for a new strategy of upward mobility in the world-economy in 1991.

Economic Integration But No Political Unification

In 1991, the GMD finally recognized the reality of active Taiwanese trade and investment in the PRC. Consequently, it relaxed its ban on direct trade and investment beginning in 1991. Only those corporations that had invested in the PRC and had failed to file a report with the government would be punished. By June 1991, some 2,600 Taiwanese companies had reported on their investments in the PRC. In addition, the GMD also modified its policy toward the PRC. A quasi-cabinet-level Commission on Mainland Affairs was established, and a semi-governmental Straits Exchange Foundation was organized; both were responsible for future policy-making and implementation at official and civilian levels. The Straits Foundation, in particular, is charged by the GMD with a mission of "front line" contact with PRC officials in dealing with civilian and business disputes that have occurred or might occur in the future.

What explains this official endorsement of economic integration with the PRC? In retrospect, the GMD may simply have followed the big capitalists' initiatives. It was only after the big capitalists entered into PRC investment and developed vested interests there and had begun to exert pressures on the GMD that the GMD shifted its mainland policies to more pragmatic ones. Unlike President Chiang Ching-Kuo's antibusiness ideology, the present president, Lee Teng-Hui, is known for his favorable attitudes toward business. President Lee has a list of close Taiwanese business friends, and he often consults with them on economic issues. The close relationship between the GMD and big business is also revealed by the fact that many influential capitalists are donors to the Straits Exchange Foundation and serve on its board. These Taiwanese big capitalists are the ones pushing the GMD toward a more flexible policy toward the PRC, with more economic, cultural, and civilian contacts between the two states.

Therefore, economic integration with the PRC can be seen as a pragmatic strategy that may allow the GMD and the capitalists to solve Taiwan's developmental bottlenecks and to achieve upward mobility in the capitalist world-economy. Still, economic integration should not be taken as a definite step toward political unification with the PRC. Taiwan has been a *de facto* state for the past 40 years. In addition, the Taiwanese state is not in a strong enough bargaining position to have an equal share in the ultimate unification structure because of its small size and relatively weak political and military status. Thus, political unification is not a good deal for the Taiwanese state.

In this respect, economic integration can be interpreted as the politics of postponement, a tactic by which the GMD gains more room to maneuver vis-à-vis PRC by not upsetting the CCP. While the CCP wishes to incorporate Taiwan by means of economic integration, the GMD wishes to use economic integration to defer and halt the threat of political unification with the PRC.

In mid-1991, the Taiwanese state formulated a three-stage model in its "National Unification Guideline" to counteract the PRC's "One Nation, Two Systems" model. This guideline pointed out that the timing and the ways of national unification should first consider the benefits, rights, security, and welfare of Taiwanese residents and proceed according to rational, peaceful, equal, and mutually beneficial principles. Three stages of unification were proposed: (1) In the short term, the first stage would consist of mutually beneficial communication, aiming to lessen the hostility of each side; each side should also recognize the other as a legitimate political entity. (2) In the middle term, the second stage would reflect mutual trust and cooperation. Direct mail, direct transportation, and direct trade would be developed. In particular, both states should jointly develop the PRC's coastal region so as to bridge the existing gap in living standards between the two sides. Both sides should also assist each other by participating in international organizations. (3) In the long term, the third stage would bring unification talks, which should be governed by the principles of political democracy, economic freedom, social justice, and compliance with the wishes of people in both Taiwan and the PRC. Since the GMD has defined the present period as still in the first stage, it is, of course, unwilling to engage in any political unification talks with the PRC.

Impact on Taiwan's Development

Since it was only in 1988 that Taiwan started to trade and invest with the PRC on a large scale, it is still too early to draw any solid conclusions on how this economic integration may affect Taiwan's development. It is likely, however, that integration with the PRC may strengthen Taiwan's competitiveness in the world-economy because integration provides new opportunities for Taiwanese capitalists to obtain cheap labor and raw materials, to escape environmental regulations, and to utilize their huge foreign currency reserves.

Although economic integration should have a positive impact, it also complicates the internal politics of Taiwan by deepening its social divisions. At one end of the political spectrum, there are the right-wing GMD conservatives, who still yearn for the defeat of the communists and for their "glorious return" to the mainland. At the other end, there is the radical New Tide faction inside the Democratic Progressive Party, which advocates Taiwanese independence (Hsiao, 1989b). The independence option appears to be unrealistic because it could provoke military aggression from the PRC, heighten Mainlander-Taiwanese ethnic conflicts, and lead to repression from the right-wing GMD conservatives.

Recent democratization has further complicated the issue because the Taiwan electorate, through various social movements, has now entered the unification game as an important player (Hsiao, 1990). The opposition party, for instance, has criticized the GMD's three-stage model for not giving priority to the Taiwanese people, including them as major players, and granting them veto power for any policy concerning national unification with the PRC. The opposition party, Taiwanese small businessmen, and many professionals may agree to develop economic relations and trade linkages with the PRC, but they do not consent to be unified under CCP rule. Small export manufacturers in particular worry that their privilege of doing business in the PRC (like many other back-door tactics) may disappear once the communication between the two sides is officially institutionalized.

It seems that all these political forces have compressed the Taiwanese political spectrum toward the vital center and strengthened the moderate elements within the GMD. Thus, the most likely short-term scenario appears to be the continuation of the present policy of economic integration without political unification. Economic integration, then, should be seen as a strategy to defer political unification and to divert any military threat in order to buy more time for the Taiwanese state to use "flexible" and "dollar" diplomacy to upgrade its relationships with core states and to regain political legitimacy in the interstate system.

HONG KONG'S STRATEGY IN THE 1980s

National Separation

Before the 1980s, the government of Hong Kong pursued a strategy of national separation. It was argued that the economic prosperity and political stability of Hong Kong owed much to its status as a British colony, since the colonial government was efficient and committed to economic growth. Indeed, Hong Kong's separation from the Chinese mainland enabled the colony to avoid the economic chaos of the Great Leap Forward and the political turmoil of the Cultural Revolution. For the sake of Hong Kong's economic prosperity and political stability, therefore, the colonial government wanted to maintain the status quo of national separation from the PRC (Castells, Goh, & Kwok, 1990).

Still, although the island of Hong Kong and the Kowloon Peninsula were permanently ceded to Great Britain, the hinterland of Hong Kong (the so-called New Territories) was leased to Britain for only 99 years. Since the lease on the New Territories was going to expire in 1997, capitalists were reluctant to make long-term investments in the colony. Hence, the government of Margaret Thatcher was pressured to enter into negotiations with the PRC for the renewal of the lease in order to boost business confidence in the colony. If worse came to worst, the Thatcher government reckoned that Britain could still keep Hong Kong Island and the Kowloon Peninsula, even if the New Territories' lease were not renewed.

This belief explains why Thatcher was shocked to find out, in late 1982, that the PRC wanted to take back not just the New Territories but also Hong Kong Island and the Kowloon Peninsula. It also explains why the negotiations were so heated and why they lasted for almost two years. Britain was finally forced to back down and drop its strategy of national separation, largely because after Thatcher's highhanded policy had gotten nowhere, she asked diplomats in the Foreign Office to conduct the negotiations. These diplomats could be described as more pragmatic, and they gave the Hong Kong issue a lower priority than the development of a long-term relationship between Britain and the PRC (Scott, 1989). Moreover, colonialism was not popular in the 1980s, and the British colonial policy did not receive much support from the Hong Kong Chinese. While the Hong Kong Chinese did not like the socialist PRC government, they also wanted an end to colonialism and the right of self-determination.

Decolonialization Policies

In late 1984, Britain signed the Joint Declaration with the PRC, agreeing to relinquish sovereignty over Hong Kong by 1997. As such, the colonial government was immediately turned into a lame duck. No longer pursuing the strategy of national separation, the colonial government quickly adopted the strategy of decolonialization, promising democratization, the construction of infrastructure projects, and the right of abode in Great Britain to many residents in Hong Kong (Cheek-Milby & Mushkat, 1989; Wesley-Smith & Chen, 1988).

① First, the colonial government speeded up democratization in Hong Kong, declaring that there would be direct elections to the Legislative Council in 1988. Democratization could be interpreted as a means for the Thatcher government to rebut criticism that it had sold Hong Kong out to the communists. If democratization is successful, the Hong Kong government will be run by the people of Hong Kong in 1997. As such, the Thatcher government would be able to claim that it had returned sovereignty to the people of Hong Kong rather than to Beijing.

② Second, in order to boost business confidence in Hong Kong, the colonial government unveiled a proposal for massive state expenditure on new infrastructure projects. There was a $16 billion (U.S.) proposal to construct railways and a new airport with subways and to expand the container port. There was also a proposal to foster higher education by adding a new Science and Technology University, increasing the enrollments at the two universities in Hong Kong, and upgrading several private colleges to university status (Shive, 1990).

③ Third, after the Tiananmen incident in 1989, the Thatcher government proposed a nationality package to grant the right of abode in Britain for 50,000 Hong Kong families. The aim of the nationality package was to provide a kind of insurance to the bureaucrats in Hong Kong so that they would remain in their posts until 1997. The package also aimed to attract Hong Kong entrepreneurs and new middle-class professionals to Britain.

These decolonialization policies have failed to attain their goals. First, there was a setback to the democratization process. Due to strong opposition from Hong Kong capitalists (who feared that democratization would bring about more taxes, more state regulations, and less business freedom) and from the PRC government (which feared that democratization would lead to a truly autonomous local government that could not be controlled), the lame-duck colonial government suddenly withdrew its promise to have direct elections in 1988. This change angered the new middle-class professionals who were the strongest supporters of the democracy movement, causing them to emigrate rapidly from Hong Kong, with the number of emigrants rising from 20,000 in 1984, to 40,000 in 1988, and to 60,000 in 1989 (Skeldon, 1990).

In addition, the proposed infrastructure projects and the nationality package backfired due to challenges by the PRC. These policies were perceived by the latter government as British conspiracies to weaken PRC control after 1997. For instance, the PRC complained that the post-1997 Hong Kong government would be in deep financial difficulty because the British would have used up all the monetary reserves of the Hong Kong government on the expensive airport package. Furthermore, the PRC accused the British of wanting to extend its colonial influence in Hong Kong after 1997. The nationality package ensured that most high-ranking officials in Hong Kong would still hold British passports after 1997, ensuring their loyalty to Britain rather than to the PRC. As a result of these policy disputes, there has been increasing hostility between the PRC and Great Britain since 1989, serving to intensify the crisis of confidence and to hasten the flight of the new middle class.

Under the shadow of the 1997 issue, however, a new actor has been emerging within Hong Kong. The Chinese capitalists in Hong Kong, who had been largely excluded from participating in the colonial government, began to formulate a strategy of connections with the PRC so as to enhance their economic and political power in Hong Kong (Rafferty, 1991).

Strengthening the Mainland Connections

Since the colonial government has pursued a "positive nonintervention" policy and failed to expand the scientific and research facilities in Hong Kong, and since most of the Hong Kong firms are small- and medium-sized, there is little possibility of upgrading industries from labor-intensive to technology-intensive or information-intensive enterprises. Due to this structural weakness of the economy, it is imperative for capitalists in Hong Kong to develop connections with the PRC so as to relocate their labor-intensive industries to the nearby Pearl River Delta. Only after they get access to the cheap and docile labor forces of the PRC will their labor-intensive industries be able to remain competitive in the world-economy (Scobell, 1988; Sit, 1989).

Besides geographical relocation, there is also a plan to develop Hong Kong as a service center for the PRC. Having been involved in international trade for over a century, Hong Kong is well known for its strengths in entrepot trade, its financial connections, and other services. Thus, it could be developed as a facilitator or intermediary for PRC trade and investment, providing valuable channels of information to China, "serving as a contact point for China's trade, financing China's modernization, acting as a conduit for technology transfer, and providing a training ground where China can learn and practise capitalist skills in a market environment" (Sung, 1985: iii).

The deepening economic connections with the PRC have empowered the Chinese capitalists in Hong Kong. While they were treated as "nobodies" by the colonial government, they have become the "VIPs" of the PRC government. They have been appointed to represent Hong Kong in the National People's Congress, the highest political organ of the PRC; they have been asked to draft the Basic Law—the mini-constitution of Hong Kong; and they have frequently been asked to be the honored guests at the National Day Celebration in Beijing (Lau, 1988). As a result, an "unholy" political alliance has developed between Chinese capitalists in Hong Kong and the socialist government of the PRC.

With backing from the PRC government, these Chinese capitalists have begun to participate in Hong Kong politics. In the recent elections of the District Board and Legislative Council, the "leftist" newspapers, banks, department stores, and unions mobilized their support for the election of these pro-PRC capitalists into office. Thus, these Chinese capitalists, together with the middle-class professionals, have emerged as new political forces to challenge the hegemonic domination of the pro-British ruling class (which was usually recruited from big British corporations) in Hong Kong.

Impact on Hong Kong Development

Economically, connections with the PRC have promoted the economic growth of Hong Kong. Despite the shadow of 1997, Hong Kong has still achieved a respectable average annual growth rate of around 7 percent throughout the 1980s (Asian Development Bank, 1990: 51). Its exports have kept rising, its real estate market has still done very well, its stock market has been highly robust, and it has experienced not unemployment but labor shortage.

Still, economic growth in Hong Kong has taken place side by side with political uncertainty. The decolonialization policies of democratization, infrastructure projects, and the nationality package have produced the unintended consequences of greater tension between Hong Kong and the PRC, a crisis of confidence, and new middle-class emigration. It seems that the prospect of national unification with the PRC has produced a political typhoon that will be at its height in 1997. An interesting research agenda for the near future, then, will be to examine whether this political typhoon of 1997 will generate enough force to destroy the bright future of Hong Kong that has been created through its economic integration with the PRC.

CONCLUSION: BUSINESS PARTNERS OR POLITICAL RIVALS?

This chapter shows that various actors in the PRC, Taiwan, and Hong Kong have pursued economic integration as a strategy of upward mobility in the world-economy. This economic integration seems to be mutually beneficial and has greatly enhanced the competitiveness of the PRC, Taiwan, and Hong Kong in the world-economy. On the one hand, the PRC has helped to solve the developmental problems of Taiwan and Hong Kong by providing them with cheap labor, resources, and investment opportunities. On the other hand, Taiwan and Hong Kong have contributed to the development of the PRC through providing employment opportunities, market stimulus to local enterprises, and the vital information and contacts to reenter the world market. In the 1980s, state managers in the PRC successfully developed close business partnerships with the capitalists of Hong Kong and Taiwan. If such economic integration should continue in the 1990s, this Chinese triangle may evolve into a new regional economic power, challenging the domination of Japanese and American capital in East Asia.

The prospects for this Chinese triangle are highly uncertain, however, because economic integration has also produced significant political divisions within the PRC, Taiwan, and Hong Kong. In the PRC, economic integration has led to regional differentiation, democratization, and serious policy conflicts within the CCP. In Taiwan, the prospect of political unification has deepened the divisions between the right-wing GMD conservatives and the radical Taiwan independence faction. And in Hong Kong, the 1997 issue has led to massive emigration and a crisis of confidence.

In addition, the prospect for a Chinese triangle is endangered by the political rivalries among the PRC, Taiwan, and Hong Kong. The PRC is always suspicious of the GMD (which may promote Taiwan's independence) and of the Hong Kong government (which may lay the groundwork for the continuation of British rule after 1997). On the other hand, the people of Taiwan and Hong Kong tend to distrust the mainland's promise of establishing highly autonomous special administrative zones after national unification. Therefore, the Taiwanese government has been unwilling to enter into any negotiations with the mainland, and the new middle class in Hong Kong has protested the mainland's impending takeover by emigrating.

In sum, Mainland China, Taiwan, and Hong Kong are not just significant business partners. They are also key political rivals. The future development of the Chinese triangle, then, depends on whether economic interests or political sentiments will triumph in the end.

PART IV

ANTISYSTEMIC MOVEMENTS

9

THE SOCIAL AND POLITICAL CONSEQUENCES OF CHINESE REFORM: THE ROAD TO TIANANMEN

Mark Selden

THE POLITICAL ECONOMY OF REFORM

In 1978, China embarked on the boldest and most far-reaching reform of an economy and society that had ever been attempted under the auspices of a ruling communist party. This chapter examines the social consequences of a decade of transformations of the core economic and social institutions and of shifts in China's global posture for clues as to the rise, demise, and character of the democratic movement of 1989.

China's post-Mao reform leadership was motivated by many of the same factors that impelled Mikhail Gorbachev and his associates to press for *glasnost* and *perestroika* in the Soviet Union: In each instance, a new administration that was seeking to consolidate its power recognized the limits of statist and collectivist approaches for "catching up" and surpassing the economic, technological, and military achievements of capitalist rivals; each also confronted the necessity of addressing popular discontent with low levels of income and consumption and the ruling party's loss of legitimacy. Reformers in the two socialist giants, moreover, shared certain common goals and perspectives. They saw the need to defuse tensions with major international enemies and rivals, particularly those with the United States and with one another. Both placed high hopes on the benefits that could be derived from transforming (but not eliminating) the state and collective economies by expanding the scope of the market and the private sector. And both looked to the West for technological assistance, expanded trade, loans, and investment.

In practice, however, the roads to reform differed in essentials. Soviet reforms began in the realm of politics and ideas. Gorbachev and his associates encouraged the emergence of an opposition politics that in due time cracked the Communist

Party's political monopoly and paved the way for the proliferation of powerful nationalist, separatist, and fundamentalist—as well as democratic—movements in the Soviet Union and throughout Eastern Europe. Six years into the Gorbachev administration, however, the attempts to transform the core Soviet economic institutions in both city and countryside had for the most part proved abortive. In China, by contrast, the institutional innovations that were pressed from above and below profoundly reshaped the economy and society from the start. Deng Xiaoping's leadership had come to power following a decade of political turmoil by making use of democratic critics to discredit its own Cultural Revolution adversaries in the democracy movement of 1978–79. His leadership stressed political stability. The regime maintained that its tight grip on politics and ideology was indispensable to the success of economic reform, "modernization," and income gains. For Deng, a new authoritarianism was the prerequisite for rapid economic advance, just as it had been, he asserted, in Japan, Taiwan, South Korea, and the other newly industrializing economies of East Asia that China more or less explicitly emulated in the 1980s (Deng, 1984: 302–325; Oksenberg, Sullivan, & Lambert, 1990: 123–150).

China's reforms may be assessed against the achievements and limits of the preceding era of mobilizational collectivism (1953–73). In the course of 25 years, China emerged from a century of disintegration, foreign occupation, and a succession of costly wars, as a regional and, from some perspectives, even a global power but one whose political and strategic reach contrasted sharply with its economic weakness. With per capita incomes of less than $350 (by World Bank reckoning), China in the late 1970s ranked among the poorest nations in the world. Yet two decades of institutional transformation and heavy investment had produced significant growth, including rapid and sustained industrialization. If the debt-ridden economies of Eastern Europe and the Soviet Union showed powerful tendencies toward stagnation throughout the 1970s and after, the Chinese economy recorded respectable growth levels, with notable gains in industry and foreign trade; nor were China's gains limited to the productive sphere. China achieved basic food self-sufficiency for nearly one billion people in a society with a class structure that yielded a relatively egalitarian distribution of income and services, particularly in the cities. Moreover, by the early 1980s, China's social profile resembled that of countries with far higher income levels in important respects, with an average life expectancy of 68 years, an average daily diet of 2,600 calories, and high levels of literacy and health care (World Bank, 1990: 202, 258, 260).

To grasp the urgency of the reforms of the post-Mao period, we need to look closely at Chinese performance in the 1970s. The salient issues in my view are three:

First, a quarter-century of collective agriculture had produced impressive growth rates but no discernible gain in per capita peasant income; indeed, measured in terms of the return to labor, the peasantry, which comprised 80 percent of the population, experienced a substantial long-term per capita income decline between 1955 and 1978.

Second, the elimination of property-based class inequality, which was associated with the elimination of the former landlord, gentry, and capitalist classes, was the rise of new forms of inequality, hierarchy, and control. Between the early 1950s and the late 1970s, the per capita income gap between workers and peasants and between urban and rural people grew from approximately 1.5:1 to somewhere in the range of 4-6:1 (Selden, 1991). By every standard of income, security, opportunity, and welfare, a deep and widening gulf separated city and countryside, industry and agriculture, and worker and peasant. Mao Zedong had pinpointed the city-countryside issue in the early 1950s, but two decades of mobilizational collectivism under his leadership only magnified the split. A second major cleavage derived from the disjuncture between the rhetoric of class struggle, self-reliance and equality, on the one hand, and the emergence of a rigid hierarchy on the other. This hierarchy concentrated power in the hands of a cadre stratum exercising control over a peasantry that was bound to the land and workers who were virtually bereft of job mobility—a hierarchy that had survived the tumultuous Cultural Revolution of the 1960s and, in certain ways, was intensified by it (Selden, 1991; Friedman, Pickowicz, & Selden, 1991).

Third, significant industrial growth rates and a rising international political status masked the growing technological gap between China, with its 1950s-style, Soviet-derived heavy industrial technology, and the cutting edge electronic technologies that define international competitiveness in the 1980s. With an industrial structure that rewarded stability over innovation, with higher education and research crippled by the Cultural Revolution, with intellectuals who were held in low esteem and had been cut off from world technological and intellectual currents for decades, and with slender resource allocations for higher education, research, and technological innovation (with the important exception of the military sector), China confronted the prospects of economic and technological obsolescence and declining global competitiveness.

This was the background for the far-reaching institutional reforms that began in the late 1970s and continued throughout the decade. Table 9.1 highlights the priorities and approaches of the reform agenda, as contrasted with those of the political economy of mobilizational collectivism that preceded it.

This chapter explores the implications that reform had for social change, cleavage, and conflict, with particular reference to the urban areas, to workers and intellectuals, and to city-countryside relations, as a basis for exploring the logic and limits of the democratic movement. The reforms precipitated the most dramatic institutional changes in the countryside, where household-centered agriculture, diversification, rural industrialization and commercialization, and large-scale population movement transformed China's grain-first collective agriculture and all other aspects of the rural economy. By contrast, a comparable reform agenda that threatened to undermine the security and relative privilege of the working class and to weaken state control over the most lucrative and commanding sectors of the economy—through selling off state enterprises, replacing lifetime employment with short-term contracts, eliminating subsidies,

Table 9.1
The Political Economy of Mobilizational Collectivism and Reform

	The Political Economy of Mobilizational Collectivism (1953–1978)	The Political Economy of Reform (1978)
I. Development Priorities	Industry (notably heavy industry) & cities; subsistence agriculture; inland over coastal areas.	Greater emphasis on light industry; economic crops & commerce; coastal over inland areas.
II. Agriculture	Large-scale collective agriculture supplemented by private plots.	Household-centered agriculture with equal distribution of contracted land.
III. Markets	State controls and constricts domestic markets.	State encourages markets, commodification, and the private sector while preserving control of commanding heights.
IV. International Economy	Nationalization of foreign capital; acquisition of Soviet technology prior to 1960; subsequent expansion and diversity of trade.	Foreign investment & technology from core capitalist economies; rapid expansion of foreign trade, loans, & investment.
V. Accumulation & Consumption	High accumulation in state and collective spheres; transfer of rural surplus to industry & cities; low income & consumption.	Moderate accumulation in state, collective, & private spheres; broadly based gains in income & consumption.
VI. Mobility	Population movement restricted, binding peasants to land, barring urban migration & transfer of population from city to countryside & coastal to inland areas.	Population controls relaxed, permitting intrarural & rural-urban migration; continued spatial hierarchy based on limited access to urban registration & benefits.
VII. Class & Spatial Differentiation	Two-class society based on the privileged position of state-owned industry & subordinate position of collective agriculture; elimination of exploiting classes & property-based income inequality but growing urban-rural inequality.	Mixed state-collective private economy gives rise to new & fluid social classes, including a bourgeoisie & a proletariat in the private sector; growth of property-based inequality among classes restricted by equal land ownership; reduced urban-rural inequality.

and other measures to stimulate market forces—was stillborn or diluted. Nevertheless, as we will show, the cities and the industrial working class were by no means spared certain whiplash effects of reform.

The security and limited privilege formerly enjoyed by the core of the Chinese working class who held state-sector jobs was undermined by the social changes sweeping the countryside. In the course of the 1980s, the nature of China's urban population and labor force changed dramatically. The urban collective and private sectors grew far more rapidly than did the state sector. The number of state-sector workers increased from 75 million in 1978 to 100 million in 1988, while the number of collective workers shot up at more than twice that rate, from 20 to 35 million. The small private sector grew from 150,000 workers to 7 million, the latter number undoubtedly representing only a small fraction of the actual number of those working in the private sector (*Changes and Development in China (1949-1989)*, 1990: 98, 223). Moreover, these figures exclude the millions of unemployed and family members who flocked to the cities throughout the decade.

In the 1980s, the urban population, which had long been suppressed by population control measures and forced rural migration, grew at a breakneck pace. By official reckoning, between 1978 and 1988, the population of China's cities and towns shot up from 172 million to 541 million, 301 million of the total being located in the cities. A significant but unspecifiable portion of those newly counted as city dwellers appeared as a result of statistical legerdemain in changing the official definition of cities and towns to include farming areas within city borders. But the figures do reflect the rush to the cities throughout the decade that was made possible by the combination of relaxed population controls and new economic opportunities. The figures require careful interpretation. The 541 million city and town dwellers accounted for 49 percent of the total 1988 population of 1.1 billion. However, those with full entitlement to the benefits reserved for the officially registered nonagricultural population of urban areas, such as state subsidies for food and housing, numbered only 201 million people. In short, as of 1988, just 18 percent of the total population constituted the officially recognized urban population (*Changes and Development in China (1949-1989)*, 1990: 96, 98; Parish, 1990: 6-8; Lavely, Lee & Wang, 1990: 824). This 18 percent with urban entitlements constituted the apex of a pyramid of privilege that was analogous in certain respects to the multilayered hierarchies of contracting and subcontracting described in other chapters of this volume with respect to Japan. The reforms released a flood of rural migrants to China's cities without changing the official registration category that consigned tens of million of these "urban villagers" to an administrative limbo in which they were bereft of essential rights of those who enjoyed the official imprimatur of urban residence (Selden, 1991; Cheng, 1991).

Throughout the 1980s, state-sector industrial workers experienced the erosion of their economic and social position vis-à-vis both the peasantry and the intellectuals. On the one hand, workers were pressed to give up the "iron rice bowl" of lifetime employment as the state implemented 1986 legislation stipulating

Table 9.2
China's Urban Population and Labor Force, Selected Years, 1955–88

	Total Population	Population (millions)						Labor Force (thousands)			
		Total Population in Cities and Towns			Non-agricultural Population in Cities and Towns			Total Labor Force in Cities & Towns	State Workers	Collective Workers	Individual Workers
		Total	Cities	Towns	Total	Cities	Towns				
1955	615	94	59	35	--	--	--	28,000	19,080	2,540	6,400
1961	659	148	103	45	106	70	36	53,360	41,710	10,000	1,650
1971	852	145	100	44	107	73	34	68,680	53,170	14,690	810
1978	963	172	119	53	124	84	40	95,140	74,510	20,480	150
1984	1,039	330	196	134	167	115	52	122,290	86,370	32,160	3,390
1988	1,096	541	301	240	201	140	60	142,670	99,840	35,270	6,590

Note: Totals may not add up exactly due to rounding.
Source: Changes and Development in China (1949–1989), 1990: 96, 98, 223.

that all new workers be hired on temporary short-term contracts. The reformers succeeded, however, in denying lifetime employment only to newly hired workers in the state sector through the use of such contracts. The great majority of workers who were already employed retained lifetime job security and benefits. In this respect, as in the rush to hire more temporary and contract workers from the countryside and in the changing patterns of income distribution, state-sector workers confronted direct threats to their privileged position.

Looking out from their cramped apartments at the two- and three-story mansions constructed by peasant entrepreneurs in the suburbs, workers on fixed salaries experienced declining relative status and position, a perception substantiated by national data. Throughout the 1980s, the growing income gap, which had once favored state employees and the cities, was reversed; the urban-rural income gap narrowed as rural residents made substantial income gains. From a spatial perspective, the gains were largest in the suburbs of large cities, where peasants and entrepreneurs could take advantage of new market opportunities. The rise of the suburban *nouveau riche* class especially brought home to the urban working class the decline of its position with respect to the peasantry.

Workers also experienced declining status with respect to intellectuals. Intellectuals, who had been repeatedly degraded, brutalized, jailed, or worse in the course of political campaigns from the early 1950s through the Great Leap Forward and the Cultural Revolution and up to the death of Mao in 1976, were suddenly valued by the reform regime as a stratum whose role would be critical to the technical change and international networking required for modernization. With the government sending tens of thousands of students and scholars abroad for study or to participate in missions, with higher education and research in China beginning to recover from the ravages of the Cultural Revolution, and with the spotlight on technological and managerial expertise and linkages to the international economy, the state courted higher intellectuals more avidly than at any time since the 1950s. Yet even as intellectuals achieved significant gains, the reforms fueled a deep malaise among them. It was they, with antennae tuned to the economies and societies of the West, who were most keenly aware of China's poverty and primitive technology. They also experienced most acutely the frustration of subordination to party cadres who had minimal educational and technological backgrounds and of low material rewards for their services at a time when exposure to the West was raising apocalyptic expectations. In short, if intellectuals were both the proponents and beneficiaries of the reforms, their growing familiarity with the glitter and power of core capitalism generated deep discontent with the pace of China's progress and with their own position in a society where Communist Party claims to monopolize power appeared increasingly illegitimate.

These sources of discontent among urban workers and intellectuals were exacerbated by two important factors impinging on livelihoods and consciousness in the 1980s. Both factors were integral to the reform agenda. The first was inflation. The combination of an overheated economy, skyrocketing budget deficits, and partial price reforms generated sharp inflationary pressures. Understated official reports listed the rate of inflation at 19 percent in 1988 and 28 percent in the first quarter of 1989. Such rates, while hardly unusual for nations of the periphery, were the highest that China had experienced since the late 1940s, when inflation had been a major factor in precipitating the collapse of Guomindang rule. Wang Houde, a vice-chairman of the All China Federation of Trade Unions, has estimated that, in 1988, more than half of urban families suffered declines in real income, and even the State Statistical Bureau acknowledged declines for 35 percent (Wilson, 1990: 58–59; Wang, forthcoming). Workers and intellectuals, as recipients of state salaries, shared the common experience of seeing their modest incomes sharply eroded by inflation.

The second corrosive factor at work in the late 1980s was the growing perception of widespread official corruption and of the use of official position to secure illicit profit and privilege. The mixed economy, the opening to foreign capital, and the production and distribution of costly consumer durables in an economy that retained powerful command features, gave rise to highly visible forms of official corruption, especially when combined with the increased involvement of officials and former officials in the private sector. The result was a deepening public malaise, fed by a series of widely publicized scandals involving official malfeasance on a grand scale—many of them involving free trade zones and foreign goods. The fact that so many of those who were most obviously prospering in the reform era were the children of leading officials further undermined the legitimacy of the system.

STUDENTS, WORKERS, CITIZENS: THE MAKING OF THE MOVEMENT OF 1989

Of the problems spawned by reform, inflation and corruption had the deepest and most corrosive effects on urban residents. Urban people, including workers and intellectuals, who lived on fixed state or collective salaries, felt not only that they had been bypassed by the benefits of reform but that they were unfairly bearing the brunt of the inflation, corruption, and declining status that were among its by-products. This was the volatile situation in which student activists planned to commemorate the seventieth anniversary of the May Fourth Movement of 1919, the preeminent moment of patriotic student activism.

Throughout the decade 1978–88, citizens, workers, entrepreneurs, and most intellectuals stood aloof from the successive student-initiated protests demanding democratic rights. In 1989, however, student activists galvanized significant support from all of these groups, touching off protests in scores of cities across the country and placing issues of representation, legitimacy, and empowerment at the center of Chinese politics. In Beijing, the movement occupied Tiananmen Square for nearly a month, securing control of the symbolic center of national power and virtually immobilizing important state functions. It displayed an extraordinary repertoire of strategies that competed successfully with the state on the terrain of political ritual, the preservation of public order, and the legitimate representation of the national interest. The movement riveted public attention in

China and throughout the world—never has there been a better made-for-world-TV movement—and built both popular and elite support in major Chinese cities. In Nanjing, Chongqing, Xian, Shanghai, Shenyang, and Changchun, to name but a few of the better documented cases, significant popular movements challenged the party-state's monopoly on power and its claim to speak for the public (Unger, 1991; Lufrano, 1992; Esherick & Wasserstrom, 1990; Saich, 1990).

The 1989 movement built on ancient traditions of remonstrance and principled protest against abuses of imperial authority. It also drew creatively on twentieth-century traditions of student-initiated mass protest, with Tiananmen as the stage, dating back to the May Fourth Movement of 1919 and the December Ninth student movement of 1935 (Des Forges, forthcoming; Nathan, 1985; Strand, 1990). In 1966, the inauguration of the Red Guards in Tiananmen Square ignited the mass movement phase of the Cultural Revolution, and protests there in 1976 led to the renunciation of the Cultural Revolution and the rise of Deng. Since the Democracy Wall movement of 1978-79, student activists have repeatedly and with increasing frequency made the square the focal point of demonstrations and protests, notably in 1984, 1986, and 1989.

The student concepts of democracy manifested in 1989 were diverse and fluid, taking shape in the course of the movement but drawing on historical and cultural predispositions. They stressed broad vision over specific institutional programs. Criticizing and ridiculing the party dictatorship as corrupt and inept, many students were drawn uncritically toward an idealized vision of democratic practices in the United States. In 1989, the most widely shared demands emphasized a dialogue with the authorities, the right to organize and protest, and civil rights such as freedom of speech and the press. Above all, the protesters emphasized "negative freedoms," such as freedom from official domination and from the monopoly on power exercised by the party-state through such institutions as the *hukou* system of population control that bound people to their native villages and cities and defined a hierarchy of urban places. Only a rare few called for free elections, checks and balances, or a multiparty system. The students' vision, which centered on expanded political rights for the educated elite, had far more in common with the century-long search for national unity than it did with conceptions of pluralist or participatory democracy (Esherick & Wasserstrom, 1990: 837).

The contradictory forces and myriad discontents that the movement tapped were manifest in the conflicting symbols that proliferated in Tiananmen. These included representations ranging from Mao, embodying worker and citizen discontent with the impact of the reforms and nostalgia for an earlier era, to the Goddess of Democracy, expressing student longings for American-style democracy and prosperity. The strains of "The Internationale" and China's national anthem mingled with those of U.S. 1960s pop songs and the pulse of contemporary Chinese rock. The students located their movement squarely in the stream of world movements for democracy and human rights that had exploded in the 1980s, notably in Eastern Europe and in East and Southeast Asia. Many emulated the white headbands worn by South Korean dissidents and flashed the "V" sign favored by anti-Marcos activists who had fought for the people's power in the Philippines. They quoted Martin Luther King, Jr. and Mahatma Gandhi on nonviolent protest and Abraham Lincoln and Patrick Henry on democracy. The mass hunger strike, a powerful tactic not previously used by the Chinese protesters, placed enormous moral pressure on the state and was instrumental in winning popular support for the students who risked health and even life for the cause.

Compared with many of the movements that coalesced in Eastern Europe in 1989, Chinese students, while challenging the party's monopoly on power, rarely questioned the legitimacy of communist rule. Whereas movements in Poland, Czechoslovakia, Hungary, and East Germany, which pitted a coalescing and diverse civil society against the party-state, eventually culminated in successfully overthrowing entrenched communist regimes, the Chinese democratic movement remained closely (if at times uneasily) associated with the Communist Party's powerful reform wing all through the spring of 1989. The student demands were compatible with the efforts by government reformers to press for economic and political change within the context of continued Communist Party rule. The strike declaration of June 2, one of the fullest specifications of the content of the democratic demands, first emphasized the spirit of tolerance and cooperation, and then called for the establishment of legitimate, unofficial organizations to form a political force as a check to government decision making. This was, in essence, a demand for consultation but far from a call to transfer or even to share power, still less for the overthrow of communist rule. Viewed in light of the cascading demands for a genuine multiparty politics that broke the ruling party's monopoly on power, questioned the fundamental character of the social system, and then swept away the communist governments of Eastern Europe one after another in the fall of 1989, the demands of the Chinese protesters were moderate in the extreme. It is, of course, a moot question whether political compromise would have generated cascading demands or led ultimately to calls for the end of Communist Party rule—that is, to a full-fledged antisystemic or revolutionary movement, as occurred in Eastern Europe.

Viewed from another angle, the student demands echoed the party's own promised agenda of political reform. At the thirteenth Party Congress, Party Secretary Zhao Ziyang had called for establishing a system of consultation and dialogue, separating party and government, improving socialist democracy, and strengthening the legal system—all within the paradigm of one-party rule. Yet even these modest political reforms had long remained stalled. From the declaration of martial law on May 20 forward, dominant groups within the party rejected compromise on political issues, insisting that stability be assured before political reform could be contemplated.

The 1989 movement was distinguished from those of the preceding decade above all by the ability of the protesters to project their voices beyond the square and to mobilize powerful and sustained urban support across boundaries of unit, class, generation, and occupation, even in the face of martial law. The breadth and depth of popular support for the student protesters were manifest in mass demonstrations, whose numbers at their peak swelled to more than one million people in the capital. Even more impressive was the formation of spontaneous popular networks that sustained the protest, preserved social order, and for a time halted the advance and sought to win over the military forces that had been dispatched to suppress the movement. For all its internal divisions over goals and strategies, the movement paralyzed and polarized the party-state and the military for the two tense weeks of martial law until People's Liberation Army forces crushed in on June 4 (Khu, 1990; Oksenberg et al., 1990).

The problem we wish to explore is why protest movements that had been spearheaded by students and intellectuals over the preceding decade made their first significant inroads in China's cities in 1989, winning the support of large numbers of workers and other citizens. How are we to explain the fact that in 1989 the movement posed the most formidable challenge to communist rule since the late 1960s, when the nation had hovered on the brink of civil war and when armies and Red Guard factions battled for control at the height of the Cultural Revolution?

In the supercharged environment precipitated by the occupation of Tiananmen, the mass protests in most large cities, and the arrival of 200,000 to 300,000 students from campuses across the country to join the demonstrators in Beijing, the students astutely linked their original demands for democratic rights to issues that broadened the base of citizen support and tapped deep urban discontent. Particularly telling were the attacks on official corruption and the state's failure to curb inflation. These themes, which were dramatized by mass hunger strikes and collective oaths by the students to sacrifice their lives for the nation, drew immense popular support for the movement. Demonstrations on May 17 and 18 brought more than one million people, including large numbers of worker and citizen participants out into the streets of Beijing. A student movement had become a mass urban movement.

Like the students, most workers, in characteristic Chinese fashion, came to the demonstrations not as individuals but in well-organized and clearly designated groups identifying their work units. Truckloads and busloads of workers from major industrial enterprises such as the Capitol Steel Corporation and the Yanshan Petrochemical Corporation entered the central city and proceeded to Tiananmen to the beat of drums and gongs. Offices and factories organized delegations and marched under their own banners (Niming, 1990: 97). One of the worst nightmares for China's beleaguered leaders—the emergence of a Solidarnosc-like alliance of workers and intellectuals—appeared imminent as the All-China Federation of Trade Unions (ACFTU) announced its support for the movement and on May 19 donated 100,000 yuan to support the hunger strikers. That same day, 400,000 demonstrators joined the sit-in in front of Shanghai party headquarters, and large demonstrations took place in other cities.

By this time, the movement had spread to dozens of major cities and to some smaller ones as well. The movement was led by students and intellectuals, but it now enjoyed substantial worker and citizen participation. Sizing up the new situation, particularly its national character, the beginnings of worker participation, and a threat by the ACFTU to conduct a general strike, the party leadership took the extraordinary measure of invoking martial law in Beijing on May 20 (Wang, forthcoming: 247). But the declaration of martial law did not prevent either students or workers from continuing to organize.

Throughout the 1980s, the state had repeatedly stepped in to crush student protests. In each case, the movements evaporated almost instantly in the face of state repression. The movement of 1989 was different not only because of the breadth of citizen support but also because the deep divisions within the party-state over the future and limits of reform strengthened the confidence of dissidents and weakened the ability of the state to crack down. On May 25, the preparatory committee for the Beijing Workers' Autonomous Federation, the first independent union federation to organize, was formed. This was quickly followed by the formation of similar labor organizations in at least 16 major cities, including Shanghai, Canton, Wuhan, Nanjing, Tianjin, Hangzhou, Xian, Zhengzhou, Lanzhou, Hohhot, and Changsha (Wang, forthcoming: 246–247; Wilson, 1990: 60). Five days later, on the anniversary of the great worker upsurge of May 30, 1925, the Beijing Workers' Autonomous Federation was formally launched. That same day, workers protested the arrest of three federation leaders, as the state moved swiftly to nip the spreading labor movement in the bud.

While these signs of worker militance and organization sent danger signals to China's leaders, the limits of worker involvement and of the student-worker alliance should be recognized. In contrast to students, workers by and large failed to build effective autonomous organizations within their own factories or beyond. The newly proclaimed autonomous labor federations were at best small and skeletal, involving a small minority of workers. The Beijing Workers' Autonomous Federation, for example, claimed 3,000 members. In many cities, the student movement either never attempted or failed to build sustained relationships with workers. Interviews make clear that many workers and citizens supported and aided the students, but they did not perceive themselves as part of a unified movement. Especially after the declaration of martial law, it became extremely difficult and dangerous for worker units to continue to demonstrate in direct opposition to state fiat.

The student-worker alliance was at all times tenuous and tension-ridden. The initial student reaction to worker offers of support was cool and even hostile. Students feared not only that worker participation might provoke a state crackdown but also that the purity of a student movement, and hence the widespread support it enjoyed as a patriotic movement, would be undermined. Even when workers associated with the federation set up tents in Tiananmen Square, they remained physically separated from the students. Likewise, the Worker Federation Headquarters was located in the northwest corner of the square, far from the symbolic center of student activity near the martyrs' monument. In this respect, the segmentation of Chinese society was reenacted in the movement. Not surprisingly, tensions and rivalry built between groups, and particularly between workers and students. Students bridled, for example, at a Workers' Federation open letter on May 21 that proclaimed that, as the "most advanced class," workers should constitute the "backbone" of the movement (Saich, 1990: 21).

Throughout the tense days of martial law, students and intellectuals retained leadership in the movement. In this respect, Solidarnosc, which had a powerful worker initiative, significant regional and national leadership drawn from the ranks of workers, and deep ties to the Catholic Church, fundamentally differed in character and strength. Nevertheless, worker and citizen involvement made it far more difficult and costly for the Chinese state to control, repress, or halt the movement. If comparison is made to Western Europe or the United States, it is difficult to find historical precedents for a dissident student movement that has enjoyed comparable levels of worker support, not to speak of participation.

The private sector also provided critical support for the movement, making perhaps its first significant entry onto the political stage (except as objects of ritualized yet often brutal struggle) since the 1950s. In Beijing, the Flying Tiger Motor Brigade provided motorcycle communication and logistical support and kept the movement apprised of troop movements. The Stone Computer Company provided access to sophisticated computer and communication networks and helped finance the movement (Saich, 1990: 47).

The movement drew inspiration and strength from the political developments then sweeping through Soviet and East European societies. Particularly important were Gorbachev's call for *glasnost* and the resurgence of Solidarnosc in Poland, from the end of martial law there to its victory in open elections. Gorbachev's visit to China dramatized the political limits of China's economic and institutional reforms just as profound political changes were under way across Eastern Europe. The ability of the students to control Tiananmen Square during the Soviet leader's visit made manifest their power to influence and challenge state policy directly at a time of maximum international visibility. Their challenge also highlighted the lack of institutional channels to translate the popular voice into power and policy. These factors suggested to China's urban residents that the democratic movement was part of an irresistible global democratizing trend.

A critical factor that allowed the movement to grow to such impressive dimensions was the deep division extending to the highest echelons of the party-state and the military, a division exacerbated by the multifaceted results of a decade of reforms and the social schisms engendered thereby. The movement continued to grow following the declaration of martial law in part because the highest ranks of leadership, right up to the Politburo and ranking military leaders, included people who favored (to greater or lesser degrees) (limited) democratizing political reform or the use of the movement to strengthen their own political positions. Political divisions at the highest level became manifest in several ways: in the public conflict between Party Secretary Zhao and Premier Li Peng over the official response to the movement; in the usurpation of the power of the Politburo Standing Committee by Deng and senior advisers of the older generation; and in the refusal of the leadership of the 38th Army to follow orders to crush the demonstrators in the weeks following martial law. Intraleadership divisions were also evident in the support that the movement received in the media, not only in such intellectual organs as the *Guangming Daily, World Economic Herald,* and *Science and Technology Daily,* but also in *Workers' Daily* and especially *People's Daily,* the organ of the Central Committee and China's journal of record (Tan, 1990; Wilson, 1990). The public support provided by significant groups of journalists, writers, and intellectuals, as well as labor leaders and government officials who marched with the protesters under banners proclaiming their unit affiliation, strengthened the confidence among demonstrators that the movement enjoyed support in high places.

It is only when we fathom the depth of intraparty leadership's divisions that we can comprehend the hiatus from the declaration of martial law on May 20 to the suppression of the movement on June 4. In the end, Deng, Yang Shangkun, and other octogenarian holders of power from the original revolutionary generation who continue to dominate China's party and army, concluded that the democratic movement constituted a direct threat to party rule and that student leaders could not or would not negotiate a settlement to end their occupation of Tiananmen and other central areas. These older leaders then succeeded in mustering the military might to crush those who sought to extend China's reforms from the realm of economic and social institutions to that of democratizing political power.

THE CITY, THE COUNTRYSIDE, AND THE FAILURE OF THE MOVEMENT

Given the depth of the social and economic crisis, the array of popular support for the movement, and the divisions at all levels of the party, army, and administration, how are we to explain the ability of the Deng leadership to suppress the movement so thoroughly after June 4 and to prevent any recrudescence of the movement in the course of the next two years? One key lies in the fact that despite four decades of rapid industrialization and despite the rapid influx of population from the countryside to the city, China's cities have remained isolated, if dynamic, islands of power and privilege within a predominantly agrarian nation. Since 1949, political initiative has shifted inexorably from the countryside to the cities. Since 1978, tens of millions of rural people have flooded into the cities, yet more than 80 percent of the population still lacks full urban entitlement and the ability of the state to control the countryside remains crucial to stable rule.

Urban students, intellectuals, and citizens established intra- and interurban networks in the course of the struggle and forged communication and financial links with supporters in the United States, Japan, Europe, Hong Kong, and Taiwan. China's burgeoning communication with the outside world through telephone, computer networks, TV, radio, and fax provided new technologies that could be utilized by dissidents—all of which had been unavailable to earlier generations of activists. But student protesters, who were tuned in so well to international currents, ideas, and networks, failed to establish—indeed never seriously contemplated establishing—organic ties to the countryside. This is hardly unusual in the global perspective of urban movements that are divorced from rural problems and perspectives, even in predominantly rural societies. This failure constitutes a break, however, from the history of the twentieth-century Chinese revolution that goes back to the May Fourth Movement that had inspired the democratic forces of 1989. The greatest triumphs of China's long revolution—the defeat first of Japan and then of U.S.-backed Guomindang forces by revolutionary armies and the carrying out of land reform and cooperation—all rested on the dynamic combination of patriotic intellectuals and a mobilized peasantry led by a party with an astute understanding of the problems of the countryside and a commitment to uplifting it.

In 1989, however, both the vision and the political activities of students and intellectuals remained unequivocally urban and modern. Like so many Third World intellectuals, their eyes were trained on New York, Paris, Tokyo, and (in rather different ways) Moscow, but certainly not on China's hinterland. Their democratizing vision and their reform commitment, which were urban and modern in inspiration and elitist to the core, were framed virtually without reference to the villages that comprise China's vast hinterland and to the rural social, economic, welfare, and environmental problems that had been aggravated by the reforms. Indeed, the rhetoric and ideals projected by the student activists suggested that many shared the view, graphically presented in the influential TV documentary series *River Elegy*, that China's peasantry constituted a great weight holding back China's modernization and democracy. Most of the democratic activists apparently saw the struggle as one of winning a share of power for intellectuals, certainly not creating a democratic system that would empower the unwashed peasantry. The extraordinary popularity of physicist Fang Lizhi, who best exemplifies the élitist strain of thought that fed the sense of superiority of the intellectuals, is one clue to the deepening divide between China's urban intellectuals and the peasantry (Kraus, 1989). To their detriment, the movements of the 1980s differed fundamentally from those of the decades following 1919, in which student activists and revolutionaries carried their messages of national subjugation and renovation to the peasantry, the countryside emerged as the major arena of contest, and the peasantry played an active role in the process.

A number of people with rural origins and who continued to have rural registration did participate in the movement, including entrepreneurs, contract workers, and recently unemployed worker-peasants in the cities. Demonstrations also mushroomed in some suburban market towns (Friedman, 1990). In the murderous crackdown in Sichuan after June 4, dozens of peasant activists reportedly paid with their lives for supporting the movement. Throughout 1989, as the movement reached explosive proportions, however, the vast majority of the peasantry remained aloof, as they had in each of the (urban) protest movements of the preceding decade. In the aftermath of June 4, despite the malaise resulting from recession, inflation, unemployment, and arbitrary cadre behavior, rural people had little reason to doubt the official denunciations of a foreign-supported, counter-revolutionary plot or the denials of any massacre, save that launched by counter-revolutionaries against China's peasant soldiers who loyally defended the nation and preserved peace.

It is tempting to see the array of contending forces in 1989 as an emerging civil society in the form of a unified popular movement confronting the party-state. China's reforms have created certain economic and social preconditions for such an outcome. The reforms of the 1980s had opened considerable space for the emergence of important elements of an autonomous civil society. These included the emergence of new social classes, mobility, and markets and the weakening of mechanisms, such as collectives and population control, that had long facilitated the party-state penetration and domination of the social, political, economic, and cultural spheres. The democratic salons of the spring of 1989 and the formation of autonomous student and worker federations outside officially designated organizational and institutional channels exemplify the fresh winds that blew through China's cities. These changing conditions created new social spaces and invite comparison with those that had emerged in the early decades of the twentieth century, only to be crushed or marginalized by the rising party-state in the years after 1949 (Strand, 1990; Habermas, 1989). In short, distinctive elements of civil society did emerge with explosive force in China's cities, permitting a host of groups and individuals to claim or reclaim autonomous space from an authoritarian party-state. At the same time, comparisons with Eastern Europe, particularly with Poland where a powerful church had long been a counterweight to the authority of the party and where Soviet-imposed governments enjoyed virtually no legitimacy, suggest the fragility of the new Chinese social forces that emerged in the course of the movement.

To conceptualize the Chinese movement of 1989 as embodying society versus a monolithic state is to miss three critical facts. First, important voices for political reform continued to be found within the Communist Party. These ranged from members of the Cultural Revolution generation, who subsequently became party members and advanced as low- and middle-echelon officials, to leading figures like Hu Yaobang, whose death ignited the movement, and perhaps Zhao, whose belated support for it and for expanded forms of participation and consultation cost him his job as party secretary (Wu, forthcoming). Second, many of the most prominent movement activists, certainly such student leaders as Wang Dan, Wu'er Kaixi, and Shen Tong, worked closely with reform currents both within and outside the party.[1] Their goal was neither to overthrow the government nor to eliminate the Communist Party. Throughout the spring of 1989, they sought the creation of a legitimate space for dialogue with authority in which to debate and shape the reform agenda.[2] Third and finally, for all its urban strength, the movement cannot be said to have captured the imagination of or to have spoken for the entire nation. Here I refer particularly to the city-countryside chasm. If China's democratic movement is to succeed in replacing state authoritarianism with a more representative or even a more consultative political system, it must ultimately embrace the countryside as well as the city and address the formidable dilemmas that confront the rural areas. This is all the more essential because of the deep rural roots of China's military, a force that will continue to shape political outcomes as it has over the last century.

In 1989, the movement demonstrated an extraordinary capacity to build organizational networks, communications, and solidarity throughout urban China and outward to Chinese abroad. The inability to build significant bridges outward from the cities to the rural areas, however, has been among the critical weaknesses of the democracy movement throughout the 1980s. In this respect, both the May Fourth Movement of 1919 and the revolution of 1949 have much to teach those who would rejuvenate the nation and inspire it with democratic ideals. Can a democratic movement address the fundamental concerns of the majority of Chinese who still till the soil and who remained bystanders through the drama of 1989? The economic reverses of the last half of the 1980s, as well as continued arbitrary cadre behavior, suggest that there was and is fertile soil in which to tap rural as well as urban discontent.

The movement of 1989 mirrored many of the deep social and political divisions in China today, where complex and often contradictory class forces and a deepening gulf between prospering and stagnant regions have emerged as a function of the reforms. The movement's history also graphically exposes the fragility of a regime torn between the desire to press ahead with problem-ridden economic reforms and the fear that these may further erode the regime's political base and deepen the crisis manifest in the combination of inflation and recession that tormented the Chinese economy in 1988–89. Yet, even as democratic activists reached out effectively to win international support and as the students (if at arm's length) joined hands with urban workers and citizens throughout China, the movement remained painfully isolated from the peasant majority. Despite the increasing mobility and rapid industrialization and urbanization of the 1980s, China's peasantry retains immense social weight. Unless and until China's democrats can build bridges to the countryside, they will be unable to lay effective claim to representing the Chinese people and will thus be vulnerable to state repression.

Economic reform, moreover, creates preconditions (and pressures) for political reform by giving rise to autonomous classes including a new bourgeoisie, by placing a premium on education and reinforcing the position of educated groups, and by strengthening ties to the outside world. The reforms nurtured the preconditions for democratization in terms of accelerating the processes of education, urbanization, mass communications, class transformation, and economic development. In addition, the passing of the original revolutionary generation may be conducive to the deepening of reform and an eventual democratic transition in China.

In the 1980s, democracy emerged as a pressing issue in China, in the Soviet Union, and across Eastern Europe, as well as in Taiwan, in the Philippines, and in South Korea, to name only some of the socialist and Third World nations where the issue has been dramatically, and often explosively, joined. Given the dual heritage of China's long imperial history and of Marxism-Maoism in a poor agrarian nation, and given the continued strength of the People's Liberation Army, the realization of democratic ideals cannot fail to be a protracted and painful process. The record of the century-long Chinese revolution clearly suggests that a viable democratic movement will require a social program that addresses the poverty and social divisions in Chinese society that emerged in new forms in the 1980s and that continue to hold back China's advance. Successful economic reform will ultimately require a democratizing political process conducive to the constitution of a civil society free from many of the social and political controls that remain intact in contemporary China.

NOTES

This essay expands on and develops themes broached in my *Political Economy of Chinese Development*.

1. East European dissidents, too, generally began with demands that could have been encompassed within the framework of communist rule. It was not until Mikhail Gorbachev clearly signaled that the Soviet Union would not intervene militarily in Eastern Europe and until it became clear that Egor Ligachev was unable to mount an effective challenge to the reformers that movements in country after country of Eastern Europe attacked the fundamental legitimacy of the ruling parties and eventually replaced them. The East European regimes, with few exceptions, lacked the nationalist aura that was a residual strength of China's Communist Party. A critical difference is that China's Communist Party continued to tap into the residual strength associated with its effective leadership of the national resistance to Japan a generation earlier, while most of the regimes in Eastern Europe suffered from their association with Soviet power.

2. In the end, as Josephine Khu (1990) and Woei Lien Chong (1990) have made clear, their inability to control militant elements among the hunger strikers thwarted hopes for a negotiated outcome as surely as did intransigents at the highest levels of the party. Negotiations collapsed when student representatives were outflanked by protesters, many of whom had recently come to Beijing from the provinces and would brook no compromise.

10

DEMOCRATIC DEVOLUTIONS: EAST ASIAN DEMOCRATIZATION IN COMPARATIVE PERSPECTIVE

Robert Schaeffer

In the late 1980s, dictators in the Philippines, South Korea, and Taiwan devolved power to civilian democrats. Movements to democratize political structures in China and Burma failed during the same period. But whether efforts to democratize East Asian states were successful or unsuccessful, they were not isolated developments. More than two dozen states on five continents have democratized in the last decade. Democratization in East Asia therefore needs to be understood in a global context.

One of the striking features of contemporary democratization is that the peaceful, often voluntary devolution of state power from military dictators and one-party bureaucracies to civilian democrats has surprised the movements pressing for an end to dictatorship. Movements and scholars specializing in different regions failed to anticipate the kind of change that actually occurred. Influenced by the modernizationist assumption that economic growth was a prerequisite for democracy, they expected that "bureaucratic-authoritarian" regimes in the periphery and semiperiphery could democratize only during an economic upturn. Instead, democratization occurred during a global economic downturn, which means that democratization was more a response to economic crisis than to economic opportunity.

Most movements and scholars predicted that economic crisis would either provoke regimes to become even more oppressive or encourage social movements to overthrow dictators by force. Instead of triggering a violent response, however, economic crises typically produced peaceful, voluntary transfers of power, which means that change was more "devolutionary" than "revolutionary."

Because they held Cold War assumptions about superpower behavior, movements and scholars expected the United States and the Soviet Union to oppose, hinder, or crush attempts to democratize states within their own spheres of influence and to abet, covertly or overtly, radical change in the other's domain. Instead, the superpowers frequently abandoned their former clients, collaborators, and compradors and assisted in the devolution of power to civilian democrats. Moreover, they refrained from intervening in the other's sphere. This means that the superpowers took a common, not an antagonistic, approach to change.

Because most movements and scholars work in or study individual nation states, they thought that political change would be contingent on particular histories and personalities, resulting in a coup here, a revolution there. Instead, democratization occurred in great regional waves, first in Latin America, later in East Asia and Eastern Europe. The scope and simultaneity of change means that this democratization was a product of systemic forces, not of idiosyncratic historical developments.

Because movements and scholars by and large failed to predict or explain the widespread change that occurred, an alternative explanation of the causes and consequences of contemporary democratization must be developed.

In general, "democratization"—the devolution of state power from military dictators and one-party bureaucracies to civilian democrats—was a political response to a generic economic crisis that took separate forms in different regions. These separate crises are expressions of the generic, global economic downturn that began in 1968–70. Although the character of the economic crisis and of the conjunctural political developments differed between regions and within states, economic crisis forced dictators and bureaucrats to devolve political power to civilian democrats representing the domestic bourgeoisie and middle class, which is composed of small-scale entrepreneurs, intellectuals, and salaried employees in public and private enterprises. By and large, the devolution of power did not extend to the urban and rural proletariat. (The rise to power of Solidarity in Poland is, perhaps, the exception.) Civilian democrats then developed a common strategy to deal with the economic crisis. They demilitarized, privatized, and demercantilized the state and the economy in an effort to resolve outstanding economic problems and to lay the basis for economic growth.

To understand democratization as a common political and economic response to separate economic crises, it is necessary to survey developments in different regions, beginning with East Asia.

EAST ASIAN DEMOCRATIZATION AND LIMITS TO GROWTH

Democratization in South Korea and Taiwan is a product of the problems associated with economic growth in ascending semiperipheral states. South Korea and Taiwan's postwar ascent is usually attributed to the ability of military dictators to initiate land reform and create a low-wage urban proletariat that could be directed into fledgling light and then heavy export industries. While these developments may have assisted annual double-digit rates of growth, they alone do not explain the success of these states. Economic growth in both countries was greatly assisted by U.S. political and economic policies that were designed to assist frontline anticommunist regimes in East Asia.

The United States supported frontline states, which until 1975 also included South Vietnam, by providing massive military and economic aid to military regimes.[1] This aid allowed the regimes to invest in infrastructure and job-creating industries while giving them the wherewithal to suppress labor militancy and keep wages low. By obtaining privileged access to U.S. markets, South Korean and Taiwanese firms found a market for their exports.

The slowly emerging U.S.-Chinese détente in the 1970s began to erode the political basis for continued U.S. aid to frontline states. By the early 1980s, U.S. political and economic policies toward both South Korea and Taiwan began to change dramatically. Continuing U.S. trade deficits, particularly those with East Asian countries, began to strain U.S. support for economically competitive dictatorships in East Asia. To deal with trade deficits, the United States after 1985 began devaluing the dollar against East Asian currencies, which forced up the value of the Taiwanese and South Korean currencies by 40 and 30 percent respectively. It also restricted access to U.S. markets and agitated for greater access to protected markets in Taiwan and South Korea (Bello & Rosenfeld, 1990b: 439). U.S. policymakers also began withdrawing support for East Asian military dictators, urging a "civilianization of politics" (Shorrock, 1988: 108).

As a result, South Korea and Taiwan were caught in a squeeze. New U.S. and continuing Japanese protectionism (imposed in response to trade surpluses with the United States and trade deficits with Japan) placed a ceiling on export-oriented economic growth in South Korea and Taiwan. At the same time, competition from lower-wage Asian countries like China, Thailand, and Indonesia, which sought to emulate South Korean and Taiwanese patterns of development, pressed on them from below (Bello & Rosenfeld, 1990b: 448). Core protectionism and peripheral competition placed real limits on economic growth for both semiperipheral states, and economic growth slowed from double- to single-digit rates (Cooper, 1986: 168; Dreyer, 1991: 57; Cumings, 1986: 162). Walden Bello and Stephanie Rosenfeld (1990b: 443) have written that "Korean technocrats [became] haunted by the specter of Korea turning into an 'Argentina,' or a country that manages to climb up to the ridge marking the transition to 'developed country' status, only to slip and fall back to the Third World."

At the same time, both states began to experience domestic problems. Small capitalists who were denied the kind of state support given to domestic monopoly firms, intellectuals denied effective political representation, highly skilled workers with few domestic job opportunities, and urban workers receiving a small share of income growth began agitating for political and economic change. In this context, leaders in South Korea and Taiwan began casting around for ways to devolve political power to some, but not all, of these disaffected groups. Military regimes saw democratization as a way to share power with the middle class and to create a multiparty political system dominated by a center-right party as a way of strengthening the state and deflecting popular protest.

Democratization in the Philippines, which resulted in the devolution of power from dictator to democrats in 1986, was a response to economic problems that differed considerably from those confronting South Korea and Taiwan. Because the Philippines was linked to the United States as a former colony and because its economic crisis had its origins in indebtedness and stagnation, democratization there has more in common with Latin American states than with other East Asian states.

INDEBTEDNESS AND LATIN AMERICAN DEMOCRACY

Although democratization in Latin America is associated with the debt crisis of the early 1980s, the crisis has its origins in U.S. efforts to cope with its own economic problems, which contributed to a crisis for Latin American dictatorships.[2]

In the late 1960s and 1970s, the United States experienced declining competitiveness in global markets, a rising trade deficit, and a lack of profitable domestic investment opportunities. To deal with these problems, the United States devalued the dollar vis-à-vis gold, and U.S. banks began lending money to private firms and public agencies in Latin America at rates higher than could be obtained in the United States. As John Walton (1989: 301) has noted, "Between 1970 and 1983, the total debt of developing countries grew from $64 billion to $810 billion . . . [and] Latin America absorbed nearly half of these loans, or $350 billion." Much of this debt was private. According to Auturo Guillen (1989: 38–39), "The region's private debt rose from $15 billion in 1972 to $58 billion in 1981," most of it contracted by "monopolistic" industrial groups to finance expansion.

Loans were used to repay old debts, finance state expenditures (subsidies for essential commodities to assist the poor or defense expenditures to expand the military), develop large-scale infrastructure projects, and increase the production of commodities for export. But profits from large-scale projects failed to materialize, and increased commodity production by producers throughout Latin America and around the world contributed to commodity gluts, falling prices, and declining profitability, which made it difficult for producers to pay back private or public loans.

Then, in 1979, U.S. policymakers began raising interest rates, both to combat domestic inflation and to attract capital from other countries to pay for increased military expenditures without raising taxes. The United States used high interest rates to borrow private capital from Latin American countries and then lent it back to Latin American states to cover the cash shortages caused by a combination of indebtedness and capital flight. Manual Pastor (1989a: 1) has noted, "From 1973 to 1987, capital flight from Latin America added up to $151 billion, or about 43 percent of the total external debt acquired during those years." Rising U.S. interest rates then made it even more difficult for private and public debtors to pay back large loans.

To forestall widespread private and public bankruptcy, U.S. officials and their factotums in international lending agencies insisted in 1982 and 1983 that Latin

American governments—still mostly military dictatorships—assume responsibility for repaying all loans made to private firms and public agencies. These governments were told, in effect, to "nationalize" private debt. The result was to reverse the flow of capital. Prior to 1982, Latin America imported more capital than it exported. After 1982, Pastor (1989b: 14) has argued "Latin America was . . . exporting capital to finance Northern economic growth."[3]

Of course, democratization was not entirely a product of economic crisis. A variety of conjunctural international and domestic political developments contributed to the process. Although the United States had long supported client dictators in Latin America and the Philippines, occasionally intervening on their behalf, U.S. officials in the 1980s began withdrawing support for military dictators. By withdrawing support for Antonio Somoza in Nicaragua in 1979, withholding it from Leopoldo Galtieri's regime during Argentina's 1982 war with Britain, escorting Ferdinand Marcos from the Philippines and Jean-Claude Duvalier from Haiti in 1986, forcibly deposing Manuel Noriega from Panama and sending him to jail in 1989, and insisting that Augusto Pinochet accept the results of the referendum and election in 1988–89, the United States signaled an end to unqualified support for military dictatorship in Latin America, even if its actions were motivated more by its cynicism about dictatorship than by its optimism for democracy (Cumings, 1989: 8).

U.S. policy changed at least in part because governments with a broader political base would be better able to guarantee debt repayment: Democracy was thus viewed as less of a financial risk than dictatorship. In Latin America, therefore, sharing political power is closely associated with sharing the economic burden.

Domestic politics also played a role in persuading Latin American dictators to devolve power. Dictators themselves frequently miscalculated both the strength of their regime and the weakness of their civilian opponents. Rulers in the Philippines (1986), Chile (1988–89), Panama (1989), and Nicaragua (1990) decisively lost elections that they had initiated. Elections provided civilian opponents with an opportunity to rally domestic and international support and to win despite the enormous advantages held by the regimes in power.

Dictatorships can usually survive riots by restive urban and rural proletariats, which were a common response to debt-related austerity programs throughout the region in the 1980s (Walton, 1989). They find it difficult to do so, however, if they cannot rely on international and domestic political allies. Faced with a profound economic crisis and deprived of regional superpower support or domestic allies, military dictators have sought constitutional ways to devolve power while retaining some prerogatives and protections from legal proceedings against them for the economic (corruption) and political (dirty wars and disappearances) crimes committed during their tenure (Hagopian, 1990: 147; Petras & Levia, 1988).

THE SOVIET AGRO-MILITARY CRISIS AND DEMOCRATIZATION IN EASTERN EUROPE

Democratization in the Soviet Union and then in Eastern Europe was a product of the economic crisis originating in the Soviet Union. According to Mikhail

Gorbachev, "By the beginning of the 1980s, the country found itself in a state of severe crisis which embraced all spheres of life" (Goldman, 1989: 329).

This crisis might best be described as an "agro-military" crisis, since it is rooted in the stagnation of collectivized agriculture and in the military-led industrialization of the postwar period. Although the collectivization of agriculture initially assisted industrial development, it eventually retarded agricultural production, which began to stagnate and then decline in the 1980s. While military industrialization had made the Soviet Union a superpower, it had also retarded commercial industrial development.

Soviet military spending placed an enormous burden on the economy. Ruth Sivard (1987: 5, 54–55) has written that military industrialization absorbed $4.6 trillion between 1960 and 1987, or between 12 and 15 percent of the annual GNP, while more recent estimates have suggested that the Soviets devoted between 20 and 28 percent of their GNP to the military in the early 1980s (Epstein, 1990: 153). Although military-led industrialization enabled the Soviet Union to expand its political influence, assist socialist movements abroad, and secure foreign sales worth $64 billion between 1973 and 1981 (Klare, 1984: 213), it did not provide substantial economic benefits at home or military advantage abroad.

Domestically, military industrialization absorbed scarce supplies of capital, skilled labor, and natural resources. The problems associated with military spending in the United States—absorbing savings and using the skilled labor, scarce inputs, and productive capacity necessary for increased competitiveness—have been even more evident in the Soviet Union, retarding economic growth and contributing to overall stagnation and decline (Gold, 1984: 195).

Overseas, Soviet military goods have repeatedly failed in battlefield competition with U.S. and Western European military goods in overseas markets, particularly in the Middle East and Afghanistan. According to Mark Kramer (1989: 351), during a 1982 air battle over Lebanon, for example, Israeli pilots "shot down 80 Soviet-made planes while losing none of their own," and during the 1991 Persian Gulf War, 4,000 Soviet tanks were destroyed by the U.S.-led coalition, prompting some Soviet military leaders to conclude that the entire Soviet military model was "obsolete."[4]

The unsuccessful war in Afghanistan and the rising costs associated with its conventional and nuclear arms race with the United States demonstrated the limits of Soviet military industrialization. The cumulative agro-military crisis forced the proponents of military industrialization to devolve power to civilian reformers led by Gorbachev, who believed that military industrialization had "exhausted our economy" (Schmemann, 1991). To deal with the twin crises, Gorbachev and the reformers sought to cut "protection costs" (Lane, 1979), by demilitarizing the budget and to jump start the economy by privatizing state industries and agriculture. Because this project antagonized both the military and the party bureaucracy, which monopolized public economic assets, the reformers needed to develop a wider political base. They therefore promoted democratization or "*glasnost*" (openness) as a way to rally wider social support for demilitarization and privatization or "*perestroika*" (restructuring).

Gorbachev withdrew the Soviet army from Afghanistan, initiated arms control agreements that actually cut conventional and nuclear arsenals, pursued détente with both the United States and China, and revoked long-standing Soviet claims to a sphere of influence in Eastern Europe. By renouncing its right to intervene militarily in Eastern Europe, as it had done in 1953, 1956, and 1968, the Soviets undercut the client dictators and one-party bureaucracies there. Like the United States in Latin America, the withdrawal of Soviet military support for East European regimes weakened them at a time when they were already experiencing serious economic problems created by agricultural stagnation and heavy military expenditures—problems compounded by weak markets for their exports, rising energy costs, and substantial indebtedness. Except for Yugoslavia, dictatorships in Eastern Europe had developed only a narrow social base since they were installed by the Soviet Union in the late 1940s. With the withdrawal of Soviet military guarantees, these weak regimes collapsed at the first appearance of organized dissent and devolved power to nascent political organizations or, in the case of Poland, to a well-organized labor movement.

DEMOCRATIZATION AND DEVELOPMENT

Contemporary democratization is a product of diverse economic and political developments. In East Asia, Latin America, and Eastern Europe, separate economic developments contributed to difficult economic crises, which slowed, obstructed, or reversed economic growth. At the same time, different political developments changed the political climate. In many states, military dictators and one-party bureaucracies were undercut by shifting superpower policies. The unexpected deaths of rulers with no apparent heirs, defeats in war, or defeats at the polls frequently undermined the ability of regimes to maintain even grudging popular support. Moreover, mass protests by dissident groups, who were infused with cosmopolitan ideas about democracy and abetted by electronic technologies that helped them organize and enlist domestic and international support, crippled the ability of regimes to contain or crush opposition to their continued rule.

Under these circumstances, military dictatorships and one-party bureaucracies sought to devolve political power in an attempt to address outstanding economic problems and to deflect incipient social protest.

Dictators and bureaucrats realized that they needed to take drastic measures to deal with economic crisis. To be successful, however, radical steps had to be broadly supported. Because their rule was narrowly based, broad support was difficult to achieve. Dictators and bureaucrats therefore had to extend political power to other social groups, who would not assume responsibility for economic problems without obtaining real political power. As Bello and Rosenfeld (1990b: 460) have written, "Economic policies that are not supported by a rough consensus forged by democratic means are likely to founder over the long run. Democracy, one might say, has become a factor of production."

Dictators and bureaucrats tried to control the devolution of political power to civilian democrats by crafting constitutions that retained residual power for military-bureaucratic groups; they also created conditions permitting the emergence of a strong, center-right political party that could broaden the social base of political power without extending it to left-oriented urban and rural proletariats. By and large, the domestic bourgeoisie, dissident intellectuals, and the middle class, long disfranchised by military rule, have been the principal beneficiaries of democratization.

Although democratization has been a common political response to the diverse economic and political crises in different regions, newly empowered civilian democrats have adopted a common approach to their separate problems. The strategy developed by nearly all democratizing states, and also by some nondemocratizing states like China, consists of policies aimed at demilitarizing, privatizing, and demercantilizing their economies.

Civilian democrats have moved rapidly to reduce defense costs by demilitarizing their economies. Demilitarization has been most dramatic in Eastern Europe. The Soviets initiated the process by withdrawing from Afghanistan and Eastern Europe and by cutting military spending and troop levels (Kowalski, 1989: 30–31). These developments made possible the devolution of power to East European civilian democrats, who promptly slashed military spending, cut troops levels, disbanded party militias, and withdrew from the Warsaw Pact, causing its collapse in 1991 (Nelson, 1991).

Demilitarization has been more extensive in Eastern Europe primarily because the economic problems associated with high levels of military spending are more acute there. Other democratizing states have also demilitarized, though less extensively. In Latin America, successive Argentine presidents have cut spending, scaled back the draft, and cut the army to one-half of its predevolution size (Wynia, 1991: 59–60). In Brazil, military budgets have failed to keep pace with inflation (Brooke 1991), and other armies across the continent have been scaled back.

In East Asia, both democratizing and nondemocratizing states are demilitarizing. South Korea has permitted the United States to withdraw some of its forces from Korean territory. Ironically, because the United States is asking South Koreans to pay a greater share of the cost of keeping U.S. forces there, demilitarization may actually increase South Korean military spending. China has also cut its army by more than one million men and cut defense spending as a percentage of the GNP by half, from 15 to less than 6 percent (Sun, 1988: Jencks, 1989: 265). This has reduced the pressure on Taiwan to maintain high levels of military spending.

Civilian democrats around the world want to demilitarize or pacify their economies for a variety of reasons. Most now recognize that high protection costs contribute little to economic growth and actually put their economies at a disadvantage in global competition with states that devote a smaller percentage of their GNP to military expenditures, like Germany and Japan. In his study of the impact of military spending on development, A. F. Mullins (1987: 103) has written, ''In general, those states that did best in GNP growth . . . paid less attention to military capability than others. This relation . . . holds right across the range from poor states to rich states and from weak states to powerful. Those that did most poorly in GNP growth . . . paid more attention to military capability.''

Not all civilian democrats have been able to demilitarize as fully as they would like. In East Asia, the divided states—China and Taiwan, North and South Korea—cannot fully demilitarize until they resolve the outstanding political and social problems associated with postwar partition (Schaeffer, 1990). In many Latin American states and the Philippines, civilians cannot cut back military spending substantially because they fear domestic rural insurgency or young military officers who use coups to demand higher wages and greater political power. In states that compete in global military goods markets, such as the former Soviet Union, China, Czechoslovakia, and Brazil, civilians are reluctant to hurt their military export industries (Randal, 1990; *New York Times*, May 3, 1991: 3).

A second common strategy developed by civilian democrats has been to "privatize" the economy by selling public assets that had previously been monopolized by dictators and bureaucrats to the domestic bourgeoisie and middle class. Throughout Eastern Europe, Latin America, and East Asia, civilian democrats have taken aim at what the Peruvian economist Hernando de Soto has called "buddy-buddy" or "crony" capitalism (Brooke, 1989) and attacked corrupt dictators and bureaucrats (many of whom now await trial on corruption charges) for ruining the economy. In de Soto's view, privatization is seen as a way to "democratize capitalism" (Brooke, 1989).

As a result, the sale of public assets has been widespread. Assets worth more than $100 billion have been offered for sale in Eastern Europe (Greenhouse, 1990), and thousands of state-owned companies and collective farms are being privatized. In Hungary, 1,600 new companies were created from state assets between 1988 and 1989 (*Economist*, April 14, 1990: 20). States throughout Latin America have announced plans to sell public utilities, airlines, roads, ports, and land. In Brazil alone, the sale of 92 "parastatal" companies and a port authority by the end of 1992 is valued at $62 billion (Pang & Jarnagin, 1991: 75). In the Philippines, the sale of 58 of 123 firms targeted for privatization has yielded $228 million (Abueg, 1991: 7).

Privatization has been less extensive in East Asia, although South Korea sold seven firms in 1990, because both South Korea and Taiwan have fewer public assets. In South Korea, the state supports large private monopolies—"*chaebols*"—that they have been unwilling to break up and sell off.

Civilian democrats hope that the sale of public assets will raise money that can be used to pay off debts, cut costs associated with heavily subsidized services and industries, and free the state from the political grasp of strong public-sector workers, unions, and political parties. Such sales are also designed to encourage the domestic bourgeoisie and middle class to invest their savings domestically rather than hoard it (as they do in Eastern Europe and the former Soviet Union) or invest it abroad (as they do in Latin America). By providing new economic opportunities and upward mobility, civilian democrats can secure the political allegiance of the entrepreneurial classes.

The problem is that the widespread sale of public assets has glutted investment markets, thereby slowing sales and lowering prices. In Poland, for instance, democrats hoped to sell several dozen state firms in 1990 but managed to sell only a handful (Engleberg, 1991: C1). Germany has managed to sell only a fraction of the 8,000 or so former East German state firms (Protzman, 1991).

Furthermore, while the domestic bourgeoisie and middle class have been able to acquire some state assets, many lack the capital or financing to buy large-scale assets. As a result, many larger assets have been acquired by old elites—former bureaucratic managers in Eastern Europe—or by foreign monopolies and consortiums.

The final economic strategy commonly advanced by civilian democrats is "demercantilization." By reducing tariff barriers, opening the door to foreign investment, loosening foreign currency controls, and reducing price supports for agricultural and industrial products, civilian democrats hope to achieve what the Brazilians call a "competitive integration" with the world-economy (Roett, 1989: 149). As Argentine President Carlos Menem has described it, "We have begun a program that will extract blood and sweat, but we do it because there is no other way to save the nation" (Wynia, 1991: 57).

As a result of opening the door to foreign investment, large global corporations are buying up privatized public assets, investing in joint ventures, and setting up production facilities to service new markets. Suzuki Motor Corporation's conversion of a former Soviet military base in Hungary into a jointly owned car factory is emblematic, taking advantage, as it does, of Hungarian demilitarization, privatization, and demercantilization policies (Bohlen, 1991).

States frequently adopt economic shocks—massive budget cuts, tax increases, sudden currency devaluations, forcible savings conversions, and huge price hikes—to make possible a transition to a demilitarized, privatized, and demercantilized economy. These one-time confiscations are "egalitarian" in that they apply equally to all classes, a sort of democratization of pain. Since some classes are better prepared to take advantage of economic opportunities and defend themselves from economic shocks, however, the effect of these shocks is unequal. A former Brazilian planning minister has said of these policies, "With these successive attacks, Brazil operates neither like a market economy, nor like a socialist economy. It works as a laboratory for a university economics department" (Brooke, 1991).

EAST ASIAN EXCEPTIONALISM?

Although democratizing states in different regions have all adopted policies aimed at demilitarizing, privatizing, and demercantilizing their economies, states in Eastern Europe and Latin America have proceeded farther and faster than those in East Asia.

In South Korea and Taiwan, but also in nondemocratizing China, demilitarization has been constrained because sibling states still confront regional, partition-related conflicts, despite the advent of a wider global détente. They have also been less eager to privatize or demercantilize their economies because state-supported private monopoly and protectionism have long been a key to their economic success. And they have democratized more slowly or, in China's case, not at all. East Asian states have been more moderate politically and economically because they are stronger than other democratizing states. In East Asia, miliary dictators and their civilian successors rely not only on the military, which has considerable legitimacy derived from the waging of anticommunist or anti-imperialist wars, but also on extensive political parties that have demonstrated a considerable capacity to mobilize the citizenry on their behalf. As Bruce Cumings (1989: 10) has noted, "The South Korean bureaucratic-authoritarian industrializing regime has a coercive capacity beyond the imagination of any South American state or leader."

In economic terms, South Korea and Taiwan have managed to achieve high rates of growth and improve their relative positions as semiperipheral states in the world-economy even during periods of systemic stagnation. Their more limited use of the strategies adopted by other democratizing states is a reflection of their relative economic strength. But while they are strong relative to crisis-ridden democratizing states and to the two declining superpowers, they are still relatively weak in relation to Japan.

Although there are important regional and individual differences, democratizing states have much in common. Generally, democratization is a political response to economic crisis. Although it is often assisted by changing superpower policy and popular protest, it is usually initiated by military dictators and one-party bureaucrats. By devolving power in a peaceful manner to some but not all social classes, elites can broaden the social base of political power and advance economic policies designed to address the crisis.

Once they assume power, civilian democrats typically demilitarize, privatize, and demercantilize the state and the economy. By demilitarizing, they can reduce the high protection costs that put them at a disadvantage in the contemporary world-economy. By privatizing, they can stimulate entrepreneurial activity and provide economic bonanzas to sections of the domestic bourgeoisie and middle class; this benefit can weld such groups politically to center-right parties that control state power. Finally, by demercantilizing, they can undercut the economic position of the rural and urban proletariat, since keeping wages low can make agricultural and industrial firms competitive on world markets.

These strategies frequently do not achieve the desired results. Demilitarization is constrained by the threat of military coups and proletarian insurrection, widespread privatization has glutted capital markets, and demercantilization has led to increased control of the economy by foreign monopolies and has exposed domestic firms to withering competition from abroad.

Although democratization has produced dramatic and positive political change, civilian democrats have not been able to resolve the economic problems that prompted the devolution of power. Because civilian democrats have not resolved these problems which may eventually cause them to lose power, contemporary democratization should be seen as a devolutionary rather than a revolutionary process.

NOTES

1. Walden Bello and Stephanie Rosenfeld (1990b: 434) have written, "Between 1951 and 1965, the United States pumped about $1.5 billion worth of economic aid into Taiwan . . . and financed 95 percent of Taiwan's trade deficit in the 1950s. Economic aid to South Korea was even larger, coming to almost $6 billion between 1945 and 1978—almost as much as the total aid provided to all African countries during the same period. More than 80 percent of Korean imports in the 1950s were financed by U.S. economic assistance."

Some estimates of U.S. aid are higher, Rep. Robert Mrazek told Congress that United States investment in South Korea had totaled "almost $100 billion since 1954" (Halloran, 1989).

2. "The return to democratic government has had less to do with the internal political situation in [Latin American] countries than with the economic crisis faced by military regimes. The military regimes collapsed primarily because of the external debt crisis that emerged in the early 1980" (Richards, 1986: 449).

3. "The reward for pliant Latin American elites is a regressive distribution that punishes the sectors that did not borrow while rewarding those that did with the socialization of their private liabilities even as their substantial private foreign assets [capital flight] remain untouched" (Pastor, 1989b: 100).

4. Marshal Dmitry Yazov has concluded, "What happened in Kuwait necessitates a review of our attitude to the country's entire defense system" (Blitz, 1991).

BIBLIOGRAPHY

PRIMARY SOURCES

British Government Documents (CO, Colonial Office; FO, Foreign Office; all located at the Public Record Office, Kew, England).
CO 852/877/1 #4. (1947). Letter from Minister of State to Deputy Undersecretary of State Sydney Caine, 26 July.
CO 852/877/1 #11. (1947). Letter from Ernest Rowe-Dutton to Burke Trend, 18 Sept.
CO 852/877/ #15. (1947). Memo from A. Crawley to Deputy Undersecretary of State Caine, 30 Oct.
CO 852/877/1 #16. (1947). Notes on item #15 by Douglas Glover (31 Oct.) and T. W. Davies (4 Nov.).
CO 852/877/1 #39. (1948). Memo, "Foreign Office position on U.S. investment in colonies," undated, Jan. or Feb.
CO 852/942/3 #28. (1949). Untitled comment on E.R.P. and stockpiling by "MEB," 2 Mar.
CO 852/1258/4. (1951). Address by J. E. Marnham (Colonial Office) on ECA assistance and technical assistance under Point A, undated.
CO 852/1366 #104. (1953). Very confidential and very private letter from Lewis Douglas to U.S. President, 14 July.
CO 852/1418/ #25. (1953). Letter from Aaron Emanuel (CO) to Fogarty (Treasury), 23 Apr.
FO 371/71822. (1948). Letter from William Gorell-Barnes to T. L. Rowan (Treasury), 5 Aug.
FO 371/71944. (1948). Various letters and memoranda on stockpiling of strategic materials, Nov.–Dec.
FO 371/82937. (1949). Letter from Oliver Franks (British Ambassador to United States) Foreign Office, 31 Dec.
Freeman, Orville. (1969). "Oral History of Orville Freeman," Accession Record 74-18; 14 Feb., 12 Mar., & 21 July; Oral History Collection, Lyndon Baines Johnson Library, Austin, TX.

Schnittker, John. (1968). "Oral History of John Schnittker," Accession Record 74-249; 21 Nov., Oral History Collection, Lyndon Baines Johnson Library, Austin, TX.

SECONDARY SOURCES

Abueg, Jose M. A. (1991, April) Selling of Marcos legacy proves difficult for Manila. *The World Paper*.

Agency of Small/Medium Size Corporations. (1990) *1990 Chusho kigyo hakusho* [1990 White Paper on Small/Medium Size Corporations]. Tokyo: Ministry of Finance Printing Office.

Amsden, Alice H. (1989). *Asia's next giant: South Korea and late industrialization*. New York: Oxford University Press.

Anderson, Kym. (1983, April). Growth of agricultural protection in East Asia. *Food Policy 8*, 327–336.

Aoki, Masahiko. (1984). Aspects of the Japanese firm. In M. Aoki (Ed.), *The economic analysis of the Japanese firm* (pp. 3–43). Amsterdam: North-Holland.

Arrighi, Giovanni. (1982). A crisis of hegemony. In S. Amin. et al. [Eds.], *Dynamics of global crisis* (pp. 55–108). New York: Monthly Review Press.

——— . (1990a). The three hegemonies of historical capitalism. *Review, 13* (3), 365–408.

——— . (1990b). The developmentalist illusion: A reconceptualization of the semiperiphery. In W. G. Martin (Ed.), *Semiperipheral states in the world-economy* (pp. 11–42). Westport, CT: Greenwood.

Asahi, Isohi. (1939). *The economic strength of Japan*. Tokyo: Hokuseido.

Asian Development Bank. (1990). *Asian development outlook*. Manila: Asian Development Bank.

Balassa, Bela. (1981). *The newly industrializing countries in the world economy*. New York: Pergamon.

Bardhan, Pranab. (1984). *The political economy of development in India*. Delhi: Oxford University Press.

Barham, Bradford. (1990, May). *Strategic capacity investments and the Alcoa-Alcan monopoly*. Paper presented at the Conference on the Political Ecology and Economy of the International Aluminum Industry, Madison, WI.

Barthes, Roland. (1982). *Empire of signs*. (R. Howard, Trans.) New York: Hill and Wong.

Basu, Sanjib. (1985). Nonalignment and economic development: India state strategies, 1947–1962. In P. Evans, D. Rueschemeyer, & E. Stephens (Eds.), *States versus markets in the world-system* (pp. 193–213). New York: Sage.

Battat, J. (1991, March). *FDI in China in the 1980s and prospects for the 1990s within the Asian context*. Paper presented at the Conference on Foreign Direct Investment in Asia and the Pacific in the 1990s, East-West Center, Honolulu, HI.

Becker, David. (1983). *The new bourgeoisie and the limits of dependency*. Princeton, N.J.: Princeton University Press.

Bello, Walden, & Rosenfeld, Stephanie. (1990a). *Dragons in distress: Asia's miracle economies in crisis*. San Francisco: Institute for Food and Development Policy.

——— . (1990b). Dragons in distress. *World Policy Journal, 7* (3), 431–468.

Bhagwati, Jagdish, & Desai, Padma. (1970). *India: Planning for industrialization*. New York: Oxford University Press.

Bhagwati, Jagdish, & Srinivasan, T. N. (1975). *Foreign trade régimes and economic development: India*. New York: Columbia University Press.

Bhatia, B. M. (1970). *India's food problem and policy since independence*. Bombay: Somaiya.

Bidwell, Percy. (1958). *Raw materials: A study of American policy*. New York: Harper Bros.

Bishop, Robert V., Christensen, Lee A., Mercier, Stephanie, & Witucki, Larry. (1990) *The world poultry market: Government intervention and multilateral policy reform*. Washington, DC: U.S. Dept. of Agriculture, Economic Research Service.

Blecher, Marc. (1986). *China: Politics, economics and society*. Boulder, CO: Lynne Rienner.

Blitz, James. (1991, March 3). Gloom for the Russians in Gulf weapons toll. *Sunday Times* (London).

Block, Fred. (1977). *The origins of international economic disorder*. Berkeley: University of California Press.

Bohlen, Celestine. (1991, April 25). Suzuki starts joint venture in Hungary. *New York Times*.

Bomsel, Oliver, Marques, I., Ndiaye, D. & de Sa, P. (1990). *Mining and metallurgy investment in the third world*. Paris: Organization for Economic Cooperation and Development.

Bosson, R., & Varon, B. (1977). *The mining industry in the third world*. Washington, DC: World Bank.

Brass, Paul. (1980a). The politicization of the peasantry in a North Indian state: I. *Journal of Peasant Studies, 7* (4), 395–426.

———. (1980b). The politicization of the peasantry in a North Indian state: II. *Journal of Peasant Studies, 8* (1), 3–36.

Brenner, Robert. (1977). The origins of capitalist development: A critique of neo-Smithian Marxism. *New Left Review, 104*, 25–92.

Brooke, James. (1989, August 8). Peru rises up against red tape's 400-year-rule. *New York Times*.

———. (1990, November 27). Peruvian with a vision gets power. *New York Times*.

———. (1991, March 24). Latin armies are looking for work. *New York Times*.

Brzezinski, Zbigniew. (1988). America's new geostrategy. *Foreign Affairs, 66* (4), 680–699.

Bunker, Stephen G. (1989). Staples, links, and poles in the construction of regional development theories. *Sociological Forum, 4* (4), 589–609.

Burmeister, Larry L. (1988). *Research, realpolitik, and development in Korea: The state and the green revolution*. Boulder, CO: Westview.

———. (1990). South Korea's rural development dilemma: Trade pressures and agricultural sector adjustment. *Asian Survey, 30* (7), 711–723.

Byres, T. J. (1974). Land reform, industrialization, and the marketed surplus in India: An essay on the power of rural bias. In D. Lehmann (Ed.), *Agrarian reform and agrarian reformism* (pp. 221–261). London: Faber & Faber.

———. (1982). India: Capitalist industrialization or structural stasis. In M. Godfrey & H. Bienefeld (Eds.), *The struggle for development: National strategies in an international context* (pp. 135–164). Chichester, England: Wiley.

Castells, Manuel. (1989). The new industrial space: Information-technology manufacturing and spatial structure in the United States. In G. Sternlieb & J. W. Hughes (Eds.), *America's new market geography* (pp. 43–99). New Brunswick, NJ: Center for Urban Policy Research, Rutgers University.

Castells, Manuel, Goh, Lee, & Kwok, Reginald. (1990). *The Shek Kip Mei syndrome.* London: Pion.

Chakravarty, Sukhamoy. (1987). *Development planning: The Indian experience.* Oxford: Clarendon Press.

Changes and Development in China (1949–1989). (1990). Beijing: Beijing Review Press.

Charvet, Jean-Paul. (1990). Cereal producer strategies in the major exporting countries in the face of collapsing world prices. *International Social Science Journal, 124,* 169–80.

Chatterjee, Partha. (1986). *Nationalist thought and the colonial world: A derivative discourse?* Delhi: Oxford University Press.

Cheek-Milby, Kathleen, & Mushkat, Miron. (1989). *Hong Kong: The challenge of transformation.* Hong Kong: University of Hong Kong, Centre of Asian Studies.

Chen, Edward K. Y. (1980). The economic setting. In David Lethbridge (Ed.), *The business environment in Hong Kong* (pp. 1–50). Hong Kong: Oxford University Press.

Cheng, Tiejun. (1991). Population registration and state control in the People's Republic of China. (Ph.D. dissertation in sociology, State University of New York at Binghamton), Dissertation Abstracts International, *52,* 1540A.

Cheng, Tun-jen. (1989). Democratizing the quasi-Leninist KMT regime in Taiwan. *World Politics, 41* (4), 471–499.

Chesley, Carol Merritt. (1985). *The demand for livestock feed in Thailand.* Unpublished manuscript. Cornell University, Ithaca, N.Y.

Chong, Woei Lien. (1990) Petitioners, Popperians, and hunger strikes: The uncoordinated efforts of the 1989 Chinese democratic movement. In Tony Saich (Ed.), *The Chinese people's movement: Perspectives on Spring 1989.* Armonk, NY: M. E. Sharpe.

Chopra, R. N. (1981). *Evolution of food policy in India.* Delhi: Macmillan

Clarkson, Stephen. (1978). *The Soviet theory of development: India and the Third World in Marxist-Leninist scholarship.* Toronto: University of Toronto Press.

The coming collapse of North Korea. (1990, June 26). *Wall Street Journal.*

Commins, Patrick. (1990). Restructuring agriculture in advanced societies: Transformation, crisis, and responses. In Terry Marsen, Philip Lowe, & Sarah Whatmore (Eds.), *Rural restructuring: Global processes and their responses* (pp. 45–76). London: David Fulton.

Cooper, John F. (1986, April). Taiwan: New challenges to development. *Current History.*

———. (1989, April) Taiwan: A nation in transition. *Current History.*

Council on Foreign Relations. (1946). *Studies of American interests in the war and the peace: Topical index.* New York: Council on Foreign Relations.

Cox, Robert. (1984). Social forces, states and world-orders: Beyond international relations theory. In R. B. J. Walker (Ed.), *Culture, ideology and world-order* (pp. 258–299). Boulder, CO: Westview.

Coyle, William T. (1989). Trade arrangements in the Pacific. In *Pacific Rim: Agriculture and trade report: Situation and outlook series* (pp. 47–52). Washington, DC: U.S. Dept. of Agriculture, Economic Research Service.

———. (1990). The changing structure of Japanese agricultural trade. In *World agriculture: Situation and outlook report: Forces for change in the 1990's* (pp. 49–55). Washington, DC: U.S. Dept. of Agriculture, Economic Research Service.

Cumberland, Kenneth B. (1956). *Southwest Pacific.* New York: McGraw-Hill.

Cumings, Bruce. (1979). The political economy of Chinese foreign policy. *Modern China, 5* (4) 411–461.

——— . (1986, April). South Korea: Trouble ahead? *Current History*.

——— . (1987). The origin and development of the Northeast Asian political economy: Industrial sectors, product cycles, and political consequences. In F. C. Deyo (Ed.), *The political economy of new Asian industrialism* (pp. 44–83). Ithaca: Cornell University Press.

——— . (1989). The abortive abertura: South Korea in the light of Latin American experience. *New Left Review, 173*, 5–32.

——— . (1990). *Origins of the Korean War* (vol. 2). *The roaring of the cataract, 1947–1950*, Princeton, NJ: Princeton University Press.

——— . (1991). The end of the 70-years' crisis: Trilateralism and the 'New World Order.' *World Policy Journal, 8* (2), 195–222.

Davis, Mike. (1990). *City of Quartz*, London: Verso.

Deng Xiaoping. (1984). *Selected works of Deng Xiaoping (1975–1982)*. Beijing: Foreign Languages Press.

Dertouzos, Michael L., Lester, Richard K., & Solow, Robert M. (1989). *Made in America: Regaining the productive edge*. Cambridge, MA: MIT Press.

Des Forges, Roger (forthcoming). Democracy in China's history. In Roger Des Forges, Ning Luo & Yen-bo Wu (Eds.), *Chinese democracy and the crisis of 1989: Chinese and American perspectives*. Albany, NY: State University of New York Press.

Des Forges, Roger, Luo Ning, & Wu Yen-bo (Eds.). (forthcoming). *Chinese democracy and the crisis of 1989: Chinese and American perspectives*. Albany, NY: State University of New York Press.

Deyo, Frederic C. (1989). *Beneath the miracle: Labor subordination in the new Asian industrialism*. Berkeley: University of California Press.

Diebold, William. (1941a). Economic war aims. *Council on Foreign Relations: War and peace studies*, E-B32. New York: Council on Foreign Relations.

——— . (1941b). Economic war aims. *Council on Foreign Relations: War and peace studies*. E-B36. New York: Council on Foreign Relations.

Dirlik, Arif. (1991, March). *The Asia-Pacific idea: Reality and representation in the invention of a regional structure*. Paper presented at a symposium on The Asia-Pacific Idea. Duke University, Durham, NC.

Dixon, Chris. (1991). *South East Asia in the world-economy: A regional geography*. Cambridge, England: Cambridge University Press.

Dreyer, June T. (1991). Taiwan in 1990. *Asian Survey, 31*, 57–63.

Drinnon, Richard. (1980). *Facing west: The metaphysics of Indian-hating and empire-building*. Minneapolis: University of Minnesota Press.

Dyck, John. (1988). Meat demand in Japan. In *Pacific Rim: Agriculture and trade report: Situation and outlook series* (pp. 53–60). Washington, DC: U.S. Dept. of Agriculture, Economic Research Service.

Eccleston, Bernard. (1989). *State and society in post-war Japan*. Cambridge, England: Polity Press.

Eckert, Carter. (1991). *The origins of Korean capitalism*. Seattle: University of Washington Press.

Economic Planning Council. (1977, 1982, 1988). *Taiwan statistical yearbook*. Taipei: Economic Planning Council.

Economic Study Group. (1942). International Control of Trade Policies. *Council on Foreign Relations: War and peace studies*, E-B55. New York: Council on Foreign Relations.

Economist. (1991, March 16). The Pacific idea.

Economist Intelligence Unit. (1990). *Country report: India and Nepal, 1989–1990.* London: EIU.

Engleberg, Stephen. (1991, January 13). First sale of state holdings a disappointment in Poland. *New York Times.*

Epstein, David F. (1990). The economic cost of Soviet security and empire. In Henry S. Rowen & Charles Wolf, Jr. (Eds.), *The impoverished superpower* (pp. 127–154). San Francisco: Institute for Contemporary Studies.

Esherick, Joseph, & Wasserstrom, Jeffrey. (1990). Acting out democracy: Political theatre in modern China. *Journal of Asian Studies, 64* (4), 835–865.

Evans, J. Albert. (1988). East Asia's high-value product markets. In *Pacific Rim: Agriculture and trade report: Situation and outlook series* (pp. 66–74). Washington, DC: U.S. Dept. of Agriculture, Economic Research Service.

Evans, Peter. (1979). *Dependent development: The alliance of multinationals, state and local capital in Brazil.* Princeton: Princeton University Press.

———. (1985). Transnational linkages and the economic role of the state: An analysis of developing and industrialized nations in the post-World War II period. In P. Evans, D. Rueschemeyer, & T. Skocpol (Eds.), *Bringing the state back in* (pp. 192–226). Cambridge, MA: Cambridge University Press.

Evans, Peter B., & Tigre, Paulo Bastos. (1989). Paths to participation in "high-tech" industry: A comparative analysis of computers in Brazil and Korea. *Asian Perspective, 13* (1), 5–35.

Feuerwerker, Albert. (1983). Economic Trends, 1912–49. In J. K. Fairbank (Ed.), *The Cambridge history of China* (vol. 12) *Republican China, 1912–1949* (pt. i, pp. 28–127). Cambridge, Eng.: Cambridge University Press.

Fletcher, William Miles III. (1989) *The Japanese business community and national trade policy, 1920–1942.* Chapel Hill: University of North Carolina Press.

Frankel, Francine. (1978). *India's political economy.* Princeton, NJ: Princeton University Press.

Franko, Lawrence G. (1976). *The European multinationals.* New York: Harper & Row.

Friedman, David. (1988). *The misunderstood miracle: Industrial development and political change in Japan.* Ithaca, NY: Cornell University Press.

Friedman, Edward. (1990). Deng versus the peasantry: Recollectivization in the countryside. *Problems of Communism, 39,* 30–43.

Friedman, Edward, Pickowicz, Paul, & Selden, Mark. (1991). *Chinese village, socialist state.* New Haven, CT: Yale University Press.

Friedmann, Harriet. (1982a). The political economy of food: The rise and fall of the postwar international food order. *American Journal of Sociology, 88,* Supplement 248–86.

———. (1982b). The rise and fall of the post-war international food order. In M. Burawoy & T. Skocpol (Eds.), *Marxist inquiries: Studies in labor, class, and state.* Chicago: University of Chicago Press.

———. (1990). Family wheat farms and Third World diets: A paradoxical relationship between unwaged labor and waged labor. In Jane L. Collins & Martha Giminez (Eds.), *Work without wages: Comparative studies of domestic labor and self-employment* (pp. 193–258). Albany, NY: State University of New York Press.

———. (1991). Changes in the international division of labor: Agri-food complexes and export agriculture. In William H. Friedland, Lawrence Busch, Frederick H. Buttel & Alan P. Rudy (Eds.), *Towards a new political economy of agriculture* (pp. 65–93). Boulder, CO: Westview.

Friedmann, Harriet, & McMichael, Philip. (1989). Agriculture and the state system: The rise and decline of national agricultures, 1870 to the present. *Sociologia Ruralis, 29* (2), 93–117.

Fröbel, Folker. (1982). The current development of the world-economy: Reproduction of labor and accumulation of capital on a world-scale. *Review, 5* (4), 507–555.

Fröbel, Folker, Heinrichs, Jurgen, & Kreye, Otto. (1980). *The new international division of labor.* New York: Cambridge University Press.

Garon, Sheldon. (1987). *The state and labor in modern Japan.* Berkeley: University of California Press.

Gereffi, Gary. (1989a). Development strategies and the global factory. *The Annals of the American Academy of Political and Social Science, 505,* 92–104.

——. (1989b). Rethinking development theory: Insights from East Asia and Latin America. *Sociological Forum, 4,* (4), 505–533.

——. (1990a) International economics and domestic policies. In N. J. Smelser & A. Martinelli (Eds.), *Economy and society: Overviews in economic sociology* (pp. 231–258). Newbury Park, CA: Sage.

——. (1990b) Big business and the state. In G. Gereffi & D. L. Wyman (Eds.), *Manufacturing miracles: Paths of industrialization in Latin America and East Asia* (pp. 90–109). Princeton, NJ: Princeton University Press.

——. (1990c). Paths of industrialization: An overview. In G. Gereffi & D. L. Wyman (Eds.), *Manufacturing miracles: Paths of industrialization in Latin America and East Asia* (pp. 3–31). Princeton, NJ: Princeton University Press.

——. (1991, May). *Mexico's maquiladora industries and North American integration.* Paper presented at a conference on "Facing North/Facing South: Canadian–United States–Mexican Relations," University of Calgary, Alberta, Canada.

Gereffi, Gary, & Korzeniewicz, Miguel. (1990). Commodity chains and footwear exports in the semiperiphery. In W. Martin (Ed.), *Semiperipheral states in the world-economy* (pp. 45–68). Westport, CT: Greenwood.

Gereffi, Gary & Wyman, Donald (Eds.). (1990). *Manufacturing miracles: Paths of industrialization in Latin America and East Asia.* Princeton, NJ: Princeton University Press.

Girvan, Norman. (1980). Economic nationalism vs. multinational corporations: Revolutionary or evolutionary change? In H. Sklar (Ed.), *Trilateralism: The Trilateral Commission and elite planning for world management* (pp. 437–467). Boston: South End.

Gold, David. (1984). Conversion and industrial policy. In Suzanne Gordon and Dave McFadden (Eds.), *Economic conversion* (pp. 191–203). Cambridge, MA: Ballinger.

Gold, Thomas B. (1986). *State and society in the Taiwan miracle.* Armonk, NY: M. E. Sharpe.

——. (1987). The status quo is not static: Mainland-Taiwan relations. *Asian Survey, 27* (3), 300–315.

Goldman, Marshall I. (1989, October 14). The future of Soviet economic reform. *Current History.*

Goldstein, Carl. (1988, December 29). Asia's supermarket. *Far Eastern Economic Review,* pp. 48–49.

Gopal, Sarvepalli. (1979). *Jawaharlal Nehru: A biography* (vol. 2). Cambridge, MA: Harvard University Press.

Gordon, Andrew. (1985). *The evolution of labor relations in Japan: Heavy industry, 1853–1955*. Cambridge, MA: Harvard University Press.

Gordon, Peter Jegi. (1990). Rice policy of Japan's LDP: Domestic trends toward agreement. *Asian Survey, 30* (10), 943–958.

Gorman, William D., & Mori, Hitoshi. (1990). Competitive position of Australian grain-fed beef in the Japanese market. In *Pacific Rim: Agriculture and trade report: Situation and outlook series* (pp. 42–49). Washington, DC: Dept. of Agriculture, Economic Research Service.

Gourevitch, Peter. (1978). The international system and regime formation: A critical review of Anderson and Wallerstein. *Comparative Politics, 10* (3), 419–438.

——— . (1989). The Pacific Rim: Current debates. *Annals of the American Academy of Political and Social Science, 505,* 8–23.

Government of India. (1957). *Report of the foodgrains enquiry committee*. New Delhi: Department of Food and Agriculture, Ministry of Food and Agriculture.

Greenhouse, Steven. (1990, May 22). East Europe's sale of the century. *New York Times*.

Guillen, Auturo R. (1989). Crisis, the burden of foreign debt, and structural dependence. *Latin American Perspectives, 16* (1), 31–51.

Habermas, Jurgen. 1989. *The structural transformation of the public sphere: An inquiry into a category of bourgeois society*. Cambridge, MA: Harvard University Press.

Hagopian, Frances. (1990). Democracy by undemocratic means? *Comparative Political Studies, 33* (2), 147–170.

Halloran, Richard. (1989, July 13). U.S. considers the once unthinkable on Korea. *New York Times*.

Harris, David, & Dickson, Andrew. (1989). Korea's beef market and demand for imported beef. *Agriculture and Resource Quarterly 1* (3), 294–304.

Harris, Nigel. (1989). The Pacific Rim (review article). *Journal of Development Studies, 25* (3), 408–16.

Harvey, David. (1990). *The condition of postmodernity*. Oxford, England: Basil Blackwell.

Hathaway, Dale. (1987). *Agriculture and the GATT: Rewriting the rules*. Washington, DC: Institute for International Economics.

Hayami, Yujiro. (1989). *Japanese agriculture under siege*. New York: St. Martin's.

Hemmi, Kenzo. (1987). Agricultural reform efforts in Japan: Political feasibility and consequences for trade with the United States and third countries. In D. Gale Johnson (Ed.), *Agricultural reform efforts in the United States and Japan* (pp. 24–46). New York: New York University Press.

Henderson, Jeffrey. (1989). *The globalisation of high technology production: Society, space and semiconductors in the restructuring of the modern world*. London: Routledge.

Higashi, Chikara, & Lauter, G. Peter. (1987). *The internationalization of the Japanese economy*. Boston: Kluwer.

Hill, Richard Child. (1989). Comparing transnational production systems: The automobile industry in the USA and Japan. *International Journal of Urban and Regional Research, 13* (2), 462–480.

Hill, Hal, & Johns, Brian. (1985). The role of direct foreign investment in developing East Asian countries. *Welewirtshafteliches Archiv, 129,* 355–381.

Hillman, Jimmye S., & Rothenberg, Robert A. (1988). *Agricultural trade and protection in Japan*. London: Gower.

Hoffman, Kurt. (1985). Clothing, chips and competitive advantage: The impact of microelectronics on trade and production in the garment industry. *World Development, 13* (3), 371–392.

Hogan, Michael. (1987). *The Marshall Plan*. Cambridge, MA: Cambridge University Press.
Holmes, Colin, & Ion, A. H. (1980). Bushido and the samurai: Images in British public opinion, 1894-1914. *Modern Asian Studies, 14* (2), 309-329.
Holmes, John. (1986). The organization and locational structure of production subcontracting. In A. J. Scott & M. Storper (Eds.), *Production, work, and territory: The geographical anatomy of industrial capitalism* (pp. 80-106). Boston: Allen and Unwin.
Hood, Neil, & Vahlne, Jan-Erik (Eds.). (1988). *Strategies in global competition*. London: Croom Helm.
Hopkins, T. K., Wallerstein, I., Bousquet, N., Dyson-Hudson, N., McMichael, P., & Tomich, D. (1977). Patterns of development of the modern world-system: Research proposal. *Review, 1* (2), 111-45.
Hsiao, Hsin-Huang Michael. (1989a). A social perspective on the 'Golden-Coast.' (In Chinese). *The Earth: Chinese Geographic Monthly*. January, 98-99.
———. (1989b). *Social forces: Taiwan moving forward*. (In Chinese). Taipei: Zili Evening Newspaper.
———. (1990, July). Emerging social movements and the rise of a demanding civil society in Taiwan. *Australian Journal of Chinese Affairs, 24*, 1-17.
———. (Forthcoming). Changing theoretical explanations of Taiwan's development experience: An examination. *International Journal of Comparative Sociology*.
Huang, Sophia Wu, & Coyle, William T. (1989). Structural change in East Asian agriculture. In *Pacific Rim: Agriculture and trade report: Situation and outlook series* (pp. 41-46). Washington, DC: Dept. of Agriculture, Economic Research Service.
Hughes, Helen (Ed.). (1988). *Achieving industrialization in East Asia*. Cambridge, England: Cambridge University Press.
Hunt, Michael H. (1983). *The making of a special relationship: The United States and China to 1914*. New York: Columbia University Press.
India Today. (1989, May 31). "Trade Winds."
International Monetary Fund. (1989). *Balance of payments statistics: Yearbook—part 2*. Washington, DC: International Monetary Fund.
Iriye, Akira. (1965). *After imperialism*. Cambridge, MA: Harvard University Press.
Jacot, Henri (Ed.). (1990). *Du Fordism au Toyotisme?* Paris: Commissariat Général au Plan.
Japan statistical yearbook. (1989). Tokyo: Ministry of Agriculture and Forestry.
Jencks, Harlan W. (1989, September). The military in China. *Current History*.
Jenkins, Rhys. (1987). *Transnational corporations and the Latin American automobile industry*. Pittsburgh, PA: University of Pittsburgh Press.
Johnson, Chalmers. (1982). *MITI and the Japanese miracle: The growth of industrial policy 1925-1975*. Stanford: Stanford University Press.
———. (1987). Political institutions and economic performance: The government-business relationship in Japan, South Korea, and Taiwan. In F. C. Deyo (Ed.), *The political economy of the new Asian industrialism* (pp. 138-164). Ithaca, NY: Cornell University Press.
Keesing, Donald. (1983). Linking up to distant markets: South to north exports of manufactured consumer goods. *American Economic Review, 83* (2), 338-342.
Keizai Henshebu [Editorial section of the Keizai Magazine]. (1990). *'keizaitaikoku' Nihon no Josei* [Women in Japan, an 'economic giant']. Tokyo: Shin Nippon Shuppan Sha.
Khu, Josephine. (1990). Student organization in the 1989 Chinese democracy movement. *Bulletin of Concerned Asian Scholars, 22* (23) 3-12.

Klare, Michael T. (1984). *American arms supermarket*. Austin: University of Texas Press.
Kohli, Atul. (1987). *The state and poverty in India*. Cambridge, England. Cambridge University Press.
Kolko, Joyce. (1988). *Restructuring the world-economy*. New York: Pantheon.
Kowalski, Adam. (1989, November). Swords into Chocolate Truffles. *New Scientist*.
Kramer, Mark. (1989, October). Soviet Military Policy. *Current History*.
Kraus, Richard. (1989). The lament of astrophysicist Fang Lizhi: China's intellectuals in a global context. In Arif Dirlik & Maurice Meisner (Eds.), *Marxism and the Chinese experience* (pp. 294–315). Armonk, NY: M. E. Sharpe.
Krebs, A. V. (1988). Corporate agribusiness: Seeking colonial status for U.S. farmers. *Multinational Monitor, 10* (7–8), 19–22.
Lall, Sanjaya. (1991, March). *Emerging sources of FDI in Asia and the Pacific*. Paper presented at the conference on "Foreign Direct Investment in Asia and the Pacific in the 1990's," East-West Center, Honolulu, HI.
Lane, Frederick. (1979). *Profits from power*. Albany: State University of New York Press.
Lardner, James. (1988, January 11). The sweater trade. (Part I). *The New Yorker*, pp. 39–73.
Lau, Mary. (1988). The early history of the drafting process. In Peter Wesley-Smith & Albert Chen (Eds.), *The basic law and Hong Kong's future* (pp. 90–106). Hong Kong: Butterworths.
Lavely, William, Lee, James, & Feng, Wang. (1990). Chinese demography: The state of the field, *Journal of Asian Studies, 64* (4), 807–834.
Lawrence, Geoffrey. (1987). *Capitalism and the countryside: The rural crisis in Australia*. Sydney & London: Pluto.
Lawrence, Geoffrey, & Campbell, Hugh. (1991). The crisis of agriculture. *Arena, 94*, 103–117.
Lee, Chung H., & Yamazawa, Ippei. (1990). *The economic development of Japan and Korea: A parallel with lessons*. New York: Praeger.
Lee, Kuen. (1991a). The emerging unofficial economic ties in East Asia. Research proposal submitted to the University of Hawaii–East-West Center Collaborative Research Committee.
———. (1991b). *Chinese firms and the state in transition*. New York: M. E. Sharpe.
Lee, Yong S., Hadwiger, Don F., & Lee, Chong-Bum. (1990). Agricultural policy making under international pressures: The case of South Korea, a newly industrialized country. *Food Policy, 15* (5), 418–433.
Lehmann, Jean-Pierre. (1978). *The image of Japan: From feudal isolation to world power, 1850–1905*. London: Allen and Unwin.
Li, Jiaquan. (1991). Mainland-Taiwan trade: Look back and into future. *Beijing Review*, January 28–February 3, pp. 26–29.
Lim, Hyun-Chin. (1986). *Dependent development in Korea, 1963–1979*. Seoul: Seoul National University Press.
Linder, Staffen B. (1986). *The Pacific century: Economic and political consequences of Asian-Pacific dynamism*. Stanford, CA: Stanford University Press.
Luckham, Robin. (1990). American militarism and the Third World: The end of the Cold War? Working Paper No. 94. Canberra: Peace Research Center, Australian National University.
Lufrano, Richard. (1992). Nanjing spring: The 1989 democracy movement in a provincial capital. *Bulletin of Concerned Asian Scholars, 24* (1), 19–42.

Martin, William G. (1986). Southern Africa and the world-economy: Cyclical and structural constraints on transformation. *Review, 10* (1), 99–119.

—— (Ed.). (1990). *Semiperipheral states in the world-economy*. Westport, CT: Greenwood.

Marx, Karl. *Grundrisse: Foundations of the critique of political economy* (rough draft). (Martin Nicolaus, Trans.). Hammondsworth, Eng.: Penguin.

Marx, Karl & Engels, Frederich. (1970). *The German ideology*. New York: International Publishers.

—— . (1978). Review. In K. Marx & F. Engels, *Collected Works* (vol. 10) *Marx and Engels: 1849–51*. Moscow: Progress Publishers, 257–267.

McMichael, Philip. (1987). Foundations of U.S./Japanese world-economic rivalry in the "Pacific Rim." *Journal of Developing Societies, 3* (1), 62–77.

—— . (1991). Food, the state and the world-economy. *International Journal of Sociology of Food and Agriculture, 1*, 27–42.

—— . (1992). Tensions between national and international control of the world food order: Contours of a new food regime. *Sociological Perspectives 3* (2), 343–65.

McMichael, Philip, & Mhyre, David. (1991). Global regulation vs. the nation-state: Agro-food systems and the new politics of capital. *Capital & Class, 43*, 83–105.

McMichael, Philip, & Kim, Chul-Kyoo. (1991, August). *East Asian agrarian regime restructuring from a global and comparative perspective*. Paper presented at the Rural Sociological Society Annual Meeting, Columbus, OH.

Mendelsohn, Andrews. (1988, April 4). Alvin Toffler in China: Deng's big bang. *The New Republic*.

Merrill, Dennis. (1990). *Bread and the ballot: The United States and India's economic development, 1947–1963*. Chapel Hill: University of North Carolina Press.

Mikesell, Raymond. (1979). *The world copper industry*. Baltimore: Resources for the Future, Johns Hopkins University Press.

—— . (1987). *Nonfuel minerals: Foreign dependence and national security*. Ann Arbor: University of Michigan Press.

Mills, C. Wright. (1956). *The power elite*. New York: Oxford University Press.

Ministry of International Trade and Industry (MITI). (1990). *1990 Tsusho Hakusho* [1990 white paper on trade]. Tokyo: Ministry of Finance Printing Office.

Mody, Ashoka, & Wheeler, David. (1986). Towards a vanishing middle: Competition in the world garment industry. Discussion Paper #35. Boston: Center for Asian Development Studies, Boston University.

Moore, Mick. (1985). Economic growth and the rise of civil society: Agricultures in Taiwan and South Korea. In G. White & R. Wade (Eds.), *Developmental States in East Asia* (pp. 126–207). Brighton: Institute of Development Studies Publications, University of Sussex.

Moran, Theodore. (1974). *Multinational corporations and the politics of dependence: Copper in Chile*. Princeton, NJ: Princeton University Press.

Morishima, Michio. (1982). *Why has Japan "succeeded"? Western technology and the Japanese ethos*. Cambridge, England: Cambridge University Press.

Mullins, A. F., Jr. (1987). *Born arming: Development and military power in new states*. Stanford, CA: Stanford University Press.

Nair, Kusum. (1979). *In defense of the 'irrational peasant': Indian agriculture after the green revolution*. Chicago: University of Chicago Press.

Nandy, Ashis. (1980). *The intimate enemy: Loss and recovery of the self under colonialism.* Delhi: Oxford University Press.

Narain, Dharm. (1961). *Distribution of the marketed surplus of agricultural produce by size-level holdings in India, 1950-1951.* Bombay: Asia Publishing House.

Nathan, Andrew. (1985). *Chinese democracy.* New York: Knopf.

——— . (1990). *China's crisis.* New York: Columbia University Press.

Nayar, Baldev Raj. (1972). *The modernization imperative and Indian planning.* Bombay: Vikas.

Nelson, Daniel N. (1991, April 24). What end of Warsaw Pact means. *San Francisco Chronicle.*

Newfarmer, Richard (Ed.). (1985). *Profits, progress and poverty: Case studies of international industries in Latin America.* Notre Dame, IN: University of Notre Dame Press.

New York Times (1991, May 3). Hard-pressed Czechs retain arms trade.

Nietzsche, Friedrich. (1969). *On the genealogy of morals.* (Walter Kaufman, Ed. & Trans.). New York: Vintage Books.

Niming, Frank. (1990). Learning How to Protest. In Tony Saich (Ed.), *The Chinese people's movement: Perspectives on spring 1989* (pp. 83-105). Armonk, NY: M. E. Sharpe.

Nixon, Richard M. (1967). Asia after Viet Nam. *Foreign Affairs, 46* (1), 111-25.

Noble, Kenneth B. (1991, April 13). Despots dwindle as reform alters face of Africa. *New York Times.*

O'Connor, David C. (1985). The computer industry in the Third World: Policy options and constraints. *World Development, 13* (3), 311-332.

Odaka, Konosuke. (1985). Is the division of labor limited by the extent of the market?: A study of automobile parts production in East and Southeast Asia. In Kazushi Ohkawa, Gustav Ranis, & Larry Meissner (Eds.), *Japan and the developing countries: A comparative analysis* (pp. 389-425). Oxford, England: Basil Blackwell.

Ogle, George E. (1990). *South Korea: Dissent within the economic miracle.* London: Zed Books.

O'Hearn, Denis. (1990, May). *Producing imperialism anew: U.S., U.K., and Jamaican bauxite.* Paper presented at the conference on the Political Ecology and Economy of the International Aluminum Industry, Madison, WI.

Ohno, Kazuoki. (1987). Nokyo: The "un"-cooperative. *AMPO Japan-Asia Quarterly Review, 19* (2), 25-28.

——— . (1988). Japanese agriculture today—decaying at the roots. *AMPO Japan-Asia Quarterly Review, 20* (1, 2), 14-28.

Okimoto, Daniel I., & Rohlen, Thomas P. (Eds.). (1988). *Inside the Japanese system: Readings on contemporary society and political economy.* Stanford, CA: Stanford University Press.

Oksenberg, Michel, Sullivan, Lawrence, and Lambert, Marc (Eds.). (1990). *Beijing spring, 1989: Confrontation and conflict: The basic documents.* Armonk, NY: M. E. Sharpe.

Okumura, Shigetsugu. (1988). *Gendai Sekai Keizai to Shihon Yushutsu* [Contemporary world-economy and capital export]. Tokyo: Mineruva Shobo.

Oman, Charles. (1984). *New forms of investment in developing countries.* Paris: OECD.

——— . (1989). *New forms of investment in developing country industries: Mining, petrochemicals, automobiles, textiles, food.* Paris. OECD.

Ozawa, Terutomo. (1979). *Multinationalism, Japanese style: The political economy of outward dependency.* Princeton, NJ: Princeton University Press.

———. (1979b). Japan's "revealed preference" for the new forms of investments: A stock-taking assessment. In C. Oman (Ed.), *New forms of international investment: The national perspective*, Paris: OECD Development Center Papers.

———. (1985). Japan. In J. H. Dunning (Ed.), *Multinational enterprises, economic structure and international competitiveness* (pp. 155–185). Chichester, England: John Wiley & Sons.

Pang, Eul-Soo, & Jarnagin, Laura. (1991, February). Brazil's catatonic lambada. *Current History*.

Parish, William. (1990). What model now? In R. Yin-Wang Kwok, William Parish & Anthony Gar-On Yeh, with Xu Xueqiang (Eds.), *Chinese urban reform: What model now?* (pp. 3–16). Armonk, NY: M. E. Sharpe.

Parrini, Carl P. (1969). *Heir to empire: The United States economic diplomacy*. Pittsburgh: University of Pittsburgh Press.

Pastor, Manuel, Jr. (1989a). *Capital flight and the Latin American debt crisis*. Washington, DC: Economic Policy Institute.

———. (1989b). Latin America, the debt crisis, and the International Monetary Fund. *Latin American Perspectives, 16* (1), 79–109.

Peterson, Trudy. (1979). *Agricultural exports, farm income, and the Eisenhower administration*. Lincoln: University of Nebraska Press.

Petras, James, & Leiva, Fernando I. Chile: The authoritarian transition to electoral politics. *Latin American Perspectives, 15* (3), 97–114.

Polanyi, Karl. (1944). *The great transformation: The political and economic origins of our time*. Boston: Beacon.

Post, Ken. (1981). *Strike the iron*. Atlantic Highlands, NJ: Humanities.

Protzman, Ferdinand. (1991, March 12). Privatization is floundering in East Germany. *New York Times*.

Pye, Lucian W. (1988). The New Asian capitalism: A political portrait. In P. L. Berger & H.-H.M. Hsiao (Eds.), *In search of an East Asian development model* (pp. 81–98). New Brunswick, NJ: Transaction Books.

Radetzki, Marian. (1980). Changing structures in the financing of the mineral industries in the LDCs. *Development and Change, 11* (1), 1–15.

Rafferty, Kevin. (1991). *City on the rocks: Hong Kong's uncertain future*. New York: Penguin.

Raghavan, Chakravarthi. (1990). *Recolonization: GATT, the Uruguay round & the Third World*. Penang: Third World Network.

Rainat, Joyce. (1988, November 14), Asia's corporate leader of the year; The meteoric Trail of Thailand's CP Group. *Asian Finance*, pp. 30–34.

Randal, Jonathan C. (1990, February 11). Czechoslovakia's new age: A farewell to arms? *Washington Post*.

Rath, Nilakanth, & Patvardhan V. (1967) *Impact of assistance under PL 480 on Indian economy*. Poona: Gokhale Institute of Economics and Peace.

Raynolds, Laura T., Mhyre, David, McMichael, Philip, Carro-Figueroa, Viviana, & Buttel, Frederick H. (1991). The "new" internationalization of agriculture: Critique and reformulation. Unpublished manuscript Field of Development Sociology, Cornell University.

Redding, S. G. (1988). The role of the entrepreneur in the new Asian capitalism. In P. L. Berger & H.-H.M. Hsiao (Eds.), *In search of an East Asian development model* (pp. 99–111). New Brunswick, NJ: Transaction Books.

Revel, Alain, & Riboud, Christopher. (1986). *American green power*. Baltimore: Johns Hopkins University Press.

Richards, Gordon. (1986). Stabilization crises and the breakdown of military authoritarianism in Latin America. *Comparative Political Studies, 18* (4), 449–485.

Riethmuller, Paul, Wallace, Nancy, & Tie, Graeme. (1988). Government intervention in Japanese agriculture. *Quarterly Review of Rural Economy, 10* (2), 154–163.

Riskin, Carl. (1987). *China's political economy*. Oxford, England: Oxford University Press.

Roett, Riordan. (1989, March). Brazil's transition to democracy. *Current History*.

Rotter, Andrew. (1986). *The path to Vietnam*. Ithaca, NY: Cornell University Press.

Rozman, Gilbert (Ed.). (1991). *The East Asian region: Confucian heritage and its modern adaptation*. Princeton, NJ: Princeton University Press.

Rudolph, Lloyd, & Rudolph, Susanne. (1987). *In pursuit of Lakshmi: The political economy of the Indian state*. Chicago: University of Chicago Press.

Rupert, Mark. (1990). Producing hegemony: State/society relations and the politics of productivity in the United States. *International Studies Quarterly, 34* (3), 427–456.

Saich, Tony (Ed.). (1990). The Chinese people's movement: Perspectives on spring 1989. Armonk, NY: M. E. Sharpe.

Sassen, Saskia. (1991). *The global city: New York, London, Tokyo*. Princeton, NJ: Princeton University Press.

Sayle, Murray. (1989, April 28). Bowing to the inevitable. *Times Literary Supplement*.

Schaeffer, Robert. (1990). *Warpaths: The politics of partition*. New York: Hill & Wang.

Schmemann, Serge. (1991, March 10). The sun has trouble setting on the Soviet empire. *New York Times*.

Schreiber, Harry N. (1969). World War I as entrepreneurial opportunity: Willard Straight and the American international corporation. *Political Science Quarterly, 84* (3), 486–511.

Schwartz, Sara J., & Brooks, Douglas. (1990). *Thailand's feed and livestock industry to the year 2000*. Washington, DC: U.S. Department of Agriculture, Economic Research Service.

Scobell, Andrew. (1988). Hong Kong's influence on China. *Asian Survey, 28* (6), 599–612.

Scott, Ian. (1989). *Political change and the crisis of legitimacy in Hong Kong*. Honolulu: University of Hawaii Press.

Selden, Mark (Ed.). (1992). *The political economy of Chinese development*. Armonk, NY: M. E. Sharpe.

Sen, Amartya. (1982). How is India doing? *New York Review of Books 29* (20), 41–45.

Shaiken, Harley, with Herzenberg, Stephen. (1987). *Automation and global production: Automobile engine production in Mexico, the United States, and Canada*. Monograph Series No. 26. La Jolla, CA: Center for U.S.-Mexican Studies, University of California, San Diego.

Sharp, Walter. (1942). Dependent areas in the post-war world. *Council on Foreign Relations: War and peace studies*, P-B45. New York: Council on Foreign Relations.

Shenoy, B. R. (1974). *PL 480 and India's food problem*. New Delhi: Affiliated East-West Press.

Shinohara, Taizo. (1964). *Japanese import requirements: Projections of agricultural supply and demand for 1965, 1970, and 1975*. Tokyo: Institute for Agricultural Economic Research, Department of Agricultural Economics, University of Tokyo.

Shitauke Kigyo Kenkyukai (SKK) [Subcontracting Firm Research Group]. (1986). *Kokusaika no Nakano Shitauke Kigyo* [Subcontracting corporations in the middle of internationalization]. Tokyo: Trade and Industry Research Institute.

Shive, Glenn. (1990). Hong Kong's brain drain: Can education stem the flow? *Centerviews* [East-West Center], *8* (3), 1–6.

Shizuoka Ken Chishokigyo Seisaku Kenkyukai (SKCSK) [Shizuoka Prefecture Research Group for Small/Medium Size Corporation Policies]. (1979). *Gekidoka no Chushokigyo* [Small/medium corporations in the middle of turbulent changes]. Tokyo: Gyosei.

Shorrock, Tim. (1988). South Korea: Chun, the Kims and the constitutional struggle. *Third World Quarterly, 10* (1), 95–110.

Shoup, Laurence, & Minter, William. (1977). *Imperial brain trust*. New York: Monthly Review Press.

Simon, Denis F. (1990, June). *The economic activities of Western nations in Mainland China*. Paper presented at the conference on "Trade and Investment in the Mainland," Taipei.

Sit, Victor F. S. (1989). Industrial out-processing—Hong Kong's new relationship with the Pearl River Delta. *Asian Profile, 17* (1), 1–13.

Sizzling hot chips: Asia is the source of the semiconductor industry's spectacular growth. (1988, August 18). *Far Eastern Economic Review*, pp. 80–86.

Sivard, Ruth L. (1987). *World military and social expenditures, 1987–88*. Washington, DC: World Priorities.

Skeldon, Ronald. (1990). Emigration and the future of Hong Kong. *Pacific Affairs, 63* (4), 500–523.

Smith, Charles. (1988, November 17). Cracking the whip over hand-fed politicians. *Far Eastern Economic Review*, pp. 31–32.

——. (1989, September 21). Part exchange. *Far Eastern Economic Review*, p. 73.

Smith, Gordon W., & Schink, George R. (1976). The international tin agreement: A reassessment. *Economic Journal, 86*, 715–728.

So, Alvin. (1984). The process of incorporation into the capitalist world-system: The case of China in the nineteenth century. *Review, 8* (1), 91–116.

——. (1986). The economic success of Hong Kong. *Sociological Perspectives, 29* (2), 241–258.

——. (1988). Shenzhen special economic zone. *Canadian Journal of Development Studies, 9* (2), 313–323.

——. (1990). *Social change and development: Modernization, dependency and world-systems theories*. Newbury Park, CA: Sage.

Spate, O. H. K. (1979). *The Pacific since Magellan* (vol. 1) *The Spanish Lake*. Minneapolis: University of Minnesota Press.

——. (1983). *The Pacific since Magellan* (vol. 2) *Monopolists and freebooters*. Minneapolis: University of Minnesota Press.

——. (1988). *The Pacific since Magellan* (vol. 3) *Paradise lost and found*. Minneapolis: University of Minnesota Press.

Staley, Eugene. (1937). *Raw materials in peace and war*. New York: Council on Foreign Relations.

Statistics Bureau Management and Coordination Agency (SBMCA). (1990). *1990 Japanese statistical yearbook*. Tokyo: Statistics Bureau Management and Coordination Agency.

Steven, Rob. (1990). *Japan's new imperialism*. Hampshire, England: Macmillan.

Strand, David. (1990). Protest in Beijing: Civil society and public sphere in China. *Problems of Communism, 39*, 1–19.

Strange, Martin. (1988). *Family farming: A new economic vision*. Lincoln: University of Nebraska Press.

Suehiro, Akira. (1989). *Capital accumulation in Thailand, 1855-1985*. Tokyo: Centre for East Asian Cultural Studies.

Sullivan, Lawrence. (forthcoming). The emergence of civil society. In Roger Des Forges, Luo Ning, & Wu Yen-bo (Eds.), *Chinese democracy and the crisis of 1989: Chinese and American perspectives*.

Sun, Lena H. (1988, May 2). Chinese grow cautious on reforms, CIA says, *Washington Post*.

Sung, Yun-Wing. (1985). The role of Hong Kong and Macau in China's export drive. Working paper No. 85/11. Canberra: Austrialian National University, National Center for Development Studies.

Surachai, Pattanajidvilai. (1986). Overview of Thai-Japanese trade and investment relations. In Pasuk Phongpaichit, Busaba Kunasirin, & Buddhagarn Rutchatorn (Eds.), *The lion and the mouse? Japan, Asia, and Thailand* (pp. 67-108). Bangkok: Chulalongkorn University Press.

Suthy, Prasarset, & Sonetepertkwong, Kongsak. (1986). Structural forces behind Japan's economic expansion and the case of Japanese-Thai economic relations. In Pasuk Phongpaichit, Busaba Kunasirin, & Buddhagarn Rutchatorn (Eds.), *The lion and the mouse? Japan, Asia, and Thailand* (pp. 135-208). Bangkok: Chulalongkorn University Press.

Taha, Fawzi A. (1989). Patterns of change in Japanese cereal production, consumption, and trade. In *World agriculture: Situation and outlook report* (pp. 9-14). Washington, DC: U.S. Department of Agriculture, Economic Research Service.

Tan, Frank. (forthcoming). The People's Daily and the epiphany of press reform: How the organ of the Chinese Communist Party subverted the party during the spring of 1989. In Roger Des Forges, Luo Ning, & Wu Yen-bo (Eds.), *Chinese democracy and the crisis of 1989: Chinese and American perspectives*.

Tank, Andrew. (1986, September 29). Made in Taiwan: Will Taiwan be Asia's next automotive powerhouse? *Automotive News*, pp. 29-31.

Tubiana, Laurence. (1989). World trade in agricultural products: From global regulation to market fragmentation. In David Goodman & Michael Redclift (Eds.), *The international farm crisis* (pp. 23-45). New York: St. Martin's.

Unger, Jonathan (Ed.). (1991). *The democracy movement in China: The view from the provinces*. Armonk, NY: M. E. Sharpe.

United Nations Center on Transnational Corporations (UNCTC). (1983). *Transnational corporations in world development: Third survey*. New York: United Nations.

United Nations Conference on Trade and Development (UNCTAD). (1982). *The capital goods and industrial machinery sector in developing countries: Issues in the transfer and development of technology*. Geneva, Switzerland: United Nations.

U.S. Department of Agriculture. (1977). PL 480 concessional sales. *Foreign agricultural economic report*, No. 142. Washington, DC: Economic Research Service.

——— . (1990). *Pacific Rim: Agriculture and trade report—situation and outlook series*. Washington, DC: U.S. Dept. of Agriculture, Economic Research Service.

U.S. Department of Commerce. (various years). *Highlights of U.S. export and import trade*. Washington, DC: U.S. Government Printing Office.

Upgren, Arthur. (1940a). Internal influences on imports of the United States. *Council on Foreign Relations: War and peace studies*, E-B11. New York: Council on Foreign Relations.

——. (1940b). A pan-American trade bloc. *Council on Foreign Relations: War and peace studies*, E-B12. New York: Council on Foreign Relations.

——. (1940c) Geographical directions of United States foreign trade. *Council on Foreign Relations: War and peace studies*, E-B15. New York: Council on Foreign Relations.

——. (1940d). The future position of Germany and the United States in world trade. *Council on Foreign Relations: War and peace studies*, E-B18. New York: Council on Foreign Relations.

——. (1940e). The war and United States foreign policy. *Council on Foreign Relations: War and peace studies*, E-B19. New York: Council on Foreign Relations.

——. (1941a). Economic trading blocs and their importance for the United States. *Council on Foreign Relations: War and peace studies*, E-B27. New York: Council on Foreign Relations.

——. (1941b). Problems of bloc trading areas for the United States. *Council on Foreign Relations: War and peace studies*, E-B31. New York: Council on Foreign Relations.

Vogel, Ezra. (1979). *Japan as number one: Lessons for America*. Cambridge, MA: Harvard University Press.

von Wolferen, Karel. (1989). *The enigma of Japanese power*. New York: Knopf.

Wade, Robert. (1990). *Governing the market: Economic theory and the role of government in East Asian industrialization*. Princeton, NJ: Princeton University Press.

Wallerstein, Immanuel. (1974). *The modern world-system* (vol. 1) *Capitalist agriculture and the origin of the European world-economy in the sixteenth century*. New York: Academic Press.

——. (1979). *The capitalist world-economy*. Cambridge, England: Cambridge University Press.

——. (1982). Crisis as transition. In S. Amin, G. Arrighi, A. G. Frank, & I. Wallerstein (Eds.) *Dynamics of global crisis*. (pp. 11–54). New York: Monthly Review Press.

——. (1984). *The politics of the world-economy: States, movements, and civilizations*. Cambridge, England: Cambridge University Press.

——. (1987). World-systems analysis. In A. Giddens & J. H. Turner (Eds.) *Social Theory Today* (pp. 309–324). Stanford, CA: Stanford University Press.

——. (1991a). The Cold War and Third World: The good old days? *Economic and Political Weekly, 26* (17), 1,103–1,106.

——. (1991b). Marx, Marxism-Leninism, and socialist experiences in the modern world-system. In Immanuel Wallerstein (Ed.), *Geopolitics and geoculture: Essays on the changing world-system* (pp. 84–97). Cambridge, England: Cambridge University Press.

Wallerstein, Mitchel. (1980). *Food for war—food for peace: United States food policy in a global context*. Cambridge, MA: MIT Press.

Walton, John. (1987). Urban protest and the global political economy: The IMF riots. In M. P. Smith & J. R. Feagin (Eds.), *The capitalist city: Global restructuring and community politics* (pp. 364–386). Oxford, England: Basil Blackwell.

——. (1989). Debt, protest, and the state in Latin America. In Susan Eckstein (Ed.), *Power and popular protest* (pp. 299–328). Berkeley: University of California Press.

Wang, Shaoguang. (forthcoming). Analyzing the role of Chinese workers in the recent protest movement. In Roger Des Forges, Luo Ning, & Wu Yen-bo (Eds). *Chinese democracy and the crisis of 1989: Chinese and American perspectives*.

Wanniskie, Jude. (1989, December 24). Some lines on the rest of the millennium. *New York Times*.

Watts, Michael. (1990). Peasants under contract: Agro-food complexes in the Third World. In Henry Bernstein, Ben Crow, Maureen Mackintosh, & Charlotte Martin (Eds.),

The food question: Profits versus people (pp. 149-162). New York: Monthly Review Press.

Weigand, Robert E. (1988). No open door for rice policy in Japan. *Food Policy, 13* (3), 230-234.

Weissman, Robert. (1991, March 18). The real purpose of GATT: Prelude to a new colonialism. *Nation*, pp. 336-338.

Wesley-Smith, Peter, & Chen, Albert. (1988). *The basic law and Hong Kong's future.* Hong Kong: Butterworths.

Wessel, James. (1983). *Trading the future: Farm exports and the concentration of economic power in the food system.* San Francisco: Institute for Food and Development Policy.

Wexler, Immanuel. (1983). *The Marshall Plan revisited.* Westport, CT: Greenwood.

Williamson, Harold F., & Daum, Arnold R. *The American petroleum industry, 1859-1899: The age of illumination.* Evanston, IL: Northwestern University Press.

Wilson, Jeanne. (1990). Labor policy in China: Reform and retrogression. *Problems of Communism, 39,* 44-65.

Winchester, Simon. (1991). *Pacific rising: The emergence of a new world culture.* New York: Prentice-Hall.

Wong, Siu-lun. (1988). The applicability of Asian family values to other sociocultural settings. In P. L. Berger & H.-H.M. Hsiao, *In search of an East Asian development model* (pp. 134-152). New Brunswick, NJ: Transaction Books.

Woodside, Alexander. (1991, March). *The Asia-Pacific region's prophetic culture and its idiosyncracies.* Paper presented at a symposium on "The Asia-Pacific Idea," Duke University, Durham, NC.

World Bank. (1984). *World tables,* 2 vols. Washington, DC: World Bank.

World Bank. (various years). *World development report.* Oxford, England: Clarendon Press.

Woronoff, Jon. (1984). *Japan's commercial empire.* Armonk, NY: M. E. Sharpe.

Woytinsky, W. S., & Woytinksy, E. S. (1953). *World population and production: Trends and outlook.* New York: Twentieth Century Fund.

Wu, Guoguang. (forthcoming). The issues of participation in the political reform: Pressures and limitations. In Roger Des Forges, Luo Ning, & Wu Yen-bo (Eds.), *Chinese democracy and the crisis of 1989: Chinese and American Perspectives.*

Wynia, Gary W. (1991, February). Argentina's economic reform. *Current History.*

Wysham, Daphne. (1990, December 17). The CODEX connection: Big business hijacks GATT. *Nation*, pp. 770-773.

Yoshihara, Kunio. (1978). *Japanese investment in Southeast Asia.* Honolulu: University of Hawaii Press.

Yoshino, M. Y., & Lifson, Thomas B. (1986). *The invisible link: Sogo shosha and the organization of trade.* Cambridge, MA: MIT Press.

INDEX

CONTRIBUTORS

GIOVANNI ARRIGHI is professor of sociology at the State University of New York at Binghamton and a board member of the Fernand Braudel Center. He is the author of *The Geometry of Imperialism* and coauthor of *Dynamics of Global Crisis*, *Antisystemic Movements*, and *Transforming the Revolution: Social Movements and the World-System*

STEPHEN G. BUNKER is an associate professor of sociology at the University of Wisconsin at Madison.

BRUCE CUMINGS is professor of East Asian and international history at the University of Chicago. His most recent book is *The Origins of the Korean War*, vol. II: *The Roaring of the Cataract, 1947–1950*.

GARY GEREFFI is an associate professor of sociology at Duke University. He is the author of *The Pharmaceutical Industry and Dependency in the Third World* and the coeditor (with D. L. Wyman) of *Manufacturing Miracles: Paths of Industrialization in Latin America and East Asia*.

HSIN-HUANG MICHAEL HSIAO is a research associate at the Academia Sinica, Taipei, Taiwan, and coeditor of *In Search of East Asian Capitalism*.

SATOSHI IKEDA is a research associate at the Fernand Braudel Center. He studied international economics at the University of Michigan, where he received his Ph.D. in 1990. His recent research interests include Japanese economic development from a world-systems perspective, and the inter-, intra-enterprise system of the capitalist world-economy.

ALEX IRWAN is a research associate of the Fernand Braudel Center. He has published articles in development studies and is currently doing research on social movements in the post-World War II period.

SANKARAN KRISHNA is an assistant professor of political science at the University of Hawaii at Manoa. His areas of interest include political economy, international relations, and South Asia.

PHILIP McMICHAEL is an associate professor of rural sociology at Cornell University. He is the author of *Settlers and the Agrarian Question: Foundations of Capitalism in Colonial Australia.*

DENIS O'HEARN is an assistant professor of sociology at the University of Wisconsin at Madison.

RAVI ARVIND PALAT is an assistant professor of Asian studies at the University of Hawaii.

ROBERT SCHAEFFER is an assistant professor at San Jose State University. He is the author of *Warpaths: The Politics of Partition* and editor of *War and Revolution in the World-System.*

MARK SELDEN is professor and chair of sociology at the State University of New York at Binghamton. He is the author of *The Political Economy of Chinese Socialism.*

ALVIN Y. SO is an associate professor of sociology at the University of Hawaii. He is the author of *The South China Silk District: Local Historical Transformation and World-Systems Theory* and of *Social Change and Development: Modernization, Dependency and World-Systems Theories.*

Studies in the Political Economy of the World-System
(Formerly published as Political Economy of the World-System Annuals)

Numbers 1–9 published by Sage Publications.

ISBN 0-313-28401-6

90000>

EAN

9 780313 284014

HARDCOVER BAR CODE